Garry Linnell is the author of six books, including the bestselling *Buckley's Chance* and *Moonlite: The tragic love story of Captain Moonlite and the bloody end of the bushrangers*. One of Australia's most experienced journalists, Linnell is a Walkley Award winner for feature writing and has been editor-in-chief of *The Bulletin*, editor of *The Daily Telegraph*, director of news and current affairs for the Nine Network and editorial director of Fairfax. He spent four years as co-host of the Breakfast Show on 2UE.

MOONLITE

GARRY LINNELL

PENGUIN BOOKS

UK | USA | Canada | Ireland | Australia
India | New Zealand | South Africa | China

Penguin Books is part of the Penguin Random House group of companies
whose addresses can be found at global.penguinrandomhouse.com

Penguin
Random House
Australia

First published by Michael Joseph in 2020
This edition published by Penguin Books in 2021

Cover design by Alex Ross © Penguin Random House Australia Pty Ltd
Cover images by Getty Images and Shutterstock
Typeset in Adobe Garamond Pro by Midland Typesetters, Australia

Printed and bound in Australia by Griffin Press, part of Ovato, an accredited
ISO AS/NZS 14001 Environmental Management Systems printer

A catalogue record for this
book is available from the
NATIONAL
LIBRARY   National Library of Australia
OF AUSTRALIA

ISBN 978 0 14379 578 0

penguin.com.au

MIX
Paper from
responsible sources
FSC® C009448

CONTENTS

PART I

1   Well have we loved 3

2   This shrinking world 17

3   The hunger and the madness 23

4   Guilty wretches and broken dreams 32

5   The skulls of troubled sons 43

6   'The most wicked of the wicked' 52

7   Moonlite in the darkness 62

8   His Honour 74

9   The beggar's vice 86

10 Going to the devil, headlong 94

11 Black snakes and bad cheques 103

12 Martyrdom and the legend stripped bare 110

13 Convict blood and a drop of madness 116

14 The gingerbread gaol 124

15 'I would do anything short of murder' 131

16 Murderers and misfits 140

17	Houses of hate	147
18	This terrible darkness	158
19	'A war to the knife'	168

PART II

20	Hatred of mankind in their hearts	179
21	Written in blood	187
22	The harp of David	200
23	The siege	207
24	The retreat of the troopers	213
25	The dispenser of death	220
26	The final shootout	225
27	My friends who sleep in your cemetery	234
28	Evil be to him	245
29	The trial	255
30	All the beautiful flowers	266
31	Falling from a great height	280

EPILOGUE	289
AFTERWORD	299
ACKNOWLEDGEMENTS	305
A NOTE ON SOURCES	307
BIBLIOGRAPHY	311
INDEX	315

PART I

Let us go forth, the tellers of tales, and seize whatever prey the heart long for, and have no fear. Everything exists, everything is true, and the earth is only a little dust under our feet.
W. B. Yeats, *The Celtic Twilight*

1

WELL HAVE WE LOVED

The evening of 19 January 1880

Come now. On this mild summer's night let us gaze upon two men who have known what it is to love and be loved, to hold and be held, and who now have only death for companionship.

In his small cottage near the city, with its arch of hanging grape-vines out front and lush vegetable garden out back, Robert Rice Howard takes out his clay pipe, lights it and begins to pace the floor.

Plumes of tobacco smoke fill the room with clouds of spice and sweetness. That old familiar feeling has returned. His stomach is churning. His mouth is dry. He thinks to himself. Has he done every-thing needed to hang a man? He goes through his checklist. He has already boiled the rope. He and his assistant have stretched it, too. The pair of them then sat down and soaped it, working the lubri-cant into every strand of the hessian. Bob is a craftsman who knows his reputation depends on the attention he pays to the little details. A rope not immersed in water and stretched will retain a great deal of spring. Worse, a rope not vigorously massaged with a bar of soap might prevent the noose slipping easily into place. And that could lead to all sorts of mishaps.

Bob can't have that. Too many people – *important* people, like the politicians and prison officials who keep him in his job – are counting on him to get this right. A mistake on the gallows in front of dozens of them tomorrow morning – the knot incorrectly placed behind the left ear, or the drop and the weight of the condemned man poorly misjudged – would be . . . *unfortunate*.

It would lead to even more criticism and assaults on his professionalism and character.

Bob is no stranger to the slights and cruel barbs of his fellow man. Is there a job in the world that carries more stigma than the role of state executioner? Bob likes a drink. That is true. In the days leading up to an execution nerves will sometimes get the better of him. Locals will often spy him clutching a lamppost for support after downing one too many. He's a big man with an even bigger appetite. But many pubs will no longer serve him a beer, and those that do often smash his used glass so it will not taint the lips of other drinkers.

Why, he still burns with the memory of that night not so many years ago when the Sheriff, Mr Charles Cowper, invited Bob into his home to help his wife prepare a dinner party. Bob had never been one to turn down an opportunity to earn a few more quid. He took on the role with his usual gusto and enthusiasm. He polished the silverware. Helped the cooks in the kitchen. Made sure the place was spotless. But when the guests learned the executioner's death-stained fingerprints were all over their cutlery, they rose together and angrily demanded he be removed. An embarrassed Mr Cowper was forced to ask him to leave.

A man needed a thick skin to persist in such a vocation. No point becoming bitter whenever you walked into a room and all conversation stopped, or good folk saw you coming down the street and quickly crossed to the other side.

Who could blame them? They all read the newspapers, which had been hurling insults Bob's way for years. But few, surely, had been as cruel as those that appeared in print just a few months earlier when

Bob presided over the hanging of a young man in a small country town.

Journalists are a bloodthirsty mob eager to entertain their audiences with the most grotesque details of a man swinging from a rope. But being the good bloodhounds they are, they have caught a whiff of change in public sentiment and are campaigning fiercely. Whipped into a frenzy of righteous indignation by preachers and other do-gooders, polite society has now determined that capital punishment for anything less than murder is a crime before God, the act of an uncivilised nation.

In Sydney, thousands had taken to the streets, walking solemnly in time to the beat of Handel's 'Dead March' on muffled drums. They had signed petitions and gathered in growing fury to oppose the impending execution of Alfred, an Aboriginal man convicted on flimsy evidence of the rape of a 60-year-old woman. While the crowds prayed and lit candles and called on the Governor of New South Wales to show compassion, Bob had taken a train and then a Cobb & Co coach to Mudgee to carry out the government's orders and oversee the hasty erection of the gallows.

He arrived to discover a town on edge. The governor of the local gaol was racked by guilt over the impending hanging and was drowning his self-loathing in whiskey. The local carpenters had no experience putting together a scaffold and Bob had to pay attention to every little detail, overseeing the placement of every beam and nail. Sandbags weighing roughly the same as Alfred had to be stitched together so the execution could be rehearsed and the drop for the body accurately measured.

A reporter for one newspaper opposing the hanging stole the rope that Bob's assistant had brought from Sydney. A new one had to be quickly found, stretched and soaped.

On a bitterly cold morning just after nine o'clock, Bob and his assistant had escorted Alfred to the gallows. Despite all the obstacles and setbacks, the hanging went smoothly. Alfred, baptised hastily overnight as a Christian, had been dispatched to his new

God with a minimum of fuss. Bob could once again take pride in his work.

But back in Sydney there was no respite from the attacks on his character. One newspaper gave its readers a long and brutal assessment of the execution. 'The wretched blackfellow was borne along between the frowsy executioners, who gripped his arms as though they liked their work of blood,' it reported.

Frowsy? Many readers would have had to put down their evening shandy and reach for their dictionary to discover that Bob and his assistant looked scruffy and unkempt, sloppy and dishevelled, badly dressed and dowdy . . .

And then came this: 'The hangman, 6ft. 2in. in height, broad shouldered, spider-legged, with arms like a gorilla, a flat face without a nose, and huge feet, presented a spectacle to be seen nowhere else out of Hades.'

There it was. Again. That flat face *without a nose*. The reporters never missed an opportunity to highlight his ruined features. 'Our hangman is a ghoul,' began a typical report. 'He is known as "Nosey Bob", a soubriquet earned through a disfigurement of his face. He was kicked by a horse and his nose so badly smashed as to almost obliterate all semblance of even a snout.'

Nosey Bob. The man with a gaping hole in his face. The accident had occurred years earlier, back when he was a coachman, ferrying the well-off around the streets of Sydney. He'd been a good-looking man back then, a tall, strapping fellow who could secure a second glance from even the most chaste of women. Well known, too. When the Duke of Edinburgh, Prince Alfred, had toured the colonies in the 1860s, Robert Howard had been his preferred Sydney guide, steering his royal highness through Sydney's darkened streets and toward its best brothels.

But one kick from that damn horse. It had changed everything.

Songs and poems had been crafted and dedicated to Nosey Bob. One had been published to much acclaim in one of the newspapers about his journey to Mudgee for Alfred's hanging:

The river gleams like a crystal floor
Where the track meanders beside its shore,
And, reflected upon its mirrory bed,
Goes the shade of the hangman's noseless head.

People would laugh, children would stare and all would sneer whenever he left his cottage and made his way to work at Darlinghurst Gaol. The injury had cost him his job as a coachman, because few of his regular clientele felt comfortable with a noseless driver holding the reins. He had doused his bitterness in grog for a while until the job of hangman was offered to him. It was a profession few others wanted to pursue. Everyone knew it had sent a previous incumbent tumbling toward insanity and life in an asylum.

Worse, some thought Bob's position as executioner, coupled with the constant taunts about his mutilated face, had brought about the premature death of his wife. Jane Howard had been 42 when she died. She had been the only person in his life who had stood by him, who understood him, who saw the gentle man behind the ugliness, who unquestioningly loved him and had given him three beautiful daughters and two sons.

Without Jane, who passed away two years ago, his life has become so much bleaker. And so he has retreated as much as he can from public view, hiding out in his tidy cottage in Sydney's east, caring for his children and worrying about that rope.

The executioner continues pacing the floor. Tendrils of pipe smoke curl upward, past that noseless face. A beer would be good to settle the nerves and wet the lips. Working with death can dry out a man. His guts might heave when an execution nears and those stares from passers-by might become more intense. But Bob's outer skin is now a hardened shield protecting him from all the bile and disgust flung his way. He will need it more than ever in these next few months. One of his cherished daughters will pass away. Death surrounds him. There is no end to it.

The only way to cope is to stare it down. To intimidate it. So he plays up to his reputation for eccentricity. If the newspapers want to cast him as an unflinching ghoul, a macabre figure with a gruesome appetite for death, then he will give them what they want.

'Prisoners are treated too kindly and kept too long,' he will tell one reporter. 'They get flabby. The muscles of the neck soften, and the neck gets as tender as a chicken. No man should be kept longer than a week or a fortnight if you want good work and a first-class execution.'

This is the Nosey Bob they expect, the man whose mission in life is to snuff out the light in other men's eyes with a well-greased rope and an oiled trapdoor ready to send them plummeting directly to hell.

He will not give them the man Jane knew – plain old Bob, the tender and devoted husband and father, the man who took on a job no-one else wanted because he had to provide for his family, the man who arrived home one Saturday night, face flushed with embarrassment and shame after being forced to leave the Sheriff's home by the back door, all because his fingers had touched the damn silverware . . .

No. They will never know the real Bob. No subtleties, no half-measures. Soon he will leave the city and move to a small cottage out near a sandy cliff at North Bondi. Visitors will find sets of shark jaws in his front yard, bleached by the sun and scattered on a soft bed of pine needles shed by two overhanging trees. Bob likes fishing. But he is not one for intricate lures. Not for him the delicate patience required to catch cautious snapper or skittish whiting. He will prefer one large barb forced through a chunk of fresh meat and hurled into the ocean. Then he will wait for the line to go tight and wade into the sea, pulling in the hooked shark until it is so close he can tie a rope around its tail and drag it on to the sand. 'When I hook a particularly big chap,' he will recall years later, '. . . a fellow that is too big for me single-handed, I make fast the line and get the old horse to pull him out.'

Quite often there will be a sound outside that cottage on the hill, a snort in the growing darkness. He will know it well. That old horse will pull up at the front gate and wait patiently for its master. They won't see Nosey Bob very often at his local pub, the Cliff House

Hotel down in Campbell Parade. Best to avoid the stares and insults and occasional invitations to fight. Instead, he will train the horse to walk down to the pub with a tin can strapped to its side and the right amount of coin in a satchel. The publican will fill the can with beer and the horse will amble home slowly, no sway in its hindquarters, just the way Bob likes it.

The executioner will then wander outside, collect his pail of beer – not a drop spilled, either – and go back inside to slake his thirst and think about all the things that can go wrong with a simple length of hessian rope.

Just like tonight. The clock ticks. Thomas Gainsborough's 'Blue Boy' stares at him from one of the walls, unblinking, all-knowing. Tomorrow the whole town will be waiting and watching. It will be a rare day, a moment to savour and perhaps even cherish. For once the entire city will be behind him.

On this mild evening in Sydney there are no passionate demonstrations in the streets, no candlelight vigils outside the Governor's residence, no powerful editorials in the newspapers berating the government for sending another man to the gallows at the hands of a noseless, frowsy executioner. A handful of preachers might be muttering from their pulpits about the brutality of condemning a man to death, but surely that is for appearances only.

No, this time the whole town is baying for blood and praying that Nosey Bob gets the job done. They want this bloody era of outlaws to end. They want the deep, dirty convict stain that has blemished the colonies of Australia for a century to be scrubbed clean.

Most of all, they want to know that Captain Moonlite has been hanged by the neck until he is dead.

—

Come now. Let us gaze upon this other man who has loved and been loved, a man who only two months ago wept like a child as he held his dying lover in his arms, a man now more reviled and shunned than Nosey Bob.

On this Monday evening, a half-moon hanging in the sky, Andrew George Scott is alone in his cell in Darlinghurst Gaol. A candle burns in the corner. His face, once handsome and filled with a lustrous black beard, is hollowed and flecked with several days' growth. The pits of his blue eyes, which once burned so fiercely, are now just soft embers. He is tired – he has barely slept in recent days – and fatigue has increased his agitation.

There is still so much to do. So much to say. So many letters to write. So many farewells to make. His final visitor left a while ago and now his world, which was once so large and filled with such endless possibilities, has been reduced to walls of cold brick and an iron door.

Scott turned 35 just over a week ago and in the morning he is due to die. On his father's birthday, too. But it is not so much the timing, or even the prospect of a premature death, that gnaws at his insides and forces his jaw to clench. It is the manner, the style of his execution, that disturbs and upsets him. Where is the dignity in his life ending on the gallows, arms pinioned, a cloth sack over his head, just to spare all those spectators the gruesome sight of his eyeballs bulging and his tongue hanging as the rope does its work?

Why couldn't they simply use a bullet? His heart is already broken beyond repair. Just a small piece of lead shot straight through it would at least allow him to die with some semblance of honour.

Honour.

It's a word Andrew George Scott uses often. He clings to it like a capsized sailor clutching driftwood because it is all he has left. His *honour*. His *dignity*. It was not the bullet from *his* gun that had killed the policeman during that bloody siege and shootout a couple of months before. He thought he knew who had fired the fatal shot. But honourable men who had been raised to believe in the ideals of gallantry did not stand before a belligerent judge and a hostile courtroom and identify a friend as a murderer. So he had refused to reveal the truth.

Not that it really mattered. They were always going to hang him. What else could they do?

The whole town – and if you believed the newspapers, the entire bloody country – has been calling for his head. He had seen the hatred and spite in their eyes as the train carrying him to Sydney for his trial stopped at all those small bush towns. They had pushed and shoved and crowded their way on to the small platforms throughout that dark night, red faced and sweating in the early summer heat, trying to catch a glimpse of the man they called Captain Moonlite. One of the last of the bushrangers. Ruthless killer of a brave policeman. Slayer of a courageous officer who had been father to a young boy and husband to a devoted wife.

He knew then that it could end only one way. They would hastily put together a sham trial to show justice had been done. The jury would include a madman who could barely comprehend English. They would appoint a bellicose judge with a strong connection to the Wantabadgery Station where one of the gunfights with the police took place. They – the politicians and the corrupt police – would make sure the verdict was never in doubt.

He goes to his death an innocent man with his honour intact. Another member of the Moonlite gang, Tom Rogan, will also swing alongside him. Didn't that tell you everything you needed to know about the farce this whole affair had become?

Poor old Rogan. He hadn't fired a single shot in anger. In fact, he'd had no idea how to use a gun and had spent 24 hours during and after the siege hiding beneath a bed, crying and praying to his Catholic God.

Scott had joined others in pleading for Rogan's life, hoping they might commute the death sentence as they did for two younger members of the gang – Graham Bennett and Thomas Williams.

But the government is determined. It is time to end the era of bushrangers. Ned Kelly and his gang might still be at large in Victoria, constantly embarrassing and humiliating the authorities, but the colony of New South Wales will set an example the rest will be forced to follow. For too long these outlaws have roamed outlying areas, raiding farms, murdering innocent people and, quite incredibly, earning fame and even admiration among the lower classes. Surely the nation is old enough to shrug off its convict past and all the lawlessness that went with it. A message must be sent.

So Scott had reluctantly given up the battle to save Rogan's life and instead turned to fight another cause from inside his cell. He wants it known that it was only his closest friend, the man he loved like no other – his soulmate who died in his arms with blood spilling from his temple from a policeman's bullet – who had stayed his hand and prevented him from taking the lives of half a dozen officers.

Scott had met James Nesbitt in Melbourne's notorious Pentridge prison when the legend of Captain Moonlite was already growing and he was serving time for one of the most audacious bank robberies Australia had seen. From the start he had loved the man. To others it seemed Nesbitt was like so many other young and broken men prone to falling under Scott's charismatic spell. Nesbitt came from a home where neighbours cringed every time they heard screams, a sure sign the old man had embarked on one of his regular drunken, wife-bashing sprees. The son had become a petty thief because life offered little else.

But there was something more to young Jim, something Scott believed only he could sense. A deep-seated decency. An innate desire to do the right thing. With his jug ears and full lips and honest stare, Jim Nesbitt knew how to calm and placate the man he always called George. If Scott was an unbroken stallion, wild and untamed and with more than a glint of madness in his eyes, Nesbitt was the patient, softly whispering horse-breaker.

During the final gun battle, during those awful minutes as bullets flew and men screamed and the air filled with the acrid stench of gunpowder, it had been Jim who told Scott to stop firing at the police. He had placed his hands on Scott's shoulders and drawn him gently toward him. And then he had looked his friend in the eye and pleaded with him. Enough was enough. This madness had to end.

'George, for my sake, shed no more blood,' Nesbitt had told him. 'Promise me not to.'

Scott, his Irish blood coursing through him so hard he could almost hear it, his ego urging him to go outside and take on the entire force, had stopped and listened and obeyed.

And then a bullet had splintered a nearby window and pierced Jim's temple.

So for weeks, and even during these last few hours left to him inside this cell, Scott has been furiously writing. There are pages everywhere: statements protesting his innocence, courtesy notes thanking those who have helped him, and letters – so many letters – telling the world about the man he loved and lost, and with whom he will so soon be reunited.

The hour grows late. Every so often a guard passes by and looks in, only to find Scott still hunched over a piece of paper, doing his best to keep his handwriting legible despite the soreness in his hand and the exhaustion sapping his strength.

Here is one letter he has just finished to an old friend in Victoria: 'I had a few friends who were kind (you were one). I had one friend, my own dearest Jim (James P. Nesbitt). He comforted me and supported me in sickness and sorrow. We were friends for years and never one feeling of unkindness ever was in one of our minds to the other. We were one in heart and soul. He died in my arms and I long to join him where there shall be no more parting, no more injustice.'

Another letter to another old friend: 'My dearest Jim in his death showed the noble charity of his nature. He kept me from shedding blood and shed no blood himself. When he died my heart was crushed. I never found a better friend, or a truer man. My fondest hope is to be with him in eternity and that I may share his grave.'

And another: 'Nesbitt was educated by the order of Christian Brothers and his life was influenced by his early training . . . At his death he did credit to it. This spirit, which for a while slumbered, shone forth at his death with renewed power and brilliancy; that spirit which saved the police, saved me from being a murderer, cost his life and robbed me of the best friend [who] ever lived.'

Scott will go on like this long into the night, his words becoming more hunched and slanted, weaving almost drunkenly across the page, the ink smudging as the hours tick by and his time runs out.

But he worries less about tomorrow than he does about the years to come. There are legacies to be forged on this night, opportunities to ensure history does not just remember Captain Moonlite and his gang as outlaws and villains, but as men who had also been wronged, who had been forced by necessity to take extreme measures. For George Scott, it is also a chance to correct all the slanderous lies that have done the rounds about his life.

A chance to maintain a semblance of *honour*.

But there is one letter that will stand out. Back in November when the siege near Wantabadgery Station had finally reached its horrible conclusion, the police found Scott slumped over Jim Nesbitt's body, crying and kissing the young man's slack, blood-smeared face, as though his breath and grief might somehow conspire to bring him back to life.

When they finally hauled Scott to his feet, handcuffed him and led him away, Scott took with him a lock of Nesbitt's hair. In the years to come, as legend and myth and fact all merged into one, it would be said that Captain Moonlite went to the gallows with that lock of hair forming a ring on the wedding finger of his left hand.

But Scott is now prepared to surrender the last physical reminder he has of James Nesbitt. He no longer has any need to cling to the hair because soon he is going to join the man he loved like no other. He will have all of him, again.

So Scott takes up his fountain pen, dips it into what is left in the inkwell, and writes to Jim Nesbitt's mother on one of the last sheets of blue prison paper he has been given. She is a woman who has known more pain than most. The only peace she seems to enjoy these days are the weeks and occasional months when her vicious husband is sent away for one of his regular stints in prison.

'My dearest Mrs Nesbitt,' writes Scott. 'To the Mother of Jim, no colder address would be true. My heart to you is the same as to my own dearest Mother. Jim's sisters are my sisters, his friends my friends, his hopes were my hopes, his grave will be my resting place and I trust I may be worthy to be with him where we shall all meet to part no more, when an all-seeing God who can read all hearts will be the Judge. When intentions will be known and judged of.

'As to my dearest Jim I have felt that the love and friendship – true, pure, real friendship that blessed our union – demands that I should defend his name to the last. My efforts are but weak, yet in time it will be known that he was an honour to all connected with him.'

Scott pauses and reaches into his prodigious memory, searching for better words that might tell Mrs Nesbitt just how strongly he felt for her son. He has always loved poetry. Others have always marvelled at his ability to summon passages from even obscure works. Raised in a small town in Northern Ireland by a well-off family that lived in a manor, nothing had been spared when it came to young Scott's education. He had devoured all the classics and immersed himself in the poets of the Romantic Age, startled at how their words and rhythms could touch and move a person's soul.

Now he recalls a verse from 'The Lady of Provence', an elegiac lament by the English poet Felicia Hemans about a lost lover. He begins writing again.

'I have won thy fame from the breath of wrong;
My soul hath risen for thy glory strong;
Now call me hence by thy side to be;
The world thou leav'st has no place for me.
Give me my home on thy noble heart.
Well have we loved – let us both depart.'

'These lines speak from and to my heart,' Scott explains. 'I know that before long his memory will be blessed, and his bright example pointed to. I will not be long before I am with him and in his grave. Mrs Nesbitt, mother of my Jim, may the great God enable you to bear the great loss you have suffered.'

Before he signs off, Scott takes the lock of Nesbitt's hair and places it on the page. 'I send you some of his hair and will try to send you anything else I can get . . . farewell my dearest Mrs Nesbitt. I am ever to you a loving son in spirit. A. G. Scott.'

And with that, the long work of the man they call Captain Moonlite is all but over. Soon the sun will rise. Come now, let us leave him to rest, to lie on his hammock, to say his prayers to a God he is no longer sure exists, to remember the good times, and hope, like everyone else, that Nosey Bob has paid attention to all the little details.

Robert Rice Howard, a man who also remembers what it was to love and be loved, to hold and be held, has an important job ahead.

He must carry out the orders of the court and the government and obey the wishes of the people.

But most of all, Andrew George Scott is counting on Nosey Bob to send him back to the loving arms of James Nesbitt.

2

THIS SHRINKING WORLD

Open your eyes. Use all your senses. Observe how this world George Scott will soon farewell is changing.

You can smell it wafting from the open windows of the little tenement houses. Where candles once flickered, kerosene lamps now fill the air with their acrid scent.

You can feel it where those homes give way to small tin-clad factories and passers-by are assaulted by the heat of blast furnaces, tended day and night by men stained black with oil and sweat.

You can see it on the outskirts of town in the giant steam engines, pistons screaming, ravenous iron bellies endlessly gorging on shovel loads of coal and perspiration, spewing black grey plumes into the sky to block out the sun.

And you can hear it in the voices in the saloons and taverns, full pitched and lusty, bellowing with the fervour that drink and hope does for a man. This land they call Australia, a confederation of colonies founded less than a century earlier on the sweat of convicts, is now starting to feel like a true nation.

No wonder they raise a glass to their new-found progress and sing. The verses are tinged with humour and optimism – and more than a little honesty.

We are all moral men – we repeat that again –
For we're always at church on the Sunday,
Impressed with the notion that outward devotion
Will cloak all our misdeeds in one day.

There's a raucous note to the songs, an everyday pragmatism that carries echoes of hope. These past two decades have seen wool replace gold and bust replace boom. Some have risen from obscurity to wealth and power and more have been broken and left to struggle. But they all sense there is more to come, that this world will continue to sweep them forward.

In the outback, where clumps of spinifex and shrubs of sandalwood cling to the thin red dust, thousands of telegraph poles stand like crucifixes on the Appian Way, wires pulsing in a language of electrical dots and dashes, bringing news from around the world. It won't be long before they carry reports that sound like feats of magic and alchemy; of men transmitting their voices using electricity and of glowing lamps that require no gas or oil. Soon will come news that in a small sheet-metal factory in Mannheim, funded by the dowry of his new wife, a young German with a fashionably drooping moustache, Karl Benz, is tinkering with a small two-stroke engine that will power the world's first automobile.

Years later they will call it the Second Industrial Revolution, an era that will make the planet glow at night and tremble with the shock of huge bombs and artillery. It will turn a quiet world into a place of endless rumble and clatter. It will shrink it, too. Even a vast continent like Australia, an ancient land of empty spaces and overwhelming silence, is not immune.

Information, once supplied by the bush telegraph with its system of whispers and exaggerated rumours and tired men on exhausted horses, now moves with astonishing speed and far greater accuracy.

The Age of Exploration is almost over. Enormity has been diminished; the infinite reduced to something imaginable. Places to hide are becoming fewer. The fringes and isolated pockets of the bush now offer the only refuge to those who cling to the past.

Who would have thought that bushrangers – those outlaws of Australia who have spent decades roaming and terrorising the countryside – would now be pushed into its distant edges?

—

There are so few of them left. Those that remain must sense their era is drawing to a close, that some kind of calamitous conclusion is coming for them, because their desperation has turned to recklessness.

On his last night on earth, George Scott, a man who stumbled accidentally into bushranging, seethes and bristles at his plight, frustrated by his inability to take revenge on a world that refuses to recognise his brilliance. In the heavily forested north-eastern ridges and valleys of Victoria, a gang led by Ned Kelly, the stubborn son of an Irish convict, plot and scheme their next move. They have now moved beyond their mundane beginnings stealing horses, duffing cattle and feuding with the rich squatters. Their long-running enmity with the local police – the much-loathed *traps* – has now exploded into a series of violent ambushes. They have murdered three policemen but not even this outrage has prevented the Kellys from becoming shrouded in myth and lionised as heroes.

This has always been the story of Australia's bushrangers. For more than two generations petty thieves, escaped convicts and castoffs of society have been taking to the bush, often on horseback. On the run in an often grim and unforgiving landscape, they live off what they can scrounge and steal, and re-emerge to find they have been transformed into legends.

The newspapers have been busily burnishing their stories, breathlessly detailing their exploits for years. They have taken the high moral ground, of course, complaining about these outbreaks of lawlessness and the often comical inability of the authorities to end their outrages. But their reports have still been tinged with the same breathless prose normally used to regale readers about stage actresses eloping with their leading men.

The trial of Captain Moonlite and his gang for the murder of a police officer transfixed the country and consumed endless pages of newsprint. At its height, a letter to the editor of a top-selling Sydney publication puzzled over the attraction outlaws still held for the public.

'Sirs,' said the writer, 'Will you do your best to stop the issue of these reports about the Moonlite gang? I am a quiet family man with three grown-up daughters . . . Anastacia is an excellent girl and very accomplished, and I am able to make a handsome provision for my children. But I enjoy my morning paper and, of course, wish to post myself up in the news before going to town.

'Since the reports of the Moonlite trial have appeared, I never get a read at the paper at all. Anastacia . . . seizes the paper directly it arrives, and she and her sisters read the report of the trial of these bushrangers right through, so that I have no chance of more than a sight at the paper.

'I don't want to disturb the amusement of my daughters; but, as I find other people similarly situated, I do wish you would interfere. There is a fascination about this kind of reading which we do not understand.'

But this fascination, this almost daily obsession with their lawlessness, is entirely understandable. The white people of Australia have no myths, no legends handed down to them by previous generations. They have no Beowulf or King Arthur striding through time's mist wielding a sword and shield, no demi-gods like Achilles with superhuman strength and a rage that could split armies. It is far too early for that. This is a nation so starved of heroic figures that a man on horseback who has not changed his clothes or bathed for months, who has held communities at gunpoint and stolen the savings of innocent travellers, suddenly finds himself hailed as a champion of the people.

Not all the people, of course. Polite society regards them with abhorrence and disdain. But few are not curious about this breed of outlaw. Even in these times, with their dominance waning and their world contracting, the last remaining bushrangers are celebrities.

Moonlite has fascinated them because he is so different. No other criminal in the country boasts such an educated pedigree as George Scott. No other outlaw is as articulate and artful when speaking in public. One moment he might refer to ancient Egyptian irrigation techniques and the science of hydrolysis, the next he is quoting the classics and expounding on the latest theories of light and matter. One morning he might be mounted on a stallion, soaring over fences, pistol tucked in his belt. That night he might be striding to a public podium, turned out in the finest of suits with a handkerchief folded in his top pocket, his skin scented, hair oiled and combed perfectly into place.

All the other notorious criminal figures of this era are so much easier to define. To them, the world that moulded Captain Moonlite is almost unknowable. Men like Ned Kelly, Mad Dog Morgan, Captain Thunderbolt and the desperate Clarke brothers were pulled from their mothers' wombs in dirt floor shacks and had a distaste for authority passed to them with the first drop from the nipple. Some have barely known how to scratch their name. Their universes have been small and bound by the limits of their horses and their own stifled imaginations. If they loathed polite society and the growing sophistication of city life, they were also intimidated by it.

Scott, though, is a conundrum. He has waltzed with the rich and powerful at crowded Saturday night dance halls and been capable of charming the prettiest girl in the room and convincing her father he is genuine marriage material. But he has also strolled the prison yard and mingled with those from the dirt shacks and inner-city tenements; young men like James Nesbitt, scarred from watching their mothers being beaten by fathers who in turn had been beaten by life.

Another paradox. Like so many bushrangers, Scott is Irish. But he is burdened with little of the resentment and bitterness toward the English empire that drives so many of his former countrymen. They will say in future years that the bushrangers and the Irish helped forge the national character. 'The distinctive Australian identity was not born in the bush, nor at Anzac Cove,' will write one historian. 'It was born in Irishness protesting against the extremes of Englishness.'

But Scott's rage and frustration is reserved for something much larger, something even he struggles to comprehend.

He needs to be recognised, to be respected, to be loved. He is, truly, a man from another world.

3

THE HUNGER AND
THE MADNESS

Ireland, 1845

These rolling green pastures. Those endless granite mountains. That cold blue-grey sky. This world has been rich and lush for centuries, steeped in fables, watered with blood and fertilised with the bones of believers and heretics, soldiers and civilians.

It has become nothing more than a mass grave for the guilty and innocent. But it is never enough.

This little patch of earth they call Ireland, the spiritual home for so many Australian bushrangers, is always hungry for more bodies. Now it is tired and worn and demanding to be fed again. It won't have to wait long. A poison is working its way through the soil, unseen and unfelt. Soon, it will produce a ruinous crop of such utter misery and hopelessness it will change the Irish character forever.

All the old gods and giants, even powerful Crom Dubh, the dark stooped one who brought the first people to Ireland, are long gone. No use turning to the new God, either. He may be an all-knowing, all-seeing deity, but even He will be forced to look away when more than a million of His starving flock stuff dirt and grass and tree bark into their mouths, a final desperate meal before their hollowed bodies are sent deep into the mud.

The pestilence is coming, a fungus-like microorganism they will one day call *phytophthora infestans*. It will infect everything it touches. It will turn the Lumper potato – the only food source for so many of the poor – into a putrid black mush reeking of rot. It will transform the bucolic countryside into fields of disease and despair. And it will force another two million Irish, already ground down by their landed English masters, to turn their backs on their homeland and seek out new worlds.

The Great Famine is beginning and the only supernatural being in Irish lore who will show any interest in its pain and suffering will be the Dullahan. Those who cling to the old tongue call him *Gan Ceaan*, the headless harbinger of death. He drives a black horse, urging it forward with a whip made from a human spine while sitting hunched atop a wagon filled with skulls and candles and the souls of the dead. If the Dullahan pulls his horse to a stop outside a house, someone inside is about to die. Gold – even the smallest amount – is the only way to keep him at bay, for the Dullahan is terrified of the precious metal. But he has little to fear in these parts, apart from being overworked, for most of these villagers and small farmers boast nothing of value.

'It would be impossible adequately to describe the privations which they habitually and silently endure,' writes William Courtenay about the Irish poor. 'In many districts their only food is the potato, their only beverage water . . . their cabins are seldom a protection against the weather . . . a bed or a blanket is a rare luxury . . . their pig and a manure heap constitute their only property.'

Courtenay, the 10th Earl of Devon, has just spent the past two years conducting a royal commission for the British government into Irish land leases. In other words, he has been examining the almost feudal system of English landowners squeezing their poor tenants with excessive rents on small plots of land that have been farmed to exhaustion.

It is a key reason why Ireland is now so vulnerable to famine. The Lumper might pass for a small rock, its light brown skin pocked and knobby and straining to contain the thick yellow flesh within. But it also flourishes in poor, overworked soil and can feed many mouths. The Irish population has been soaring in recent years and the gentry have been reaping the benefits while sowing the seeds of a calamity: sub-dividing their land into smaller and smaller plots where the poor can barely produce even enough of the Lumper to survive.

Once disease strikes – within a year 90 per cent of the potato crop will be lost – there will often be no other food for the wretched. Because their God above refuses to answer their prayers, they will turn to what lies beneath their feet. Some of the dead will be buried with green mouths frozen in a rigid grimace, their guts still filled with undigested grass.

Men like Courtenay may sympathise with their plight, but many others see it as an act of retribution by God. Consider Sir Charles Trevelyan, the bureaucrat responsible for overseeing famine relief. The potato blight, he believes, is 'the judgement of God . . . [an] effective mechanism for reducing surplus population. The real evil with which we have to contend is not the physical evil of the Famine, but the moral evil of the selfish, perverse and turbulent character of the people.'

It has been like this for centuries, long before the Irish refused to surrender their allegiance to Catholicism. At their closest point the two islands are separated by just 12 miles. But a yawning gulf of derision and suspicion has long divided England and Ireland. A young Benjamin Disraeli, the conservative British politician who will serve two stints as prime minister, thinks the Irish 'hate our order, our civilisation, our enterprising industry, our pure religion. This wild, reckless, indolent, uncertain and superstitious race have no sympathy with the English character. Their ideal of human felicity is an alternation of clannish broils and coarse idolatry. Their history describes an unbroken circle of bigotry and blood.'

In turn, Irish hate for the English has become ingrained. Secret societies of Irish labourers and farmers have flourished for years. They are often known as White Boys because of the smocks they wear in night raids where they level fences and hamstring cattle in retaliation against oppressive landowners.

Some go by the sobriquet of 'Captain Moonlite', others as 'Captain Rock' and 'Captain Right'. Many have been caught and transported to colonies like Australia. But the pestilence will weaken their strength and resolution, too. By 1847 the horror will increase with a series of mass evictions across the country when thousands of the poor are unable to pay their rent. One landlord in County Mayo, Lord Bingham, will be dubbed 'The Exterminator'. He commands more than 60,000 acres and, faced with rising rate costs because his tenants can no longer pay, will turn his kingdom into grazing lands by expelling 2000 people from the parish of Ballinrobe and demolishing more than 300 of their homes. Within a few years he will be promoted to a major-general in the English army.

Few will capture The Exterminator's inhumanity better than the Catholic Bishop of Meath, Thomas Nulty. 'Seven hundred human beings were driven from their homes in one day and set adrift on the world,' he will write. 'The horrid scenes I then witnessed, I must remember all my life long.

'The wailing of women – the screams, the consternation of children – the speechless agony of honest industrious men – wrung tears of grief from all who saw them. I saw officers and men of a large police force, who were obliged to attend on the occasion, cry like children at beholding the cruel sufferings of the very people whom they would be obliged to butcher had they offered the least resistance.'

The Irish will bury their dead and never forgive. They will carry their grudges across the world, to places like Australia, where they will continue to simmer.

'The Almighty, indeed, sent the potato blight, but the English created the famine,' John Mitchel, an Irish nationalist, will write. Mitchel will soon find himself in Van Diemen's Land after being transported for 14 years for his seditious and treasonous criticisms of English policy in Ireland. It will be a long journey from the small northern Irish town of Newry where he was raised. There must be something else apart from misery and distress lying in wait in the dirt of this region, for it also produces more than its share of malcontents and rebels.

Just 10 miles to the north-east of Newry in County Down sits the hilltop village of Rathfriland. Set amid all those rolling green pastures and with those endless Mourne Mountains in the distance, it will become the first home of Andrew George Scott.

He enters this world on the eighth of January 1845, just as the spores of *phytophthora infestans* begin their work in the dank and dark earth of Ireland.

It is an appropriate beginning because for much of his life George Scott will find himself out of step with the world around him. When the despair of the Great Famine settles across much of the land of his birth, he will enjoy a childhood protected by wealth and privilege.

—

Poison in the soil. A hint of madness in the blood. The Scotts of Rathfriland might know little of poverty and hardship as the blight takes hold, but there is a darkness that stains the family, a shadow that creeps just beneath the surface of one of the most eminent households in the district. The locals whisper that the Scotts have 'a wild drop in their blood'.

It is nowhere to be found in the father, Thomas, who is a justice of the peace and soon to become Seneschal of the Manor – a powerful local position where he will sit in judgement on local criminal and financial disputes.

But Thomas' brother is said to be far less stable, well known for having hurled a pile of dried peat at a stagecoach driver who was about to announce his arrival in town by blowing his bugle. The assault never made it to the courts and assumptions will be made – as they always are in a village of just a few hundred people – that a little of the Scott wealth changed hands to keep the matter quiet.

Thomas and his wife Bessie are good Protestants, God-fearing people who take their two boys, Thomas and the younger Andrew, to church each week and provide the best education available in the district. They live in a large house on the crown of a steep hill that was once a mediaeval fortress, aptly looking down on the world below. The view takes in the ever-present plots of potatoes but also includes large fields of cereal – one reason why Rathfriland will be spared the worst of the famine. When it does strike, the local market house will be turned into a soup kitchen and Thomas and Bessie will help organise many of the local charity drives.

Just a few miles to the south lie the mountains – a dozen giant granite peaks bearing names like Slieve Donard, Pigeon Rock and Buzzard's Roost. They are sprinkled with heather and gorse and pale butterwort, and are home to large hares and red squirrels. Peregrine falcons and ravens soar above, watching the ghosts of old chieftains and Celtic heroes said to haunt the open grasslands and small lakes. When the light is soft and the sun is setting, it becomes a place laced with magical possibilities that will inspire songs and poems. In a little over a century, the writer C. S. Lewis will be inspired by them to create the realm of Narnia in a series of hugely popular novels, recalling that: 'I have seen landscapes which, under a particular light, made me feel that at any moment a giant might raise his head over the next ridge.'

Perhaps it is the region's capacity to stimulate such flights of imagination that conspire to create so many of the wild stories about Captain Moonlite's early years. They will be numerous – most of them undocumented and far-fetched, some quite possibly invented by Scott himself. One tale will see him taking up arms as a teenager under Giuseppe Garibaldi, the general whose campaigns throughout the mainland and Sicily help unify Italy. Another will have him fighting in the American Civil War and joining the Californian gold rush. One historian will display a clear disregard for mathematics and logic by claiming Scott leaves Rathfriland for London in 1856. There, he will begin training as a civil engineer, rub shoulders with the rich and famous and embark on a raucous affair with the wife of a well-known merchant. The 19th century is certainly an era when boys are thrust into adulthood at an early age, but it's unlikely even the silver-tongued Andrew George Scott could pull off such feats at the age of 11.

He does, however, have a capacity when young for finding trouble. He is said to be close friends with two orphaned boys taken in by their uncle – Rathfriland's main physician, Dr McClelland. Scott is a frequent visitor to their home and the doctor will often be heard declaring: 'That boy ought to be given a latch key – he is here every blessed day.'

One evening the young Scott is 'interfering' with one of the gas lamps that serve as streetlights in the town. The worker responsible for their care catches him in the act and gives Scott 'a sound spanking'. That wild drop of blood simmers, along with thoughts of revenge.

Scott has seen a pair of old flint-lock duelling pistols in Dr McClelland's home and asks if he would be allowed to polish them for the physician. When the doctor agrees, Scott takes them away, loading one with a charge of powder and a lead bullet. He then lies in wait for the gas man's return and, after watching him mount a ladder, walks up and fires the gun, striking the man in the buttocks.

What is said to follow highlights the gap between the rich and poor in rural Ireland. The son of a potato farmer would have been whipped and his parents fined. The young Scott is no doubt reprimanded. But the gas man is paid compensation, Dr McClelland treats the injury and the affair is quietly dispensed with.

—

Insulated from the famine and protected by wealth and privilege, Scott is only four years old in 1849 when Ireland's other ancient curse – sectarian violence – touches his family. A Catholic-Protestant divide has existed since Henry VIII's reformation in the 1500s and ever since the last Catholic rebellions were put down in the 17th century, families like the Scotts have been arriving from Scotland and England and turning Northern Ireland into a Protestant stronghold.

Each year on 12 July the local Orangemen – a Protestant order sworn to uphold their domination of Ireland's political, economic and social systems – stage a march to commemorate the victory of King William III's army over the Catholic forces of James II in the Battle of the Boyne in 1690.

In 1848 local County Down magistrates, including Thomas Scott, had persuaded them to stay away from Catholic areas amid rising tensions exacerbated by the famine. But a year later, taunted as cowards by local Ribbonmen – a movement of poor Catholics similar to the White Boys – the Orangemen are determined to stage their parade along the traditional route that will lead them through a tight pass several miles north of Rathfriland known as Dolly's Brae.

Thomas Scott will later tell a formal British government inquiry that he had travelled to Dublin in the weeks before the march to warn officials about his fears of a possible violent altercation between the Orangemen and the Ribbonmen and to ask for police reinforcements. He will say he had 'apprehensions . . . that serious work' would take place during the procession and had told other magistrates he feared a riot would result.

He is right. Late on the afternoon of the 12th, the Orangemen – more than 1200 strong and at least half of them armed with guns and other weapons – are on the return leg of their march when they are confronted at the Brae by hundreds of armed Ribbonmen and other local Catholics wielding scythes and pitchforks. A few shots are fired before the police charge the Catholic crowd gathered on a hill that overlooks the pass, forcing them to disperse.

It is then that Thomas Scott's worst fears are realised.

The Orangemen begin to riot, firing at their retreating enemies, vandalising their properties and setting homes on fire. Within hours government officials estimate that more than 30 Catholics lie dead, some of them pulled from their burning cottages and beaten to death. Others put the death toll as high as 80.

A year later the British government will ban marches, parades and even songs that 'tend to provoke animosity'. Thomas Scott will be praised for his attempts to stop the violence. But not a single Orangeman will be charged with murder.

Isn't this the real story of Ireland? All that rich folklore littered with stories of fairies and leprechauns. All those frightening tales of the Dullahan and other malevolent spirits. They are no match for reality.

Below these rolling green pastures and endless granite mountains lie nothing but broken bones and dashed hopes and a poison turning crops black. Above ground, hate, hunger and vengeance fester in their usual forms.

Little wonder it is the spiritual home of so many of Australia's bushrangers.

4

GUILTY WRETCHES AND BROKEN DREAMS

August 1861

Damn fine ship, this one. In years past they would cram hundreds of fleeing Irish into small, leaking boats and send them on to the roiling high seas with nothing but barrels of dried meat, bags of weevil-ridden flour and an endless supply of prayers. But this *Black Eagle* – the largest wooden vessel ever built on the shores of the Mersey River, a 1400-ton clipper made of oak and American hackmatack – is a vessel of speed and elegance.

Craftsmanship is on show everywhere. There's an intricately carved majestic eagle about to take flight on the prow. The stern is finished with gilt. There are state rooms and spacious, airy cabins below. No dank caverns, no musty, disease-breeding holds for this mob of free settlers. Still, the surrounds must be of little comfort for the Scotts. The ship will be their final taste of luxury and privilege. Ahead lies only uncertainty and anguish.

Hard to believe it has come to this. A decade earlier Thomas Scott had been appointed Seneschal of the Manor of Rathfriland, an exalted position that involved adjudicating on criminal and financial disputes, hosting dinners for various lords and overseeing the day-to-day routine of the manor house. But it all began falling apart in 1858 when the English government abolished positions like his across Ireland. Not long after, and no longer enjoying the income or prestige to which his family had grown accustomed, several land titles bequeathed to his wife Bessie became mired in expensive legal challenges.

It quickly became clear the Scotts had no alternative but to leave Rathfriland and grasp the first available lifeline. The colony of New Zealand, convulsed in a series of bloody conflicts with the Maori, has been offering employment and large plots of farming land to free settlers from across the empire in a bid to boost the white population and secure the future of the two islands.

A few weeks before the Scotts board the *Black Eagle*, a large gathering of the elite of Rathfriland and its surrounding towns had gathered to farewell Thomas, Bessie, their two sons and Bessie's two unmarried sisters. A silver plate and a purse of sovereigns had been given to the family, along with speeches marking the warmth with which the family was regarded.

'As an active Magistrate of this County, almost twenty years, and Seneschal of the Manor of Rathfriland ten years, your just and upright conduct has won for you our confidence and respect,' Thomas was told. 'We must also regard your departure as a private bereavement, as you have endeared yourself to all classes by your sympathy with the poor, your courtesy to your equals and your hospitable kindness to all.'

It was a sombre occasion. There was no disguising the family's reluctance to leave. 'While not concealing my own sentiments, political or religious, it has ever been my aim not to obtrude them unnecessarily,' Thomas told them. 'It has been my happiness to live on terms of amity and cordiality with my neighbours of all classes and denominations.

'I need not allude particularly to the reverses which have occasioned my emigrating. It is painful to me to see no more the familiar scenes of my native land . . . if you do thus sometimes think of us, much more shall we, in new scenes, think often of those that we have left.'

Andrew George Scott is 16 when he boards the *Black Eagle* with his family. Another passenger will regale the travellers during the journey with tales about his adventures fighting in Italy with Garibaldi – stories the young Scott possibly appropriates for himself in later years. While most of his family have never been at sea, the young Scott is familiar with ships; British records will show he was nominated for a cadetship in the Royal Navy at the age of 13 in 1858 and probably spent at least 12 months on board the HMS *Britannia* when it was commissioned as a training vessel the following year. He will tell a court hearing in Australia many years later that he also served a stint on board the HMS *Excellent*, a gunnery training vessel based near Portsmouth that instructs generations of gunners in combat and firing skills. It makes sense. Scott will be known as a keen shot who often carries a collection of guns with him.

More than a decade later a tattered Bible will be found among belongings left behind by him in Sydney. Inside will be the inscription: 'From Bessie Scott to her son, A. G. Scott, wishing that he may read, mark, learn and digest these blessed contents.' Scrawled in a bolder hand will be the line: 'H.M.S ship Britannia.'

That he has seafaring skills is not in doubt. But how did that wild drop of blood cope with the rigid discipline of cadet life under the *Britannia*'s legendary training skipper, Captain Harris? The initiation rites? The bullying? The crowded sleeping decks and the early morning long drum rolls accompanied by sharp cries of 'Turn out, sir, turn out, if you please!'?

There would have been months filled with the monotony of learning the difference between standing and running rigging and the techniques of reefing and furling. Cadets would learn how to slide down the topsail halyards, grabbing hold of two ropes running parallel a foot apart, twist them around both legs and then plummet to the deck, sometimes inflicting nasty burns on the leg.

In early 1861 – seven months before the *Black Eagle* departs the United Kingdom – the cadets and officers of the *Britannia* gathered on the poop deck for an historic photograph. The bearded officers appeared stern and uncompromising. Only a few of the cadets managed a smile. Most of them were young boys lost in oversized navy monkey jackets, staring ahead with the pale, unfilled faces of prepubescence.

—

This sleek *Black Eagle* takes only three months to make the journey to New Zealand. It will be an unremarkable crossing for the passengers, except for those unfortunate enough to witness a sailor die after falling from the foreyard arm.

But many years later the Scotts will be remembered as a tortured and disturbed family by at least one of the crew of the *Black Eagle*.

George Harrison, the ship's chief steward, will tell newspapermen feverishly trying to flesh out the details of Captain Moonlite's past, that the Scotts had shown 'in all their poverty, all the signs of good breeding'.

But . . .

'The father and two sons were all regarded as not right in the head. Moonlite, then 17 years old, showed himself to be a bright, intelligent lad but suddenly, at intervals of two or three days, he would go off, and the officers of the ship and the sailors in consequence all regarded him as "soft in the head" or as being "a shingle short".'

Harrison's comments (another passenger, Edward Allen, will remember the young Scott as 'high spirited') will come amid a frenzy of speculation in the Australian colonies about Captain Moonlite, his background and his motivations. And while competing reporters sifting through his past will treat like gold nuggets any fresh claim suiting their narrative that George Scott is inherently wicked, it will be difficult to ignore a pattern of mental illness.

There will be the time he is hauled from court after giving evidence on behalf of another prisoner, shouting and threatening gaol officials. That wild drop of blood is a potent, simmering explosive. Stress is its detonator. Seeking attention for several of his complaints, he will corner a prison governor and hold a knife to his neck. He will shoot an uncooperative horse in the head. He will stage a mock trial of a man he takes prisoner during a siege and threaten to hang him. And faced with the pressure of speaking before hundreds of people, he will lie in bed for days citing 'anxiousness' and exhaustion.

Thomas Scott is steering his family into a new life on the other side of the world and is burdened with an intelligent, charismatic and untamed younger son. The Scotts will take up a 40-acre parcel of land just north of Auckland after they arrive. But plans for a farming life are soon set aside when Thomas' background as a justice of the peace earns him the role of resident magistrate for Maungakaramea.

Finally, after several years, a little stability. Thomas quickly forges a reputation as an even-handed magistrate. He oversees plans for a new church and becomes a pillar of the local community, the sort of man the newspapers have been gushing about since the arrival of the *Black Eagle*. 'Many of her passengers have already been absorbed into our population and are regularly employed,' will note one journal. 'They appear to like the country and adapt themselves readily to their altered circumstances. The frequent arrival of immigrants is greatly to be desired because it will tend to strengthen the hand of the authorities, and lead more readily to a peaceful and speedy solution of our political difficulties.'

—

Those *difficulties*. Those *troubles*. If Britain has conquered the world's oceans and dominated its lands – one in four of the earth's inhabitants now fall under its rule – it is also the undisputed master of the euphemism. These *difficulties* with native inhabitants in countless countries have been consistently annoying hurdles on its path to becoming the greatest global power in history. It has dealt with them in its usual consistent fashion, too – feeble attempts at peace followed by blunt and often bloody force.

The Maori will give these *difficulties* another name, something a little more direct. *Te riri Pakeha*, they will call them – the white man's anger. Since the early 1840s an uneasy peace has existed between

New Zealand's colonialists and the people from the Polynesian islands who had claimed it as their own centuries earlier. Skirmishes and bloody battles have been fought. But now the settlers, torching extensive forests and planting grass seeds in the ashes, have gone too far. Government seizures of large tracts of traditional Maori land for more farmland have triggered full-scale conflict in what will become known as the New Zealand Wars. Thousands of British troops have been engaged to track resistance leaders and remove any of their undermanned opponents who refuse to take an oath of allegiance to Queen Victoria.

The most defining campaign will take place with the invasion of the Waikato and the three-day Battle of Orakau. Rewi Maniapoto, one of the leading Maori resistance leaders, will reluctantly build a *pa* – a type of fortified hill fort – in a peach grove that will lack water and can be easily surrounded. Maniapoto's worst fears are soon realised when he and 300 followers – about a third of them women – run out of food and are encircled by a 1400-strong force.

The Empire's forces demand their surrender. Maniapoto is said to have replied: '*Ka whawhai tonu ahau ki a koe*' – 'I shall fight you forever, and ever, and ever'. On the third day the Maori decide to break out of the *pa* and make a run for it. Pursued by cavalry and hundreds of foot soldiers, more than a hundred fleeing men, women and children are shot and bayoneted in some of the most gruesome atrocities of the wars.

Somewhere amid all this carnage and mayhem is a wounded 19-year-old Andrew George Scott. In February he had sought a commission in the Waikato militia and had later transferred to the Auckland Volunteer Engineer Corp. Years later he will say he reached the rank of major and that other soldiers jokingly referred to him as 'Captain Moonlite'. But right now he is in bad shape. A bullet has entered his lower right leg and will force his foot to turn in, forever leaving him with a limp. In the years to come he will also carry the scars of gunshot wounds on his other leg, his chest and a shoulder. There must be other scars, too, deep lacerations in his psyche that will never heal. During his recovery allegations of malingering will hang over him. For a man who treasures the notion of *honour*, who will go to the gallows complaining that dying at the end of a rope lacks dignity, such charges must shroud him in shame and embarrassment.

There is resentment, too. Three years later he will apply for a commission in the New Zealand armed constabulary. He writes to the defence minister telling him he hails from a respectable family and is enjoying good health. 'I would make it my constant endeavour to discharge with zeal and discretion the duties that may devolve upon me.' The letter is supported by a recommendation from almost a dozen eminent Auckland identities saying Scott is a 'gentleman well suited to an office of command'. But the minister rejects the application, telling him he has 'no hope' and does not have 'a sufficient claim' on the colony to justify such a role.

Scott is surely devastated by the reply. He knows his adopted country could do with men who are fine horsemen, know how to handle a gun and are keen to uphold the law. If New Zealand does not already have enough troubles with the Maori, it is also experiencing difficulties with a problem imported from nearby Australia.

Lured by a gold rush in Otago on the South Island, the bushrangers have arrived.

—

Richard Hill commits his first real crime at the age of eight in London's West End. A fellow pupil at his junior school is showing off by placing a sharpened pencil in his nostril. Hill uses his hand to drive the pencil so deeply into the boy's nose a doctor is called to extract it. The incident brings his education to a premature end and propels him into a world of petty theft that, by the age of 18, sees him transported to the Australian colonies.

Hill will rarely rate a mention in the annals of Australia's outlaws, despite embarking after his release on a sadistic spree of murder and robbery on the Victorian goldfields and rubbing shoulders with some of Australia's most notorious bushrangers, including Harry Power, who will soon take on a young lad named Ned Kelly as his apprentice.

Hill admits slaughtering two diggers near Ballarat. But it is a botched burglary that sends him to the Pentridge stockade and on to one of Melbourne's infamous prison hulks anchored in Port Phillip Bay. It is overseen by the merciless inspector-general of Victoria's prisons, John Price, a man so reviled for his harsh treatment of convicts that in 1857 a group of them will beat him to death with picks and shovels as he stands listening to their grievances on the side of the bay.

Hill is a violent sadist, a monster even by the standards of his time. In the early 1860s, after winning his freedom again, he leaves Melbourne and heads to Otago calling himself Richard Burgess. There, he joins with several old mates from Australia, including Thomas Kelly, a friend he had made in Pentridge years earlier. The gang prey on local miners, assaulting and robbing them before going on to murder several others – Burgess throttles one to death – in a rampage that causes outrage across New Zealand.

But it is only when they are captured and sentenced to hang that Burgess displays a less violent talent. He can write. Claiming to have found God, he begins scribbling in his cell, confessing on paper to all his crimes. There are so many admissions they end up merging into one of the most comprehensive and detailed autobiographies of a 19th-century criminal.

Life of Richard Burgess, the Notorious Highwayman and Murderer is a clinical insight into the mind and actions of one of the most violent outlaws the southern hemisphere has experienced. 'Written in my dungeon drear this 7th of August, in the year of Grace, 1866,' writes Burgess. 'To God be ascribed all power and glory in subduing the rebellious spirit of a most guilty wretch.'

The American writer Mark Twain will call it 'a remarkable paper. For brevity, succinctness and concentration, it is perhaps without its peer in the literature of murder.'

Convinced salvation awaits him, Burgess smiles as he approaches the scaffold in front of a large crowd. 'I have no more fear of death than of going to a wedding,' he says. A large smile spreads across a face dominated by a receding hairline. 'Indeed, though this is the morning of my death, I greet it as though it were my wedding morn!'

You can always rely on a bushranger for a theatrical flourish. It must be the months and sometimes years of hiding out from the authorities, often with only their horse for company. Give them an audience and they are suddenly transformed from stagecoach robbers to stage veterans. In his final moments on earth Burgess gives the performance of his life. He walks across the scaffold, stands beneath the noose and reaches his face to it and kisses it.

'I greet you as a prelude to heaven,' he says. Glorious final words. But it will be his confessions that will echo for more than a century.

—

The trial and execution of Burgess captivates New Zealand, but for the Scotts it must be of only passing interest. If a curse hung over the family in its last few years in Ireland, it has followed them to the other side of the world. Their youngest son is covered in bullet scars, walks with a limp and, despite fighting for his country against the Maori, is not regarded as good enough to serve in the constabulary.

At about the same time, Thomas Scott loses his job as a magistrate when the colonial government decides to abolish his position as part of widespread budgetary cuts. The man must feel trapped in a twilight zone where history keeps repeating. It's Rathfriland all over again. The people of Maungakaramea – including a delegation of local Maori – launch strong protests against the decision and their disappointment is taken up by the local newspapers.

'What has led to this measure on the part of the Government is, no doubt, an anxiety for stringent economy and the condition of the colonial finances,' says one. 'We are aware retrenchment is being carried out in nearly every direction, and, in some cases, we suspect with a very questionable policy.

'It is a matter of regret that a magistrate such as Mr Scott should be set aside, judging from the repeated testimonials in his favour, both since and before his coming to the colony . . . on the occasion of a critical period in Northern Ireland, in connexion with the celebrated affair at Dolly's Brae, when the animosities of so-called religious parties ran very high, Mr Scott received the special thanks of the authorities at Dublin Castle . . . we hope that the Colonial Government do not intend thus abruptly to set him aside, especially as his only demerit seems to have been that he was too successful in his exertions to keep his district as free as possible from breaches of the peace and litigation.'

Once again father and son are forced to look for new opportunities. Thomas turns to his final hope – God – and begins training as a reverend. Andrew George Scott has been studying civil engineering under Samuel Harding, one of the most prominent engineers in the colony. Harding has helped design one of the biggest infrastructure projects New Zealand has seen – the construction of the Auckland-Drury railway line – and his bright student proves to be a quick learner.

George Scott also serves as a teacher during a stint as a junior master at a newly opened private college for boys – the Collegiate School – run by Dr Robert Kidd in Karangahape Road in Auckland.

Years later, when that frenzy over the origins of Captain Moonlite is in full swing, those who were with Scott at the Collegiate School will hint at the presence of that wild drop of blood, and how money and alcohol may have brought it to the surface.

'Dr Kidd and I discussed his fate . . . and we knew that Captain Moonlite's criminal career was very brief,' will recall the Reverend John Haselden, a former student who goes on to become the Canon of Auckland Cathedral. 'The reason probably was that he had given way to drink.'

Another former student of the school will allege Scott is forced to leave the college in disgrace after borrowing money from several wealthy students and failing to repay it.

So many stories, so much conjecture. In Scott's last days on earth he will rail against all the lies and distortions about his life. From the dock in the courtroom and in his manic last nights in his death cell, he will denounce and condemn those who speculate about his past. But many will come to believe the man protests too much, that in fact he deeply craves attention and is one of those individuals whose self-worth is based only on the recognition he receives from others.

If he arrived in New Zealand as a complicated teenage boy in 1861, he leaves seven years later an even more complicated man. In May 1868 he boards the *Ethan Allen*, a well-travelled barque that plies the Pacific between San Francisco and Sydney, and heads for Australia in search of honour, respect and somebody to love. It will be the last time his family sees him.

5

THE SKULLS OF TROUBLED SONS

Gently run your fingers over the head of George Scott. He won't mind. It is well-proportioned, is it not? In life it was covered by thick dark hair, a well-groomed beard and trimmed eyebrows. It had boasted a rather handsome face in an era when blackened teeth and faces pocked with scars and warts rarely drew a second glance. But in death this head is smooth, hairless, cold. The phrenologists and medical men will scrutinise it for years, caressing the bumps and indentations of the skull, peering into its nooks and crannies, nodding knowingly as every bulge and prominence reveals all the evil that lurked within.

This plaster cast death mask is all they will need to help explain why Scott became one of the most hated men in the colonies. All they need do is follow the rules and teachings of a Viennese physician and the secrets of a man's inner self are quickly revealed.

Franz Gall begins collecting more than 120 human skulls at the start of the 19th century as part of his investigation into the mysteries of the mind. Gall – and all his devout followers in the decades to come – is convinced the brain is an organ of the mind. The skull, therefore, is nothing more than a topographical map, its contours and curves a guide to its owner's personality and intelligence. He first begins to suspect the link in school when he notes a classmate with advanced reading skills also has an oddly shaped head. Gall, himself the owner of a large wide head, becomes further convinced about his theories at university when he observes many fellow students with high intelligence also tend to have prominent eyeballs.

Gall's theories are denounced by the Catholic church, the Austrian government and even the French emperor, Napoleon Bonaparte. But they gain currency when the English, with their class distinctions and eagerness to highlight the supremacy of the aristocracy, embrace and popularise them.

The science of phrenology quickly gains popularity throughout the British Empire because it helps explain why the criminal classes continue to flourish and why so many are destined to a life of lawlessness. Crime, it turns out, has little to do with injustice or inequality. It is determined by nature. Scott's head, the phrenologists become convinced, indicates a man who found it impossible to tell the truth, a man so caught up in his lies and deceit he would believe them to be true and defend them to the death.

By the end of the 19th century Franz Gall's theories will become unfashionable, replaced by the conjectures of another prominent Viennese medical expert, Sigmund Freud.

Freud will have no time for the pseudoscience of phrenology. He will believe his clinical method of psychoanalysis sheds greater insight into the inner workings of the mind. Had he been given an opportunity to study George Scott he might have noted traits of narcissism and paranoia, as well as a tendency toward histrionics and exaggeration. But he might also have shrugged his shoulders and declared it all too hard because there will be an exception to his theory. The complex Irish, Freud will supposedly say, are a 'race of people for whom psychoanalysis is of no use whatever'.

But this much is certain. Wherever George Scott goes in life, conflict follows. And this new country he is about to call home is already reeling from the act of another Irishman with a wild drop in his blood.

—

Troublesome sons. For almost a century Australia has been their destination. Many have arrived in ships to be punished, others have come for salvation, to flee the famine or to escape from expectations that can never be met. When Thomas Scott bids goodbye to his second boy in 1868 in New Zealand and prays that the raucous cluster of colonies he is heading to might finally be the place to calm his son's wild drop of blood, a mother in England – a woman Thomas admires – shares the same fervent wishes. Her second boy, too, has proven hard to control and she hopes that a visit to the outer reaches of the Empire might also be the making of him.

Queen Victoria has not had much luck with the men in her life. In 1861 her ailing husband, Prince Albert, died just weeks after journeying to Cambridge to admonish their first son, Edward, for spending several nights with an actress. Both parents had been growing increasingly disillusioned with Edward's behaviour. He was reckless and immature, a poor prospect to inherit the crown. Victoria was devastated by her husband's death. She began to withdraw from public life, tiring of the throne and believing Edward, not typhus, had broken his father's heart. 'I never can, or shall, look at him without a shudder,' she tells her eldest daughter.

Seven years after the death of her German husband, the Queen still dresses in mourning black. Always an enthusiastic participant at the dinner table, she has turned to comfort eating and not even her flowing charcoal dresses can disguise her burgeoning weight. She insists her servants continue carrying out the daily rituals of her husband. Under her orders they still set out hot water for his morning shave and visit his prized herd of cows.

Now her second son is proving to be just as big a disappointment as the first. Prince Alfred, the Duke of Edinburgh, is almost surpassing his older brother when it comes to leading the sort of boorish, privileged lifestyle enjoyed by so many royal children across Europe. A year earlier the royal brothers had been partners in a drunken and debauched spree through Paris, their days filled with official functions, their nights spent in the city's most exclusive and exotic brothels.

Victoria has just sent Alfred on what will become a 17-month world tour taking in much of the Empire's outer reaches. His arrival in Australia in command of the *Galatea*, a steam-powered frigate, is the first visit by a royal to the colonies. Despite all his mother's hopes, the Prince's journey to this land of troubled sons has not been going well. There have been some damn *difficulties*. What started as an opportunity for the Prince to present a more regal attitude to the world, and for the colonies to prove to London they are no longer a motley collection of uncouth ex-convicts, has been turned into a bloody and embarrassing mess.

And who else to blame but the Irish?

When the Prince arrives in Melbourne a local chapter of the Orangemen decorate a public hall with images of King William putting the Catholics to heel at the Battle of the Boyne. It is only a few months after the local papers breathlessly reported on unsuccessful attempts by the Irish Republican Brotherhood to seize Dublin and end British rule. Sectarian sentiments are running high. When many of Melbourne's Catholics hear of this provocation, they gather outside the hall and start hurling stones and singing nationalist songs. Shots are soon fired from inside the hall and a teenage boy is killed.

A public banquet welcoming the Prince a few weeks later descends into another riot when 40,000 people – four times the expected crowd – turn up to discover his royal highness has cancelled his appearance. He's like that, of course. If he does turn up he's usually late and his coach will hurtle past those lining the sides of roads longing for their first view of royalty, presenting them with nothing but dust and stones for souvenirs. In Geelong, the organising committee for another banquet flees the scene when crowds larger than expected arrive. In Bendigo, three young boys find themselves trapped inside a model of the *Galatea* and are burned to death when they set off fireworks stored inside it.

The Sydney press reports on these shambles and tragedies in sombre tones. But its editors cannot disguise a note of delight in the misfortune and embarrassment suffered by their Victorian cousins. The two big mainland colonies are riven by rivalry and distrust. There is nothing like watching those southern newcomers squirming in discomfort. But the hubris and sense of superiority in New South Wales will soon be shattered and replaced by humiliation and then outrage when the Prince finally makes it to Sydney in early 1868. Another troubled Irish son is waiting to kill him.

—

Come now. Let us be reminded of that other man who will love and be loved, who will hold and be held, but who will also be treated with scorn and contempt within a few years, a man to be handed the task of extinguishing the light from those steel blue eyes of Andrew George Scott.

Robert Rice Howard is a strikingly good-looking coachman in 1868, driver of a fine Hansom cab, the immensely popular two-wheel horse-drawn carriages that fill the streets of big cities from New York to London. He's not Nosey Bob just yet, even though there is a horse somewhere out there in the streets of Sydney just biding its time, waiting for the moment when Bob is not paying attention so it can send its iron shoe deep into his face. Right now he is only known as Robert Howard, a man you can trust to get you to the other side of the town – in one piece, on time and with the utmost discretion.

He almost owns the cab beat in Darling Point – a privileged part of town that provides him with an endless list of passengers including lawyers, politicians, judges and other high-ranking government officials and their wives. In his job you get to meet all sorts and in the busy days leading to the arrival of Prince Alfred, Howard has been carting nervous officials all over town.

Perhaps that is how his name is slipped to the courtiers accompanying the Prince when they arrive in Sydney. It becomes another part of the Nosey Bob legend – Robert Howard personally guiding Queen Victoria's son through the rough streets of town, expertly navigating the muddy puddles and piles of horse shit, swerving to avoid oncoming traffic, dropping off the 'Dook', as Howard calls him, at the front door of the city's high-class brothels, protectively keeping watch outside for any potential problems, or taking him all the way down to Castlereagh Street 'where lived a fair Jewess, of whom Alfred was enamoured'.

But where is Bob on this Thursday afternoon, the 12th of March? The Prince has been persuaded to make an appearance at a fundraising picnic at the picturesque suburb of Clontarf on the shores of Sydney Harbour. More than 1500 of the town's elite have paid over a pound each – more than the average weekly wage – to rub shoulders with his highness. The Prince is impeccably turned out in top hat and tails, his piercing eyes casting a worn glance over the devoted crowd, no doubt counting down the hours until he is free of these official duties and allowed to indulge in his preferred pursuits. A strong man like Robert Howard, with his keen eye for trouble in the distance, would prove invaluable. He might even be able to spot the mad Irishman making his way toward the Duke of Edinburgh with two guns concealed beneath his coat.

———

Henry James O'Farrell is his name. A troubled son of Ireland, to be sure. He's the youngest child born in Dublin to a butcher who took his family to Melbourne in 1841, back when the settlement was little more than a rambling collection of sod huts overflowing with old convicts, drunks and fortune seekers. The O'Farrells prospered just as the colony began to mature – an older son became a lawyer and Henry trained to join the priesthood. But family fortunes were squandered, Henry fell out with a powerful figure in the Catholic church and his life has now spiralled into bouts of depression, mania and alcoholism.

A year earlier he suffered a complete mental breakdown, waving guns in the air and complaining about attempts to poison him. In recent months he has developed an obsession with Fenianism, an all-embracing term used by the English to describe any kind of Irish republican sentiment. He has been reading the reports about the new wave of rebellion taking place in Ireland and the hanging just a few months earlier of the Manchester Martyrs – three Fenians convicted of killing a police officer during an attempt to free members of the Irish Republican Brotherhood. In January he grew excited at the news that a Fenian warship was planning to intercept a convict ship carrying Irish rebels to Western Australia.

Months ago he arrived in Sydney and began staying in a series of hotels. Yesterday he went to a vacant lot near the Waverley Hotel with a six-chambered Smith & Wesson and a smaller Colt and used his handkerchief for target practice. Today he has made his way to Clontarf. He has weaved through the crowd wearing a hired black suit and white waistcoat. Now he is just a few feet away from the Prince. O'Farrell takes aim and fires into his back.

There are screams and shouts as the Duke slumps to the ground. O'Farrell manages to fire another shot that ends up going through someone's foot. He shouts 'I'm a Fenian – God save Ireland' before he is swallowed by an angry mob intent on tearing him to pieces. In the chaos another sound will soon be heard – a collective wailing throughout the colonies, followed quickly by the mortifying fear that all those hopes of being regarded as equals within the Empire, that all those attempts to shroud that stained convict reputation, have been dashed.

It's one reason why the crowd at Clontarf turns feral so quickly. While dozens of nearby men and women faint or begin sobbing, red-faced old barristers with bellies filled with sherry are transformed into sober and fit young men, running ropes over makeshift gibbets and urging the mob to drag O'Farrell to them to be hanged. Old women are screeching and demanding scissors so they can slash the fiend to pieces. And who should rise above this orgy of fury and violence? What man has the strength and resolve to become a voice of reason? Why, it's none other than the Chief Justice himself, Sir Alfred Stephen, the hanging judge fresh from sending two bushrangers, the Clarke brothers, to their doom.

Sir Alfred calls for calm and helps steer the bloodied and beaten O'Farrell through the mob and down to the shore to a waiting steamer that, despite the urgings of its sailors to hang the man from the ship's main mast, will rush him across the harbour before he is taken by a cab to Darlinghurst Gaol.

The Prince, bleeding but still conscious, is hauled off to Government House where nurses who happen to have been trained by Florence Nightingale will discover the bullet has entered his body just to the right of his spine. Fortunately, his double-strength trouser braces had slowed its path and a day later it will be extracted, his highness stoically propped on a chair as an incision is made and the lead bullet removed.

In days to come spontaneous 'gatherings of indignation' – heavily tinged with colonial embarrassment – will attract tens of thousands around the country. Henry Parkes, the Colonial Secretary of New South Wales and the man the nation will come to regard as the 'Father of Federation', will personally lead an investigation into O'Farrell's assassination attempt. He will also add fuel to a national outpouring of loathing against the Irish, people he regards as 'jabbering baboons and disruptive trouble-makers'. It will partly result in funding being withdrawn from Catholic schools and trigger recriminations and resentment against the Catholic Irish in Australia for decades.

The Prince will quickly recover and take his leave of the colonies. In just a few months the body of Henry O'Farrell will be swinging from a rope at Darlinghurst Gaol. It will then be cut down and examined by Dr Thomas Guthrie Carr, fresh from a stage performance of mesmerism the night before.

Carr is a tireless self-promoter who stands almost seven foot tall and has a sexual appetite that matches his frame. He holds séances for the wealthy, practises as a physician with a skill for amputating damaged limbs and will soon be charged with the rape of a young woman he hypnotises. But right now he is immensely popular in Sydney. That Second Industrial Age might be ushering in an era of science and rationality, but it's as if Carr, with the strength of his towering figure and the power of his charisma and charm, is personally holding it at bay for as long as he can while he extracts small fortunes from the pockets of the wealthy and the impressionable.

The man also happens to hang out his shingle as a skilled phrenologist, another man accomplished in the science of analysing the shape of a person's skull to deduce their personality traits and intelligence.

The skull of Henry O'Farrell, he finds, indicates a troubled man. He tells reporters that: 'The constitution of the brain exhibited very small hope and showed, in connection with a highly nervous temperament, a person subject to extreme reactions, to periods of deep melancholy – faith struggling with despair.'

His lengthy analysis also finds 'A man of extraordinary impulses, acting without thought, or rather deciding with little thought . . . very sensitive to the least annoyance . . . forming hasty conclusions, false ideas of honour, irritable of temper, having indomitable will, great personal conceit . . .'

In other words, a very troubled son.

Just a few weeks later another young man born in Ireland hobbles down the gangplank of a ship that has just brought him to Sydney from New Zealand. He, too, has an irritable temper and struggles with ideas of honour and personal conceit.

He too possesses an indomitable will and a desire to be remembered. Andrew George Scott, with that well-proportioned head and thick brown hair, is about to embark on an adventure that will see him, like Henry O'Farrell, leave an indelible mark on the colonies and bring this rough and wild era to a bloody close.

6

'THE MOST WICKED OF THE WICKED'

It must have come as a shock to many of the well-heeled guests at Clontarf to see Sir Alfred Stephen guiding Henry O'Farrell to safety, refusing to surrender him to the seething mob and their hastily erected gallows. Even his greatest admirers will quietly admit they think he is far too stern and strict for the times. *Severe* will be one of the words they whisper.

But the man is a stickler for the law. Better to ensure O'Farrell received the trial he deserved and its subsequent penalty than allow the masses to dispense justice. Sir Alfred has sat on the bench for almost four decades and as his hairline recedes and those enormous mutton chops grow thicker and whiter, he has become more resolute and adamant that stiff punishment is the only deterrent to serious crime. But he also knows what those very same people baying for O'Farrell's blood are really like. They may shudder at the assassination attempt on the Prince's life, but many of them are the same damn idiots captivated by the exploits of the nation's bushrangers.

It is an issue that grieves the Chief Justice to his core. All those frustrations over the fame accorded the outlaws had spilled over the previous year when he sentenced the notorious Clarke brothers to death.

'How many wives have been made widows and children made orphans, what loss of property, what sorrow you have caused,' Sir Alfred had lamented, '. . . and yet these bushrangers, the scum of the earth, the lowest of the low, the most wicked of the wicked, are occasionally held up for our admiration!'

Sir Alfred had sat in judgement on grieving widows with babies growing in their bellies and broken men weeping for mercy and not one of them had managed to tug at his heart, much less his head. So the two grizzled men who stood before him with their lank hair and deep-set eyes in 1867 knew what was coming. Brothers Thomas and John Clarke – Sir Alfred's scum of the earth, the lowest of the low, the most wicked of the wicked – had never quite managed to get their hands on a bag of that mythic dust that turned so many bushrangers into local legends and heroes. Their work had been too bloodthirsty and too brutal to become the stuff of folklore. They personified the other side of bushranging, the *real* side Sir Alfred knew the public preferred to ignore.

Thomas and John were the sons of Jack Clarke, a pig thief and shoemaker from County Down, the same region that has given the world Andrew George Scott. The brothers were killers of at least one policeman and suspected in the murders of four other officers. They had also dispensed with several other victims, including a disgruntled member of their gang. Perpetrators of more than 70 hold-ups, they had terrorised the south coast of NSW for more than three years.

Such had been their wave of lawlessness that Sir Alfred had led a coalition of like-minded politicians and magistrates two years earlier to draft and implement The Felons Apprehension Act. It was a law that declared men like the Clarkes outside the law and able to be captured or killed by members of the public without fear of themselves being charged with murder.

Sir Alfred might be characterised as a one-dimensional hanging judge by his critics, but he is a complicated man who is difficult to pigeonhole. He has fought for law reforms, first in Van Diemen's Land and now in New South Wales. He has defended Aboriginals when charged under English law for involvement in traditional revenge killings. But he is no soft touch when it comes to hanging the guilty.

If Sir Alfred cannot comprehend the nation's infatuation with bushrangers, he will also struggle to understand the changing public mood toward capital punishment.

He had his first taste of it in 1855 when he sentenced a young woman to the gallows for the murder of her husband. Mary Ann Brownlow, a 23-year-old pregnant mother of two small children from Goulburn, had stabbed her cheating husband after discovering he was having an affair and was planning to sell land she had inherited from her aristocratic French family. The case had held the country spellbound. Mary's husband was a proven scoundrel whose life had ended after she had 'tickled' him, according to the press, with a butcher's knife in his ribs while she was drunk. A lengthy gaol sentence was expected, particularly after Mary Ann told the court her husband's death was unintended and that she still loved him, despite his failings.

But Sir Alfred found the incident to be a 'most foul and brutal murder' and sentenced her to hang. There were petitions and public prayers. The papers railed against the decision and gave over hundreds of column inches to outraged readers. As the weeks passed, Mary Ann gave birth to a son while awaiting her sentence – and the rest of the country nervously waited for news of a reprieve.

It never came. On an October afternoon, as Mary walked to the gallows, weakened and frightened, it was said she paused only to breastfeed and say farewell to her newborn son. Moments later she was hanged. Her new baby died not long afterwards, her other two children orphaned and placed in the care of the government.

But if there were many who had harboured doubts about Sir Alfred's capacity for sympathy, few were dissatisfied to learn he had been appointed to sit in judgement on the Clarke brothers. The 1860s explosion in bushranging across NSW and Victoria had become nothing less than a travelling menagerie of the absurd, the degenerate, the shameless and the depraved. The impunity which seemingly accompanied the outlaws as they roamed the country drove men like Sir Alfred to view their crimes as no longer simply offences against their fellow man, but actions designed to drive a wedge into the very heart of the state.

What was it about the Australian character, he asked, that so many could have empathy for scoundrels like the Clarke brothers and all their other evil comrades? There had been the crowd favourites like 'gentleman' Ben Hall, the son of convicts whose well-organised raids on outlying properties and bush hold-ups inspired the Felons Act. Hall, who doffed his hat to women and was known for a sense of humour and an unrivalled streak of courage, was given up by an informer and ambushed, shot at least 30 times by eight well-armed policemen, his body 'pierced by bullets and slugs from his feet to the crown of his head'.

His mirror-opposite had been Mad Dog Morgan, 'the most bloodthirsty ruffian that ever took to the bush in Australia', a ruthless and mentally unstable stock thief who suffered a suitably grisly ending. Shot and killed while holding up Peechelba Station in north-east Victoria, Morgan was photographed propped on a country bed like a prized trophy, his eyes kept open by a pair of toothpicks. Later, his beard and underlying skin were flayed as souvenirs and his head cut off and sent to the anatomy department at the University of Melbourne.

These men and their outrages had kept Sir Alfred resolutely committed to the death penalty. And so, as darkness descended across Sydney after a long day of hearings, he glared down at Thomas and John Clarke from the bench and delivered his verdict.

'Tell me,' he asked, 'where is the man you ever heard of who, by a course of bushranging, has gained a shilling's worth of property he can call his own? If liberated tomorrow where are their gains?'

Sir Alfred went on to recite a list of the outlaws who, in the past five years, 'have been either shot dead or hanged or imprisoned for life – a list almost of demons.

'There was Peisley. He was executed. Davis? Sentenced to death but commuted to 15 years. Gardiner – sentenced to 32 years. Gilbert – shot dead. Ben Hall – shot dead. Bow and Fordyce – sentenced to death, commuted to imprisonment for life. Manns – executed.'

On he went. O'Meally? Shot dead. Morgan? Shot dead. Dunn? Executed . . .

When he finally reached the end you could almost hear the glee in his voice.

'There is the list!' he said. 'The murders believed to have been committed by you bushrangers are appalling to think of . . . [but] better days are coming. It is the old leaven of convictism not yet worked out. But brighter days are coming. You will not live to see them, but others will.

'Others who may think of commencing a course of crime like yours may rely on it that better days are coming . . . there will be no longer that expression of sympathy with crime which some time since disgraced the country – and sunk it so low in the estimation of the world.'

And with that, he sentenced the Clarke brothers to swing.

With the 1860s drawing to a close, Sir Alfred was not alone in thinking the scourge of bushranging was drawing to a close too. If there was embarrassment and humiliation over Prince Alfred's narrow escape, there was also optimism that the outlaws were running out of time and space. There was, of course, a character called Captain Thunderbolt still at large in central NSW, but the execution of the Clarke brothers, it was felt, was a sure sign the reign of the lawless was all but over. So who could imagine a young man limping down a gangplank in Sydney's docklands would keep the bushranging cause alive for another decade?

—

After leaving the *Ethan Allen* George Scott makes his way to Melbourne where family cousins who minister at local congregations arrange an interview for him with the Bishop of Melbourne, Charles Perry.

Perry is a controversial figure. His critics see him as a pious and narrow-minded man. Struggling to find enough men to spread the Lord's word throughout Victoria's goldfields, he has just begun a program of appointing lay readers – civilians not ordained in the ministry but allowed to conduct sermons and oversee funerals.

The program has been a disaster for the church. When Scott sits before Perry and begins to charm him with his wit and intelligence, the newspapers have already been detailing successive scandals involving lay readers and ordained ministers.

'Lay members of the Church of England are humiliated by acts of clerical impropriety, bringing contempt upon the people as well as upon the priesthood,' thunders *The Age*, just a few weeks after Scott meets with Perry. 'What possible reliance can be placed upon these blind and stumbling leaders . . .? The whole body of Episcopalian clergymen are stained and lowered in their own as well as in popular esteem by the misconduct of reverend hypocrites of the same cloth.'

There have been so many outrages. A reverend has broken the leg of a helpless animal during a sermon in full view of worshippers. Despite calls for his sacking, Perry temporarily suspends him before reinstating him in the same district. As well, a lay reader has been 'guilty of excessive conviviality . . . and not only this but the additionally suspicious fact is elicited that the clergyman in question travels with an *alias*'.

Yet another, says *The Age*, has attempted 'improper familiarities' with young girls he was preparing for confirmation, a 'culminating point in the ministerial disasters of Bishop Perry's diocese'.

The bishop is under enormous pressure. The newspapers might accuse him of grossly misjudging the character of so many men he has charged with spreading the Lord's word. But surely this charming young man sitting before him – the son of an ordained minister in New Zealand – can be trusted to stay out of trouble.

Yes, this fellow seems to have everything. His family is of good standing. His own credentials speak to loyalty and an enormous capacity to learn. What do the newspapers know? Bishop Perry does not need a phrenologist's skills to know that George Scott has a mature head on his shoulders. He has found a new 130-pounds-a-year lay reader for the church, a man who, surely, will remain on the right side of the law.

—

In late July 1868, Scott arrives in the town of Bacchus Marsh, halfway between Melbourne and the goldfields of Ballarat that have so quickly helped transform the colony into a financial powerhouse.

Scott is a powerful orator. With his Irish lilt and captivating blue stare, he thunders from the pulpit of the Holy Trinity Iron Church and the crowds soon begin to fill the pews inside the chapel's tin and brick walls. He is appointed to oversee the establishment of a young men's association. He hosts morning teas for the town's respectable women, charming them with his manners and tales of derring-do. He acts as producer and director for a play at the church, and has to rescue a rather overweight woman who falls through the flimsy stage floor during rehearsals. He befriends one of the town's most prominent and respected landowners, James Crook, lodging with him at his Manor House, a mansion built decades earlier by the founder of Bacchus Marsh, William Bacchus.

Who cannot help but fall under his spell? Scott is a gifted conversationalist with a vast bank of knowledge and experience for someone so young. That dragging right foot of his might be a damn nuisance but the man is an expert horseman, roaming the plains to spread the Good Lord's word in neighbouring towns like Ballan and Melton. He always has a Bible and a fine gun packed by his side. The heights of the gold rush might be over, and brutal thugs like the highwayman Richard Burgess no longer as common, but a man can never take his safety for granted.

In fact, everything seems to be going wonderfully well for Scott. There is only one issue that arises in the first few months of his arrival, and even he is not to blame for it. Scott had reached Bacchus Marsh in the company of John Connell, a young man he called his groom.

Here, surely, was another example of Scott's panache, not to mention a talent that will soon become apparent for drawing young men around him. It also contained a trace of his affluent upbringing, for few other lay readers roamed the colony with a personal groom. In August, Connell had gone out drinking. He hadn't taken a drink for a while and the liquor soon began taking hold. By the end of the night he had broken a window and when two police officers arrived to arrest him, he staged a violent struggle that eventually ended with his wrists roped behind his back. He was locked up for two days and heavily fined.

But that had hardly been the fault of Scott. He, too, is known to like a drink and he will become a regular figure in the smoke-filled saloons and drinking holes of the area. But first there is work to be done and a new reputation to forge.

Bacchus Marsh is placed between two major waterways – the Lerderderg and Werribee Rivers – and water supply for the town is a major issue. He might only be in his mid-20s, but Scott, never shy to parade his talents, is a man who has always sensed and seized upon opportunities.

Within months he is advertising in the local newspaper: 'Mr A. G. Scott, C.E (Licenced Government Surveyor, Auckland, N.Z),' declares the ad, 'is about to open an office in Bacchus Marsh where he may be consulted on all works of Surveying and Engineering.

'Mr Scott, having served his time as a pupil with Samuel Harding, Esq., Member of the Institute of Civil Engineers, one of the most celebrated hydraulic engineers of the day, is specially competent to survey and report upon irrigation schemes, waterworks &c.'

To underline his credentials he holds a public meeting at the Mechanics Institute hall. To his disappointment, attendance is small. But it doesn't stop him from getting to his feet and showing off his engineering knowledge. He explains to the small crowd the meaning of hydrostatics and hydraulics. He gives them a scientific explanation of water and describes how it is almost 'incompressible'. Barely drawing breath, he then takes them on a tour through the great waterworks in history; how the ancient Romans supported one of their aqueducts with 7000 arches; how Peruvians managed to have water journey 300 miles to irrigate a town smaller than Bacchus Marsh; how the ancient Egyptians developed water-diverting technology that he believed would still be appropriate for his newly adopted town.

The thing about Scott is that when he gets to his feet and builds a little momentum, he finds it almost impossible to stop. He feeds off his audience – and his own adrenaline. It is a Wednesday evening – the middle of another busy week – and no doubt some in this sparse crowd are already wondering what time they will get home. But Scott is only warming up. After just a few months in town he believes he has seen enough – and carried out enough experiments – to justify calling for the erection of a weir across the Werribee Gorge. The wall for this dam would be more than 100 feet high and might cost 30,000 pounds to build.

Of course, he would need to take a few more readings and test the quality of the lime in the soil, but if the good people of Bacchus Marsh could only start the works at once 'they might have irrigation for the district next summer'.

A round of applause and a few complimentary remarks follow from the man chairing the meeting – Scott's wealthy new friend James Crook. But if the attendees heading for the door think they have politely heard the last of the matter, they will stand corrected. Within a few days A. G. Scott, always an avid letter writer, is filling newspaper columns with his theories about hydrology and how this new dam wall can be quickly built.

But that inability of Scott to avoid conflict? Even here, nestled in this quiet valley of market farmers, a discussion about irrigation can quickly turn personal. One of the local papers, *The West Bourke and South Grant Guardian*, scoffs at Scott's ideas and says he is far too dismissive of plans for other dams in the region.

Scott once again takes pen in hand and writes a lengthy discourse to the *Guardian*'s rival, *The Bacchus Marsh Express*. He begins by showing off his Latin, starting his letter with *nemo me impune lacessit* – 'No one provokes me with impunity' – and then launches an equally scathing attack on the paper that has criticised him. 'I need scarcely reply to the rabid and scurrilous remarks made by the editor of the *Guardian* . . . as the abusive character of that journal is well known by all in this neighbourhood, and does not require any proof from me.'

His letter – almost 2000 words long – includes a note of apology halfway through 'for using your valuable space and wearying your readers'. But the man is simply clearing his throat. On he goes, defending his theory as if it were scripture itself. There are dense paragraphs filled with mathematical formulae to lend weight to his argument – 'An acre contains 4840 square yards. A square yard contains 9 square feet. 4840 by 9 is 43,560 feet (the number of square feet in one acre), multiplied by 12,000 (the number of acres in watershed) is equal to 522,720,000 square feet, which at six inches deep is equal to 261,360,000 cubic feet, equal to 1,633,500,000 gallons . . .'

It is a taste of the George Scott to come, a man with a tendency to obsess over details and minutiae, a man who can't help but show off. For those who manage to get to the end of the letter, Scott finishes with an emphatic Latin flourish: *Magna est veritas et prevalebit* – 'The truth is great and shall prevail.'

But truth and George Scott are only occasional companions. Within a few months the reputation of the budding engineer with a talent for Latin and equations will be questioned in court. At about the same time, the aspiring preacher on a small salary who always seems to be borrowing money from those around him will become involved in one of the country's most famous bank robberies.

Flectere si nequeo superos, Acheronta movebo.

George Scott surely knows the phrase. If I cannot move Heaven, I will raise Hell.

7

MOONLITE IN THE DARKNESS

Ludwig Wilhelm Julius Bruun is a blond 18-year-old with a sore throat and a gun to his head. It is a dark and moonless Saturday night in early May 1869. The chill mist is doing little to improve the cold Bruun has been struggling with for the past week. But the steel muzzle of the Colt pistol just behind his neck has become a more immediate problem. So, too, the man holding it.

Bruun is the local agent for the London Chartered Bank in the mining town of Mount Egerton, deep in the Victorian goldfields. He sleeps in a small room at the back of the bank and has just returned after visiting a friend.

It is about 10pm. The light from a nearby tavern has cast the street in the soft pale yellow of a near ripe lemon. Bruun has just moved to unlock the bank's front door when a masked man slides up behind him on his left side and grabs him on the shoulder.

'He told me to be quiet or he would shoot me,' Bruun will recall later. 'At the same time I heard him cock the pistol.'

The man orders Bruun to open the bank. 'I don't know the way about this bloody place,' he tells Bruun. 'Go behind the counter.'

There's something familiar about the robber, thinks Bruun. But as he trembles in the shadows of the bank's porch before a thief in a black coat and a black crepe mask across his face, Bruun, usually known as Julius and who is the son of a well-off Danish immigrant, is having a difficult time trying to think straight.

Bruun unlocks the door and walks inside. The man orders him to hand over his firearm – a Dean and Adams revolver resting in a buttoned leather case.

'When I gave him the revolver he said: "Now open the safe and give me everything you have in it, or I will shoot you."'

Bruun hands the bandit a haul of banknotes and a collection of gold and silver coins. 'Have you given me all now?' he asks Bruun. 'If not I will shoot you.'

Bruun opens another drawer and hands over a cake of gold. He can't be sure exactly how much he has surrendered. He had balanced his books late in the afternoon and normally the takings would have been transferred to the larger branch in the nearby town of Gordon. But with Mount Egerton being a mining town, and miners oblivious to normal office hours, there had been several transactions after that. So he had locked the bank's doors just after 6pm before leaving for dinner at a friend's home. Still, he knows the haul is worth more than 1000 pounds. There are men nearby who spend weeks and months at the bottom of deep shafts breathing nothing but dust who can only dream of such a fortune.

With the cash and gold secured in a bag, the thief orders a blind-folded Bruun out of the bank. They wander past a dam and Bruun is told he is to be taken into the bush, tied and gagged.

'I asked him not to do so as I had been suffering from a sore throat, and I commenced crying.'

At Bruun's suggestion they end up at the local schoolhouse where the man dictates a note that Bruun scribbles by matchlight on a piece of paper.

'I hereby certify that L. W. Bruun has done everything in his power to withstand our intrusion and the taking away of the money, which was done with firearms.'

The man then wanders over and signs the note 'Captain Moonlite', before tying up Bruun and leaving with the bag of gold and cash.

Bruun will soon cut through the ropes securing his hands with a pen knife he grabbed during the robbery. He will quickly race off and alert the town that the main bank of Mount Egerton has just been held up.

But Bruun will do more than just that. He's almost certain he can identify the man who did it. The young man's nerves might still be jangling, his face stained with tears and his throat still raspy. But as lights suddenly go on around the town and the police are summoned, Bruun has realised why the robber seemed so familiar.

He had an Irish accent, that was for sure. And there was no doubting the peculiar way he walked. He dragged one of his feet every time he took a step.

—

It's a decent day's journey on a good horse from Bacchus Marsh to Mount Egerton. By the end of February in 1869 George Scott had been more than happy to undertake it. Despite the reputation his sermons had gained, despite advertising as an engineer and telling the locals the best way to build a dam, despite having been in town for barely six months, trouble – as usual – had managed to find him.

He had struck up a friendship with Robert Crook, the son of James, the self-styled lord of the Manor House. The Crooks had been involved in a long and simmering feud with their neighbours, the James family. In mid-February in 1869, the James family laid a charge with police accusing Robert Crook of vandalising their fences and stealing sheep and cattle from their farm.

Scott appeared at the trial as a defence witness and told the court Crook had not even been in Bacchus Marsh on the night of the alleged theft because he had been visiting a friend in the nearby town of Ballan. The prosecutor suggested Scott had been approaching people before the trial looking for witnesses – 'any witness would do, even a swagman' – who would, in exchange for 10 pounds, also back up the claim that his friend was out of town.

Scott denied the allegation – although a few months later he would confirm he had attempted to procure an alibi for Crook. But then a 13-year-old Sunday school student of Scott's, Jane Wells, gave testimony that contradicted his evidence. She was certain she had seen Scott and Robert Crook together between 10 and 11pm on the night in question. 'I was going to bed and lifted the curtain and heard them laughing and talking and going down the road. They were riding on horseback. They came from Mr Crook's way.'

The evidence from a young teenage girl contradicting Scott's claims about his friend's whereabouts propelled the *Guardian* – the local newspaper that had already sniffed that something was amiss with Scott and scoffed at his recommendations for a dam for the region – to quickly leap into print.

'A.G. Scott and Jane Wells have sworn positively to facts the opposite of each other,' thundered the *Guardian*. 'We trust that a sense of what is due to the Church with which this young man is connected will induce him to refrain from performing any duty with its ceremonials until the bench has discharged the prisoner . . .'

In the end the charges against Crook were dismissed. But Scott's time was up. Sensing another potential scandal with a lay reader, the Church of England had ordered its new recruit to head further inland to Mount Egerton. By the end of February Scott had ridden into this mining town and a young blond man was one of the first to catch his eye.

Gold had turned Mount Egerton from sleepy farming land 14 years earlier into a thriving boom town. A chunk of gold in the hands of a man calling himself Captain Moonlite is about to make it famous.

—

If the rattling of convict chains was the constant soundtrack in the first half century of the Australian colonies, the 1850s and '60s had seen it replaced with the shouts of sweaty miners and their cries of 'Eureka!'

Gold had changed everything. Beneath the soil of north-west Victoria and into central New South Wales, what appeared to be endless seams of the precious metal lured hundreds of thousands to Australian shores, swelling the population with the promise of quick fortunes even greater than the treasure unearthed during the Californian rush in the late 1840s. There, the town of San Francisco had been transformed within a decade from a backwater settlement of 200 people huddled by a windswept bay into the financial hub of the United States with a population of more than 150,000.

The transformation of New South Wales and Victoria was just as abrupt. In February 1851 Edward Hargraves, an English settler who had unsuccessfully plied the Californian goldfields, found five specks of alluvial gold near Orange. Five months later, on the same day Victoria was recognised as a separate colony to NSW, James Esmond, the son of an Irish merchant, found alluvial gold 20 miles north of Ballarat. Australia's population at the time was little more than 450,000. Over the next two decades that number soared to almost two million. The human stampede came from everywhere – from the outer reaches of the Empire and Europe, from Russia and China and the dwindling American goldfields – spilling off ships and trekking inland, filling the night with songs and accents, the exotic scent of foreign dishes mingling with the smoke from thousands of meagre campfires.

It also brought inevitable conflict. The Eureka rebellion in Ballarat in 1854, which years later will be regarded as the birth of Australian democracy, resulted in 27 deaths when miners rebelled against rising licence fees, their lack of a voice at parliamentary level and the brutality of colonial armed forces. In the early 1860s the Lambing Flat riots in the Burrangong goldfield of NSW culminated in a mob of 3000 European and Australian-born miners attacking 2000 Chinese miners, bashing them and burning their tents. Racial tensions became a common feature of the goldfields. If the dwindling mobs of Aboriginals living on the edges of the gold settlements provided sport for the miners when plied with grog, the Chinese were viewed with hostility and contempt. Many came from poor rural areas and were accustomed to the gruelling field work that sifting for gold required. They also worked communally in large groups, were content with smaller returns and covered more ground than other miners.

There were fortunes to be made. But a man did not need to uncover a sizeable nugget to secure his future. The real winners were the grocers who tripled their prices for flour, mutton, tea and sugar. The candlestick makers enjoyed a thriving trade. And a man with an unlimited supply of whiskey and rum needed only to spend a year hocking his wares to never work again.

But there was another business that enjoyed even better returns courtesy of the goldfields. This profession did not require a man to squat for hours with an aching back and throbbing legs, hunched over a sieve and dish, straining his eyes to find just a speck of gold. All a man required to enter the business of bushranging was a gun, a horse and a desire to benefit from the hard work of others.

The road between Bacchus Marsh and Ballarat, worn down by so many weary feet, had seen more than its share of outlaws plying their trade through the years. Richard Burgess, that self-proclaimed guilty wretch who would go on to terrorise the South Island of New Zealand, shot and strangled several men along the route before burying the bodies in shallow graves.

And not long after George Scott rode down it on his way to Mount Egerton in early 1869, his criminal career about to begin in earnest, a father and son had a narrow escape when they encountered another two bushrangers, one of them old and already a household name, the other destined to become the most infamous in Australian history.

—

The old one is Harry Power. You don't see many bushrangers like Harry. Most never live to see grey strands speckling their beards, or squint at the world with puffy bags forming under their deep-set eyes. The business does not lend itself to longevity and the getting of wisdom. But then, Power, another proud son of Ireland, is considered a bit of a late starter. Did his best to stay on the straight and narrow for years, roaming the bush and trading in horse flesh, much of it legal, some of it not. But he watched and he learned and now he has become such a natural in the saddle you can see the bow in his legs whenever he gets down and struts about on his stumpy limbs.

He's not long past 50 and even though he remains a magnificent horseman, he sits uncomfortably in that saddle these days. A chronically twisted bowel gives him no end of trouble; when he squats in the bush and those contractions begin tightening his guts so bad it feels like his shit is turning to stone, you can hear his bellowing from miles away. And Harry has a loud voice. He'll proudly tell you he can 'cooey louder than any man in the bush'. One day in the years to come, as he lies on a small cot in a prison cell wrongly believing he is about to die because of that bloody bum of his, he will boast to a visitor about those vocal cords.

'You wouldn't think it to see me lying here with a voice like a child's,' he will say, a shine appearing in those old blue eyes. 'I frightened the people with my voice and of course I cursed and swore, and everyone thought I was going to kill them. I'd got myself a bad name and it was worth a good deal to me.'

Harry might never become a rich man because his robberies rarely produce big plunder, but he understands just how important theatrics are in the business of bushranging. Truth be told, he fancies himself as a bit of a performer. You can usually find him wearing old leather boots that turn up at the toes, a look so ridiculous a man might laugh if there wasn't a gun pointing at him while being bailed up on a lonely bush track.

Harry and his young apprentice have come down from the heavily forested hills and valleys of north-east Victoria and ended up on the Bacchus Marsh-Ballarat road, pursued by a posse of troopers. Back in February, as George Scott scouted this same area for a swagman happy to earn 10 quid to provide an alibi for his new mate Robert Crook, Harry had broken out of Pentridge prison courtesy of a forged pass and a fortuitous hole in the wall.

Harry Power is familiar with prison walls. He'd been shipped to Australia back in 1840 for stealing a bridle and saddle in Lancashire. Since then he's had stints in gaol for wounding a drunken trooper and stealing horses. Now, at an age when most outlaws are rotting beneath the ground, his career as a bushranger has begun in earnest. He has set himself up in a hideaway in almost impenetrable forest near Glenmore, where the squawking of a local peacock sitting atop his crude bush shelter warns him of any approaching intruders.

Harry is a natural bushman, unlike many outlaws with little affinity with the Australian landscape apart from overwhelming gratitude for the cover it provides. The thought of being a free man in those hills will almost bring a tear to his blue eyes in later life. 'Ay!' he will reminisce, a smile exposing his missing front teeth. 'It's grand to be on the ranges and to breathe the beautiful pure air, and to see Mount Feathertop far above ye, and down below for miles and miles the beautiful country. There's water all the year round and it's always cool and pleasant. That's the place for a man to live.'

Harry's plan since his escape has been to stage a few hold-ups and earn enough to get himself to America and live out his remaining years as an honest man. After all, as the man says, 'I've led a very wicked life.' But there's only so much you can do as a solo bushranger. The pickings so far as a highwayman have been slim and Harry has often lamented his lack of a partner, someone to hold the horses and point a menacing gun on the passengers and drivers of passing stagecoaches while he rifles through their possessions.

Well, now he's found himself one, even though the lad is a young'un and will need plenty of training. Still, 15-year-old Ned Kelly has shown some promise, despite turning to jelly when he first came under fire. Harry has taken him on as a favour to Ellen Kelly, an Irish-born widow scratching out a living on an 88-acre selection of tired soil at Eleven Mile Creek, near the road that carries travellers from Melbourne to Sydney.

Ellen has a violent temper, fuelled by that Catholic Irish loathing for authority and a burning resentment at the difficulties life has hurled her way. Her alcoholic husband, Red, transported to Australia for seven years for pig stealing, died three years ago. She now ekes out a miserable existence with her family of seven children. Their bark hut, with its hessian walls and dirt floor and flimsy curtains separating a handful of small stuffy rooms, serves as a sly grog shop. Ellen is now carrying another child to her latest lover and has allowed Harry, a family friend, to take on her eldest boy as an apprentice.

Because he is a Kelly, Ned is no stranger when it comes to breaking the laws of the colonies. When his old man Red wasn't passed out from the grog or looking for his next batch, he was off pinching the cattle of rich squatters and getting into trouble with the police. Red's brother Jim, another regular cattle duffer, had burned down a derelict hotel in Greta with 16 people inside – most of them children – when Ellen refused to sleep with him. Everyone escaped and Jim, originally sentenced to hang for attempted murder, had been dispatched to a mental asylum.

But it will be Ned's stint as a trainee bushranger under Power's tutelage that will bring the Kelly family under closer scrutiny from the authorities. They already know Ned is on the run with Power and has helped him with several highway hold-ups. Just recently the pair had been planning to knock off a herd of horses on the 35,000-acre property of squatter John Rowe near Mansfield. As they lay on top of a bluff overlooking Rowe's property, believing they were out of view, Rowe came charging out of the house and began firing at them.

Old Harry will never forget how young Ned 'turned white and wished to surrender' when the bullets began ripping up the ground in front of them. He had to give him a whack to break him out of his frozen torpor and drag him back to their own horses hidden in the bush. But as they made their escape Harry was quickly impressed by Ned's horsemanship. The kid was a natural in the saddle. There was a reckless confidence in the way he handled his mount at full gallop, guiding it expertly down jagged gullies and ravines in thick forest, plunging down steep inclines before hitting the plains and making their escape.

Now here they are, on that road between Bacchus Marsh and Ballarat; old Harry, grey beard and painful arse, and young Ned, square-jawed with a thick head of black hair and long thin eyebrows running straight above a pair of wide-set eyes.

'Myself and young Kelly had halted near the road, the police being all out in the bush after us,' Power will say years later. 'We were on the top of the hill and could see for miles around. A buggy with a man and a boy in it came up. I took stock of them.'

Harry casts a watchful eye over the pair and thinks to himself: 'A bagman with a large family . . . that's his eldest son, a smart-looking lad. [They'll have] not many notes – all cheques; no use robbing him of a few pounds.'

As the buggy rolls past, Harry asks the man in his booming voice if the road ahead is busy and if he has seen any police about.

'The gentleman gave me fair answers and began loading his pipe. I think he knew us, but he was a cool hand. I asked for some matches and got some, and then I asked the time, though I'd a couple of gold watches in my pocket. His watch was silver and I didn't want it. After a few words he drove on, and I daresay he was glad to get off.

'But what did he do when he got to Bacchus Marsh? Why, he set the police after us and I don't think he ought to have done that when I let him go by. I'm sorry I didn't stick him up.'

It will be another of Harry Power's many regrets. And there are more than a few that will make him wince when he looks back on his wicked life. Some months ago he'd held up a large cattle station and, wrongly thinking there were armed men hiding in the house, pointed his gun at a baby sleeping in a cradle.

'If ye have any men waiting to take me I'll blow out the child's brains,' he told its frantic mother.

She had fallen instantly to her knees, begging old Harry not to shoot and assuring him through her sobbing there was no-one else around. It wasn't a very gentleman-like performance, he will concede.

He has always been mindful of women and their sensitivities, to say nothing of their chastity. Why, there had been the time he'd arrived at Ellen Kelly's clapped-out bark hut and the old girl wasn't home. But one of her young daughters happened to be there on her own. 'I was old and she young, she liked me in a friendly way.' As the girl sat in the dirt-floor room sewing together a rug made from possum skins, Harry sat smoking his pipe, watching her every move, the devil whispering in his ear.

'There was no-one round for miles, hadn't I lots of money, and couldn't I tempt the girl?' That most certainly was not the Harry Power way. 'I got up and went out, and the devil followed me. "I'll best you yet, Mr Devil," said I. It shall never be said that my mother's son wronged any girl.'

Harry likes to think of himself as a chivalrous old bugger. Certainly he has regrets – so many hold-ups he could have committed, so many riches that might have been his had he not spent so much time bushranging on his own. There was the day he bailed up a stage-coach on his own just out of Beechworth. He'd had two dozen people standing hostage in front of him and had quickly realised, cradling his single rifle in his arms, that there were far too many of them. 'Well, I couldn't do it properly and I lost no end of money there.'

But then, look what will happen after taking an apprentice like Ned under his wing. He will teach the kid as much as he can and what will he get in return?

The following year after the pair sit astride their horses high on this hill between Ballarat and Bacchus Marsh, Power will finally be tracked down by the police.

Word will get around that the traps and their blacktrackers come for him in the thick bush guided by a detailed description of Harry's hideout provided by young Ned. Even that damn peacock resting on top of Power's shack will join the conspiracy. Perched on top of Harry's hideaway, the man himself fast asleep inside, the peacock will remain mute as the troopers creep inside and arrest Harry after a short struggle.

'Young Kelly was with me for a time, but he was no good, and helped sell me at last,' Power will say. The Kellys? There was no trusting them. 'God will judge them for taking blood money.'

That was the problem with bushranging. A man could wield a loud gun and have a voice to match it. He could be chivalrous and respectful of women. He might even harbour a little respect for the undermanned troopers sent to hunt him down. But colleagues in the same line of work? There was no trusting the bastards.

8

HIS HONOUR

George Scott is prone to boasting about his background. He'll often let drop in conversation his time in the Navy on board HMS *Britannia* and his service against the Maori in New Zealand. To let you know he was well educated he might break into a sonnet from one of the Romantic poets, or perfectly quote a line from one of the classics. He likes to cultivate an air of mystery, too. One moment he's down at the saloon taking a brandy and relating one of his many exploits, the next he is suddenly mounting a horse and disappearing for a day or two, returning just in time to read a sermon or conduct Sunday School lessons.

In the years to come historians scrutinising his life will think they are tracking a ghost, a strange being who seems to live in parallel worlds, flitting between reality and some other place, leaving a trail of confusion in his wake. Meet him for the first time and you will almost certainly fall for his charm. He will be a convivial chum at the bar or around the fireplace. But the next day your greeting will be met with a cold and aloof stare. It's as if he has no recollection of meeting you.

The strangest of men will become the strangest bushranger Australia has seen. So it's only appropriate that the Mount Egerton bank robbery will become one of the most bizarre and puzzling gold heists in Australian history. Scott will go to the gallows a decade later owning up to many mistakes, but insisting he played no part in the theft. The teenage bank clerk held up by a limping masked man calling himself Captain Moonlite will insist it was Scott. The Mount Egerton gold heist will be like George Scott's life and state of mind – peppered with shifting and conflicting evidence.

At its heart lies the relationship between Scott and Bruun. They are introduced in late February when Scott arrives in Mount Egerton. The Irishman immediately follows his usual practice, cultivating a friendship that borders on the obsessive. Bruun will complain that Scott visits him constantly at the bank, a day never passing without his arrival in the flimsy building. One evening Scott suggests he should even sleep over in the bank. They quickly become inseparable. They take walks around the small town. Scott instructs his naive young companion in the art of using a gun. They dine at the home of James Simpson, Mount Egerton's schoolteacher and a renowned drunk. They drink at the local tavern.

But then, a month or so later, the relationship suddenly ends. Scott will later tell friends the pair had been walking down a street and seen an altercation between two men. He'd urged Bruun to help him break up the fight, but the younger man had been afraid and ran away, hiding behind a nearby fence. In Scott's telling, this meant Bruun was not a real man. He had no *honour*.

Bruun's version, like most recollections in the case, will be vastly different. His refusal to attend church had triggered a disagreement between the pair, he will say. After the dispute, Bruun had organised to send some clothing Scott had left in a leather valise at the bank back to him. Through it all there are hints and suggestions that Scott is consumed by being with Bruun. The young man will tell a crowded courtroom a few years later that 'Our intimacy continued until the end of March . . . [Scott] used to go into the bank office and into my private room. One night [he] proposed to sleep in the bank, but I said there was only one bed. He said: "you sleep on the floor" and the matter then dropped.'

It's tempting to believe the real reason the friendship ends so suddenly is because Bruun has grown uncomfortable in Scott's presence. Perhaps he rebuffs an advance by Scott for a physical relationship between the pair. Whatever the reason, it's clear something has taken place between the men that can never be repaired.

In the early hours of the morning after the bank robbery, that thick mist still clinging to the ground around the small township, Bruun accompanies two police officers to the house where Scott is renting a room. Scott is in the process of undressing and preparing for bed when he opens the door. He has a collection of guns mounted on the wall above his bed. Bruun tells the officer he is certain it was Scott who stuck up the bank.

'It's a vile conspiracy to injure me,' scoffs Scott. Why, he's only just returned to Mount Egerton after visiting Melbourne. He's sure he has a ticket lying somewhere to prove it. He got off at a nearby station and as he made his way to Mount Egerton, a man on a horse went riding by him very quickly – it was probably the thief making his escape.

On Sunday morning, barely 12 hours after the robbery, church-goers will never forget the prayer offered by Mount Egerton's new lay reader. 'Oh Lord, we pray Thee, in Thy great goodness, and in accord with Thine unerring standard of dealing out even-handed justice to all men, so order and direct that the efforts made by the constituted authorities in seeking after the bank robbers may be entirely success-ful, and that they may be speedily brought to justice; and that the wicked and evil done by these lawless forgetters of Thee may result in good thereafter.'

It's a curious prayer because it assumes several men have been involved in the theft. As far as Scott knows, Bruun has only identified him as the culprit. He has not told Scott that the masked man in the bank claimed to have several associates in on the job.

Scott is quick to tell all who will listen that Bruun's allegations are untrue. He is an innocent man. In the weeks to come he will stand outside the home of Bruun's father, demanding the man's son apologise for daring to suggest he had robbed the bank. According to Bruun, he threatens him with a decent horsewhipping if he does not retract his claims.

Andrew George Scott has had his *honour* questioned. And who could believe a man of God would stoop so low as to rob a bank? The police instead charge Bruun and that drunken schoolteacher, James Simpson, with the robbery.

—

There is a committal hearing in May and Scott tells the court he had been close to both men. 'I knew Bruun well and was very intimate with him for two or three weeks. During that period I saw him almost daily. I knew Simpson well. I resided with him for a week and was very friendly. A coolness took place between us about a fortnight or three weeks later, and about the same time there was a coolness between Bruun and me.'

The prosecutor then begins to question Scott about his financial situation. Scott says he resigned from his lay readership the morning after Bruun alleged he was responsible for the bank robbery. 'I am not in any employment now. I was to receive 130 pounds per annum.'

The prosecutor, like most of those associated with the case, has heard rumours that Scott, who seemed to be on the edge of poverty before the theft, has appeared financially well off since the heist.

He asks Scott: 'Then you are now a gentleman at large?'

'As much a gentleman as you are,' replies Scott.

'What are your resources?'

'I decline to answer impertinent questions.'

'You must answer the question.'

'I have money,' says Scott. He then goes on to obfuscate, giving the court a shortened history of his life and naval career. Yes, he has been in the habit of carrying a gun, as well as a knife. 'I was in the habit of carrying it amongst the Maoris – and there are some Maoris here . . .'

A titter of laughter ripples through the courtroom.

'I was a major in the volunteers. I have been called Captain Scott. I never heard Captain Moonlite until recently.'

Now that can't be right – Scott will always say his colleagues during the war in New Zealand often jokingly referred to him as Captain Moonlite. Here he is again, once more weaving in and out of reality, leaving behind his usual trail of confusion and contradictions.

Scott agrees he lied to the police about his whereabouts on the night of the robbery. 'The assertion that I came by the train on the Saturday night would have been a very bad alibi. I was out that night. I won't say where. I regret that I told a lie to the officers of justice.'

Scott is good at sounding contrite. He's also brilliant at deflecting the question of where he actually was on the night of the robbery. It's a question he will face again six weeks later when Bruun and Simpson stand trial in Ballarat. This time his refusal to answer will cost him his freedom.

—

Friday 23 July 1869. At exactly 9am the packed crowd in the Ballarat Circuit Court is asked to rise as his Honour, Mr Justice Redmond Barry, takes his seat on the bench to begin the trial of Julius Bruun. Barry's fleshy face, encased in thick mutton chops that reach to the top of his neck, is a familiar one to many in the town. In the mid-1850s he had presided over the trial of 13 men charged with high treason over the Eureka Stockade rebellion. Held in Melbourne, the hearing saw more than 10,000 people celebrate wildly in the streets when all were acquitted.

Barry looks every inch the pillar of colonial society and has a pedigree to match. He is the son of an army major in County Cork, a graduate of Trinity College, a lover of the flute, a collector of rare wine, a devout reader of the classics, the founder and chancellor of the rapidly growing Melbourne University, an enthusiastic follower of the latest breakthroughs in science and a man for whom a knight-hood is just a few years away.

In fact, is there a man in the colonies more committed to the belief that education and learning must be the foundation of any advanced society? A few months earlier he had visited Ballarat to open a new library. The crowd no doubt squirmed impatiently before finally surrendering with glassy eyes as he made his way through another of his long-winded speeches.

'Prurient tempers may skulk to gloat in private, unobserved, over base and impure thoughts perpetuated by a prostitution of the talents destined one might imagine for a more decent use,' he'd told them. 'But those who come here to read their own books, provided for them by the prudent dispensers of public funds, require no screen to hide their studies from the broad daylight of the public gaze.'

The man might be a lover of the ponderous passage but his passion for learning cannot be mistaken. Back in those early years in Melbourne in the 1840s – it had been little more than a small village of sod huts and drinking houses with the prospect of a public library simply unimaginable – he had allowed members of the public to visit his home and read from his wide collection of books.

So Redmond Barry should be comfortably ensconced in the warm bosom of the colonial aristocracy, sipping sherry with the rich and powerful. But the Establishment doesn't quite know what to do with the man. It's his private life they worry about. The Anglican bishop, Charles Perry – the man who had seen such potential in George Scott a year earlier – has been muttering about Barry's loose morals for some time. In this purse-lipped Victorian era, Barry has hardly bothered concealing a long-running affair with a woman of little education and from a far lower social class.

He first met Louisa Barrow in 1846. She was already married with a child. For Barry, such a small detail was hardly an impediment. It was more of a lure. Now, years later, Barrow has given Barry four children, all of whom he pays for and publicly acknowledges. He has bought a city house for Barrow, a short, stout woman who wears her hair severely parted down the middle, so they can spend weekends together.

This scandalous flouting of public standards might almost be forgiven if it were just a one-off example of love finding its true path. But Barry has always shown a predilection for married women. It is the reason why he settled in Melbourne in the first place. Unable to secure regular work in the overcrowded legal system back in Ireland, he had sailed for Sydney in the barque *Calcutta* in early 1839. The ship was just a few days out of London when he began flirting with one of the only married women on board – a Mrs Scott.

Immediately smitten with the 26-year-old Barry, Mrs Scott began visiting his cabin. Barry, ever the meticulous legal note-taker, recorded each encounter in his diary with the enthusiasm of a sports statistician.

Here is his diary entry on 24 July: '. . . after breakfast, Mrs S.'

Within a week his appetite for the woman had grown all-consuming. 31 July: 'Mrs S twice.'

4 August: 'Mrs S 4 times.'

Barry couldn't help himself. He rebuffed an appeal from the woman's distraught husband to end the affair. Eventually Mrs Scott moved out of the marital cabin and the captain of the ship confined Barry to his quarters to limit fallout from the scandal.

But the relationship became the talk of the ship and when it docked in Sydney it did not take long for the story to ripple through colonial society. Barry, despite a thick folder of impressive credentials and introductory letters, found doors closing. A week after being admitted to the Bar, he sailed to the settlement of Port Phillip.

But if his libido and scant regard for traditional marriage has been an endless source of gossip for polite society, no-one can fault Barry's diligence and knowledge of the law. He defies stereotypes. Like Sir Alfred Stephen in Sydney, he has been a staunch defender of the rights of Aboriginal people and has often appeared in court *pro bono* to act on their behalf. But as a judge he also has a reputation for toughness. He has never shied from sending a man to the gallows and his courtroom is known for its attention to regulations and detail.

On Saturday morning – the second day of Bruun's trial – Justice Barry looks on as George Scott is sworn in to give evidence.

Scott once again lists his background, and then goes on to contradict his testimony from the committal hearing a few months earlier.

'I have been serving as a volunteer in the New Zealand war, where I held the position of major,' he says. 'I have been called Captain Scott. My comrades used to call me jocularly "Captain Moonlite". I used to be called so at Egerton, where I have been lately.

'On the night of the 8th of May I was visited while in bed by Constable Monckton, Constable Mackston, and the prisoner, and was told that the prisoner had accused me of sticking up the bank. I said it was a conspiracy . . . they examined my firearms. I had no Colt revolver . . . I told the police that I had come from Melbourne on the previous night, as I had been at a house in Ballan on the Friday night and had remained there all night and all Saturday, leaving it at ten o'clock on Saturday night.'

Scott is asked by the Crown prosecutor, Mr Adamson, to name the person he had been visiting.

'I decline to answer.'

Redmond Barry intervenes: 'You must answer it.'

Scott hedges. 'It was a man known as Mick. I do not know his other name.'

Adamson: 'There was another person that you saw there. What was his name?'

'It was not a man, it was a woman. I decline to answer. I cannot answer the question.'

A frustrated Adamson says if Scott continues to decline to name the woman he will ask to have him committed for contempt of court.

Scott turns to the judge. 'Am I bound, your Honour, to answer the question?'

'You certainly are.'

'But I regard it as a matter of honour that I should not divulge the name.'

'You are sworn to tell the whole truth,' Barry reminds him.

'And so I will, but this is a question of honour.'

There it is again. The touchstone of Scott's life. His *honour*. But why is he so reluctant to reveal this woman's name? Years later, sitting hunched over a small table in his death cell in the early hours of the morning of his execution, he will write that he had been 10 miles from the bank at Mount Egerton when it was robbed. 'I was with a female to whom I was engaged,' he will write. 'When the robbery affair was discussed she asked me to pledge my word not to say where I was on the night and hour of the robbery. I gave her my promise and have kept it to my cost.'

It is a curious and puzzling admission. It contradicts later evidence he will give that he had spent several nights at the home of a married woman. In all his copious correspondence it is the only mention he makes of having intended to marry. The newspapers will report how, during the trial that will sentence him to death, a good-looking widow from Melbourne, a woman known as Mary Ames, arrives in Sydney and campaigns for his sentence to be commuted. She is said to have been engaged at one stage to Scott. But the man himself never speaks affectionately about this lost love of his.

It is another of those seeming contradictions in the life of Captain Moonlite. Ballan is a small town just a short ride from Mount Egerton; a betrothal between the dashing local lay reader and a woman living nearby would surely be well known in these parts. Years later, Scott will say the woman ended up leaving him for a richer man, a cliché that will add to suspicions the whole story is a crock.

Indeed. If all this is true, if Andrew George Scott is having a relationship with a woman he intends to take as his wife, why does he leave her as soon as the trial of Bruun is over? Not just leave her – but jump on a ship and head straight for the Pacific Islands?

First, though, there is this matter of his *honour*.

Scott is cross-examined by Bruun's lawyer, Mr McDermott. He concedes he had helped his friend Robert Crook try to obtain an alibi for the sheep-stealing episode at Bacchus Marsh and regrets his lie about having been in Melbourne on the night of the bank robbery. There's also another thing he'd like to clear up.

'I rode back a part of the way from the place on the Ballan road where I had been stopping. I hired a horse from Mick and, as the road was very bad, sent him home when I rode part of the distance. I have said that I saw a man riding on the road between Buninyong and Egerton, who was riding fast, and might have come from Egerton. I led Constable Monckton to infer that the horseman was seen by me on Saturday evening. I was wrong in saying so.'

Once again Scott is asked to name the woman he had been visiting. Once again his *honour* prevents him from disclosing the name.

You might think Justice Redmond Barry would sympathise with a man who would travel miles on horseback to spend a night with a woman. But this 'honour' thing Scott keeps prattling on about is a foreign concept to a judge who openly records the names of his sexual conquests in his diary.

He bangs his gavel down on the hard bench. Andrew George Scott is held in contempt of court and taken to the lock-up.

—

The trial of Julius Bruun lasts throughout the day. The jury hears confusing evidence from a so-called handwriting expert about the 'Captain Moonlite' signature – and then discovers the very same expert lodged at Scott's house and shared meals with him prior to the trial. There's an air of suspicion that perhaps Bruun, Simpson and Scott were all party to the robbery.

Justice Barry, who tells the jury 'they must assume at once that either Simpson alone or Simpson and Bruun were in the case, or that Scott independently or Scott and Bruun were concerned from beginning to end', will say years later the case against Bruun had filled him with doubts.

After four hours of deliberating, the jury agrees, returning a verdict of not guilty just before midnight. Plans to try Simpson for the robbery are dropped as a result. After months of speculation, the law is none the wiser as to who this Captain Moonlite really was, and who made off with the heist's takings.

But there are some who think they know. Before the robbery George Scott had been borrowing money, claiming he had not been paid by the church and that funds due to him from New Zealand had not yet arrived. After the theft, he has been seen paying debts with London Chartered Bank notes – the very bank that was robbed in these days when banks issue their own notes.

Scott insists he is innocent. He always will. But the press, while admiring his chivalry in refusing to reveal his whereabouts on the night of the robbery, have their doubts. One of the windbags at the *Ballarat Courier*, a newspaper where a thesaurus apparently rests on every desk, pens a ponderous editorial at the conclusion of the trial. 'It is . . . no breach of journalistic propriety to compliment that eccentric member of the church fulminant and tonitrant upon the manliness which he displayed in refusing to give up the name, although threatened with imprisonment, of the frail fair one whose seductive company kept him away from his virtuous stretcher on the night antecedent to the robbery.

'This most amiable reticence was not lost upon the gallant Sir Redmond, who, though sternly ordering the offender to await the sentence of the court, conveniently let the contumaciousness of the witness slip from his judicial memory. Were we to discuss the probabilities of Scott's complicity in the robbery, this recusance would weigh favourably in our mind . . .'

In other words, good folk from Ballarat to Mount Egerton already believe Scott is Captain Moonlite.

But Scott remains indignant. He continues demanding Bruun issue a public apology for naming him as the suspect in the robbery. It's a matter of *honour*, of course. Negotiations are conducted after the trial at the home of Bruun's father. Scott turns up one day and threatens to horsewhip Bruun if he fails to apologise. When he leaves the house Scott believes he has finally secured an admission from the young man he had taken such a close interest in earlier in the year.

But according to Scott, Bruun arrives at a meeting at a local theatre a week after the trial without a written apology. Instead, he 'handed me a parcel which I afterwards found contained the gold . . . up to this date I had no guilty knowledge or connection with the swindle. When Bruun handed me the cake of gold he immediately left me and disappeared from Ballarat for the time being.

'I followed him over two hundred miles to where I heard he was, to give him the cake of gold and make him apologise. I could not find him.'

It's a remarkable tale that ticks all the boxes for Andrew George Scott: a noble man, brimming with innocence, setting out on a journey of hundreds of miles by horse to return a stolen cake of gold and have his honour restored.

It's also highly unlikely. The truth is that Scott does indeed set out on a journey of thousands of miles, a voyage that will end in dishonour, and with his reputation firmly trashed.

9

THE BEGGAR'S VICE

Gold. Such a precious substance. It can be bent and beaten, and then do the same to those who seek it. That great Romantic poet, Lord Byron – a spendthrift who was always hopelessly falling in love – knew all about its lure and how its lustre could cloud reason and upend logic.

'A thirst for gold,' he had written, 'The beggar's vice, which can but overwhelm the meanest hearts.'

George Scott has just boarded *Pilot*, an 84-ton trading vessel leaving Melbourne for Fiji. There's a cake of gold hidden among his possessions that will soon overwhelm his heart and his senses. He also carries at least four handguns and a fine letter of introduction from his great friend in Bacchus Marsh, James Crook, lauding his character and his engineering abilities. It's a few weeks after the trial, and just 15 months since he arrived in Australia. If we can believe him, he is leaving behind a fiancée and a trail of broken friendships and suspicions.

The journey to Fiji will include stops at several other Pacific islands. So come now. While the *Pilot* ploughs through the seas over the next couple of weeks, giving Scott time to cultivate several new friendships and plot his next move in life, we have time to consider another gold robbery just as famous as the one staged at the Mount Egerton bank.

In some ways the man at the centre of the theft was a little like George Scott. He carried poetry and power wherever he roamed. He had been a butcher at Lambing Flat just before the series of brutal attacks began on the Chinese miners. But the preferred trade of Frank Gardiner, the man they called 'The Darkie' for his long flowing black hair and swarthy skin, was in horse flesh. He had once been sentenced to five years in Pentridge in the 1850s for trying to sell 32 stolen horses near Ballarat. He had escaped after a month in prison and headed into the lawless plains of south-west NSW, cattle duffing and stealing horses before going on to serve seven years' hard labour on Sydney's Cockatoo Island.

By the early 1860s Gardiner was at large again, forging a reputation as a wild and untamed bushranger, which would be matched only by Captain Thunderbolt several years later. But unlike so many of his fellow outlaws, Gardiner's colleagues ran large gangs that were efficiently organised and disciplined. He was also, unusually, literate. By some accounts the son of a Scottish convict supervisor and an Aboriginal woman, Gardiner was said to carry in his pocket a book of Lord Byron's poetry.

For years Gardiner had been untouchable. But then gold changed everything. The riots at Lambing Flat, coupled with the increasingly daring exploits of Gardiner and other bushrangers, forced the establishment of an officially organised police force that divided NSW into policing districts. Another 800 men had been recruited to fill its ranks. New six-shooter guns were issued and hopes rose that the era of bushrangers would soon be extinguished.

But if there were never enough police to cover the ground required to flush the outlaws from their bush hideaways, what was lacking in even greater qualities in this new force was imagination. Few officers, it seemed – many of them Irish or newly arrived migrants with military backgrounds – had the ability to think like the best bushrangers and anticipate their moves.

By the early 1860s this battle, avidly chronicled by the newspapers of the day, had become mired in a series of frustrating dead-ends. The police were led by Sir Frederick Pottinger, a heavily bearded son of Ireland who had squandered his inheritance on the racetracks of England and, after failing to recoup it on the goldfields, had joined the NSW police troopers and been quickly promoted because of his titled heritage.

Pottinger soon became a symbol for all the failures by police to stem the growth – and increasing popularity – of the bushrangers. These criminals, already idolised and protected in many outback areas by the speed of the bush telegraph, were epitomised by Gardiner and a gang including the charismatic Ben Hall and another long-time horse thief, John Peisley. They seemed to roam at will, staging hold-ups on bush tracks, plundering hapless miners and raiding towns from Bathurst to Gundagai.

Peisley would be hanged in April 1862 for the murder of an inn-keeper, as Sir Alfred Stephen was delighted to tell us earlier. But his loss hardly slowed the Gardiner gang. By now Gardiner was being hailed in the small taverns and makeshift corrugated tin pubs throughout the bush. Any man with a fiddle could break into a song about the Australian Dick Turpin, a courageous highway robber who always handed over a share of his spoils to the poor and needy. A few months after Peisley's hanging, the Gardiner gang, uniformly dressed in red serge shirts and scarves, hid behind a series of large rocks near Eugowra in the central west of NSW. A Cobb & Co coach protected by four police officers was making its way from Forbes to Orange laden with a small fortune of gold and cash worth 14,000 pounds.

Two bullock wagons were used to block the coach and in the shootout that followed, the gang escaped with almost 3000 ounces of gold and more than 3000 pounds in cash.

Pottinger was quickly on the scene and gave chase with a squad of his men, ultimately retrieving part of the plunder and eventually arresting three members of the gang. One of them, Henry Manns, another who was on Stephen's list of those executed, would be hanged the following year, 1863, despite growing public calls for clemency. His hanging was one of the worst botched executions in memory.

'A gleam of something white falling between the black bars of the scaffold, a dull thud, and half sigh, half exclamation from the spectators, and Henry Manns swung by the neck between earth and heaven,' reported *The Empire*. 'For a moment his limbs stiffened, and he remained motionless, and then came that horrible convulsive struggle for the life which was being so cruelly choked out by the fatal rope – choked, and yet not choked; for, from the mal-adjustment of the knot . . . it slipped in the fall round to the front, and caught the victim under the chin, forcing his head back . . . by the jerk the blood had been forced out apparently from his eyes, and had spurted about his cap, and downward to his neck, the front of which stretched blue and ghastly to its full extent.'

Eventually four men were summoned to readjust the knot and drop Manns again before he finally died slowly from strangulation. The bungled hanging became the talk of Sydney, just another example of the Establishment's ineptitude when it came to dealing with bushrangers.

Pottinger may have boasted a knighthood but after Gardiner's daring gold robbery it did little to protect him from the scorn and ridicule of the impatient Sydney public and politicians. In the months after the hold-up new songs hailing the bravery of Gardiner were being sung in the taverns of the outback. At one stage Pottinger hid behind the home of one of Gardiner's mistresses. Gardiner arrived late at night, but escaped in the subsequent shootout when Pottinger's gun misfired.

The bumbling style of the man charged with hunting down the bushrangers was cemented 18 months later when Pottinger accidentally shot himself in the lower chest while trying to jump on board a moving coach. He died four weeks later, his reputation shredded. There was one saving grace. By then, Gardiner was behind bars.

—

They found him in northern Queensland helping to run an inn about 40 miles north of Rockhampton. Gardiner had fled there with another mistress and settled into the local community. But three officers posing as miners eventually arrested him and took him back to Sydney.

Even in court Gardiner proved elusive. With no evidence to support a charge of masterminding the largest gold robbery seen in Australia, they indicted him on the attempted murder of a police officer during a shootout that had occurred back in 1861. But a bumbling prosecution left the jury with no choice but to find him not guilty. So they hauled Gardiner back into court a month later for another trial, this time for the attempted murder of another officer during the same shootout, as well as shooting with the intent of inflicting grievous bodily harm.

Who should be presiding over this second trial but Sir Alfred Stephen, the original hanging judge, a man haunted by the scourge of bushranging, flummoxed by the hero worship enjoyed by so many of its practitioners, obsessed with Gardiner's ability to avoid arrest and soon to send the Clarke brothers – 'the most wicked of the wicked' – to the gallows. No-one in the court had failed to see Sir Alfred's mouth turn down when Gardiner escaped the death penalty again on the new attempted murder charge. It was as though the judge had just swallowed a spoonful of curdled milk.

But Gardiner had been found guilty on that second accusation of shooting with intent, along with the robbery of two country store-keepers. It gave Sir Alfred something to work with, even if he could not use the rope on Gardiner. He found it hard not to sound triumphant when he began sentencing Gardiner by telling the courtroom he had very few remarks to make, 'but feel it my duty to utter some'.

And so he turned to the most famous bushranger in the colonies and unleashed an outpouring of relief mingled with anger.

'What a career you have led! You have been the captain of a band of robbers. Well, you say that you repent; if it be real I say I am truly glad, for your sake, that it is truly so. But, on the other hand, I do not see how society is to be affected by that, for you have brought this country to as low a state of degradation in character as probably any country in the world has had to suffer under.

'At this very hour, the idea entertained in England and other countries is that, from end to end, the colony is little better than a nest of thieves.'

It did not take Sir Alfred long to get to one of his favourite topics – the public's obsession with bushrangers. The judge said he was aware a relative had been passing out pamphlets supporting Gardiner in the pit of the Victoria Theatre – 'that shows to what an extent among some classes in the community this sympathy has been carried. You are a man that many sympathise with, but I think that had you have perished as some of your companions have done, it might not have been an unwholesome lesson to the community and the world.'

Now, said Sir Alfred, it was time for Gardiner to receive the just and necessary reward for a crime spree 'unequalled within my experience or reading in any other country . . . acts which would sink the character of any community on earth. And I charge you now Gardiner, with being the head, the front, the parent of all this. I declare to you on my honour as a man, speaking to you not merely as a colonist but as man to man, face to face – I would say that if I could feel sympathy with you, I should feel ashamed of myself as a member of society, as a gentleman, or as a Christian.'

They were not the words of any normal judge passing sentence on a guilty offender. Sir Alfred's 'few remarks' had become a deluge of built-up resentment against all those outlaws who had stolen from the innocent and robbed the colony of its chance to muffle the sound of those rattling convict chains.

Sir Alfred said he was aware some would believe the gaol term he was imposing on Gardiner to be too severe, but he wanted to make a stern example of him for the public. He sentenced him to 32 consecutive years of hard labour, two of them to be spent in irons. 'I hope that a better feeling will spring up – that it will be seen that crime strikes at the vitals of a country; that it saps its prosperity,' the judge noted. 'A country's prosperity is gone when its character is gone.'

Sir Alfred had no idea how far sympathy for Gardiner extended into the community. Less than a decade later a series of powerfully backed petitions will secure the early release of Gardiner, on condition he leave the colonies for good. He will arrive on the docks of San Francisco in early 1875, now a bustling city of more than 200,000 souls, to become the owner of the Twilight Star Saloon.

A reporter from the *San Francisco Chronicle* will be there to meet him and will report him to be 'a man of apparently forty-five years of age, with a full, round, English face, jet-black beard and moustache, and a quiet demeanour which sensationalists would hardly associate with the exploits of the great Australian Dick Turpin'.

The reporter asks Gardiner why he had enjoyed the support of 'three fourths' of the people of Australia. It isn't hard to picture Gardiner standing there on a crowded San Francisco pier, a wry smile forming beneath that thick beard and moustache, collar upturned against the perennial chill wind that blows in across the city's wide bay. Here is yet another chance to add to the legend, to burnish the myth of that great Australian character – the gentleman bushranger.

Why had he been so popular? 'Because I never committed any murder,' Gardiner replied. 'Because I have given away more than half my earnings on the road to poor travellers, and because I never robbed a poor person in my life.'

'A magnificent horseman, a brave man, it seems wonderful how he could have selected such a mode of existence,' gushed the reporter. 'Perhaps of all bushrangers Gardiner was the most successful and the most popular.'

Gardiner, a petty horse thief catapulted by fate into celebrity status, had arrived in a country that mirrored the Australian colonies. The Wild West was in full swing and mythmaking was all the rage. In place of any official police force, hired guns travelled from town to town – from Carson City in Nevada to Tombstone in Arizona – pursuing gangs of outlaws and bringing a warped sense of order to the chaos left in the wake of the Civil War.

The *Chronicle* reporter had clearly been charmed and possibly overwhelmed by Gardiner. The Darkie might have been the most successful and the most popular of Australia's outlaws at the time – but there were still more to come.

10

GOING TO THE DEVIL, HEADLONG

There are seven male passengers on board *Pilot* as it begins its journey across the Pacific to Levuka in Fiji in early September 1869. Only one thing is certain. They will not go thirsty. In the hold are hundreds of cases of wine and stout, 17 cases of whiskey, 52 cases of brandy and 35 cases of Old Tom gin. They will not go hungry, either. Not when George Scott is around. He might like a drink, but you're more likely to find him on deck during the day taking careful aim and shooting the large sea birds that circle above the schooner.

Pilot is a small boat. But to her owner, 30-year-old Allan Hughan, she more than compensates for her size with her ability to handle large swells. He had her refitted a year ago and journeyed to Western Australia to search for pearls, the latest in a series of fortune-seeking schemes he had hatched in recent years.

This time he was so confident of success he had insisted on taking his two children and wife, Phoebe – a thin and pale woman more at home teaching music than ploughing through rough seas in a small ship. Hughan had loved the way *Pilot* handled the conditions – 'a splendid sea boat that rides upon the large waves just like a cork and very seldom a wave washes the deck'.

But the safe performance of the schooner was one of the few positives to emerge from that trip. Not only had there been some nasty weather to contend with, but Hughan had been greatly embarrassed when two Aboriginal prisoners he had been loaned to help with the expedition escaped by swimming ashore.

The diving equipment he had added to the ship proved to be ineffective because of the strong tides. A few weeks later the ship had been forced to make a hasty retreat from Enderby Island on the remote north-west coast of Western Australia after being threatened by a hostile clan of Aboriginals furious that an earlier crew of pearlers had stolen some of their women. Hughan returned to Melbourne by the end of June with just a few pearls to show off – 'one of them, which is about the size of a pea, is valued at between two and three hundred pounds'.

But if there is an adventurous spirit that runs strong in Hughan's blood, he is also a magnet for trouble. The year before that pearling expedition he had sailed from Melbourne to Fremantle and endured 'a most unpleasant' journey that ended in court with Hughan claiming the skipper and his mate had assaulted him.

In 1865 he led a party of men driving more than 9000 sheep through the rugged interior of Queensland. One night his cook told him he was certain he had seen a famous horse thief and bushranger known as 'The Snob' camped nearby. Hughan wandered over and engaged the man in a conversation. He quickly realised as he listened to the man's bragging that he was definitely 'The Snob', otherwise known as Edward Hartigan, one of the most wanted scoundrels in the colony. On Hughan's signal, he and three other men wrestled 'The Snob' to the ground, seizing his gun and tying him up with rope.

After dispatching one of his shepherds to notify the police, an excited Hughan penned a breathless and lengthy account of the capture to the *Rockhampton Bulletin*. The newspaper rushed the letter boasting about this remarkable citizen's arrest into print.

'Since his arrival in our camp "The Snob" . . . has confessed to stealing several horses, the manner of his escape from the police, and expressed his firm conviction that before three weeks he will again be at liberty, and may then do me a "good turn",' Hughan wrote, before closing out the letter by saying 'with these facts, communicated to you whilst watching my captive, the wind playing most perseveringly with my writing materials, I will close my already long letter and remain obediently yours, Allan Hughan'.

It soon transpired 'The Snob' was not just a good horse thief but a clairvoyant as well. He *did* escape. A few weeks later *The Bulletin* ran a short paragraph following up Hughan's exploits. 'Our readers may recollect a short time ago a letter from Mr Allan Hughan of Belcombe Creek, Gordon Downs Station, announcing the capture of the notorious horse stealer "The Snob". Mr Hughan, we since understand . . . was unable to hold the rascal in his custody until the arrival of the police, and is still at large.'

Allan Hughan is a smallish man with a receding hairline. But just like his ship, he compensates for his size by refusing to be overwhelmed by circumstance and misfortune. There will be plenty more of that to come; a failed business venture will soon follow and within six months *Pilot* will be shipwrecked off New Caledonia.

Yet Hughan is an optimist, a cork that keeps bobbing along in ever turbulent seas. So it is almost inevitable that he will fall under the spell of such a mercurial figure as George Scott. He is everything Hughan aspires to be – a charismatic adventurer who seems to care little for the conventions of the day.

One night during the voyage to Fiji the passengers will conduct a séance on the *Pilot*. It will be Scott, the former lay preacher who spent six months invoking the name of God, who guides the group into the spirit world.

'Scott was eloquent on the subject,' one passenger will recall years later. 'In explaining to the circle the mysteries of the phenomena, he requested the members to ask questions and the table would rap out the answers.

'One of the passengers enquired how many pistols Scott had about him, and the answer came: "Four". Moonlite at once confessed the reply was correct, and forthwith pulled out of each pocket a miniature revolver . . . a more pleasant and polite travelling companion could not be met with anywhere.'

The spirit world, it seems, is alive and well on the *Pilot* as it nears Fiji. Allan Hughan should be taking advantage of its openness by asking a few more questions about his dashing travelling companion. The answers rapped out on the table just below the main deck might give him second thoughts about George Scott.

—

God has been forced into a strategic retreat in the second half of the 19th century. The Second Industrial Revolution is showing just how powerful science can be when its theories are put into practice. New inventions with intricate wiring and complex machinery are being unveiled at an astonishing rate. Steel and iron can now be easily bent and shaped to the will of man. Even controversial theories still unproven have put religion on the back foot. Charles Darwin's *Origin of Species*, with its suggestion that chance and necessity guides nature, not an all-knowing Creator, has helped trigger a crisis in faith.

Spiritualism first gained popularity in 1848 when two sisters in New York reported contacting the spirit of a murdered man whose body had been found in their house. Now it has become an antidote for the times and spread throughout the British Empire. Instead of the church's offering of eternal damnation or salvation, it provides a more comforting option – an afterlife where the dead remain in touch with the living.

There are ghosts and mysterious forces at work. Ethereal transmissions and spooky occurrences have become the parlour games of the Victorian age. It is perfect fodder for George Scott, a man who constantly shifts between the real world and an imaginary one. He might come from devout Presbyterian stock, have a father who is now a minister of the church, and even stood at the pulpit himself and lectured audiences on the importance of God's word. But there will be signs in the coming years that Scott is wrestling with his faith.

His behaviour over the coming 12 months after the *Pilot* arrives in Fiji will hardly be Christian-like. But then, he is not on his own. In the 1860s the Pacific Islands, with their remoteness, lack of a central government and no court system to settle disputes, have lured an army of miscreants, swindlers and fortune seekers.

The worst of them is Bully Hayes, a large, brutal American who plies its seas blackbirding – kidnapping locals – and molesting women. Hayes will be described in the years to come as one of the last of the buccaneering pirates. A bigamist and thief who is missing an ear after being caught cheating during a card game in California, Hayes has put a lengthy seagoing career to use by touring remote islands and enticing – or coercing – locals to come on board his ship. He then takes them prisoner before selling them as slave labour for plantations from Queensland to Fiji, Tahiti and Samoa.

In Fiji, cotton has become the new gold. Land is cheap, labour cheaper, thanks to men like Hayes, and taxation almost non-existent. With the Civil War in America disrupting cotton production, prices have soared. In Levuka, Hughan introduces Scott to a friend, an English immigrant called Francis Holworthy, who three years earlier had brought a large collection of cotton seedlings to Fiji hoping to ride the boom.

Scott, cashed up and looking to make his fortune, agrees to join Hughan and Holworthy in a partnership that will set up a new cotton plantation on the French island of New Caledonia, a week's sailing from Fiji.

Suddenly George Scott is no longer a poor lay reader in a cold and insignificant mining town, but a man on the cusp of making a fortune and overturning the financial bad luck that has dogged his family since those years in Ireland. He is no longer surrounded by dishevelled miners like those back in Mount Egerton, scrabbling in the dirt and relying on sheer luck to improve their lot in life, but smart men with well-laid plans who see the bigger picture. These are men who think like him and want the same thing.

Hughan and Holworthy – who will end up marrying one of Hughan's daughters – also introduce Scott to George Winter, a former politician from Victoria who arrived in Fiji in 1862 and embarked on a series of land deals that have already made him a rich man. Scott wants land of his own and agrees to purchase from Winter an archetypal Pacific island he can call his own. Vomo is 225 acres of pristine land lapped by white sands and azure seas. Scott signs a promissory note agreeing to pay 260 pounds for the island within nine months.

After several weeks in Fiji he heads to New Caledonia where his partners plan to set up their new cotton plantation. He stays at a hotel in Noumea, entertaining guests and prospective business partners, drinking beer and gin and taking in the view. The island will prove to be the one place where Allan Hughan, by now completely infatuated with Scott, will finally bring his bad luck to an end. The *Pilot* will be wrecked not far from Noumea in the coming months. But after that he will discover a role for which he has far more talent than driving sheep and searching for pearls, becoming the official photographer for New Caledonia and documenting indigenous life throughout the Pacific in thousands of sepia-washed images.

Hughan will also need the work because all those well-laid plans for a cotton plantation will come to nothing. When the man he has begun referring to as 'my little heart's treasure' and 'my joyous, innocent darling' heads for Sydney in December carrying an introductory letter from Holworthy, Scott tells his partners he will be back soon with more cotton seed and equipment so the business can officially begin.

Hughan is blinded by his affection for George Scott. He can't – or won't – allow himself to imagine that this bold, gun-slinging adventurer with the Irish lilt has a duplicitous bone in his body. So perhaps Hughan puts it down as a small oversight in the enthusiastic rush to get back to Australia for supplies when Scott departs his hotel in Noumea, leaving unpaid a bill for more than 250 francs in lodgings and drink.

—

The year 1869 has not been the finest of years in the seagoing career of Captain William Yuill. September had been particularly disastrous. Instead of earning money hauling cargo through the Pacific in the schooner *Sarah Pile*, Yuill spent several uncomfortable days in a courtroom on charges of 'counselling, aiding and abetting' a young woman to procure an abortion.

He was no stranger to a courtroom. Sailors seeking unpaid wages and police charging him with assault were just a few who had dragged William Yuill before the bench over the years. But this case had been awkward. The newspapers had dined out on the affair, regaling their readers with all sorts of sordid details; how he had gotten the girl pregnant late the previous year after being introduced to her at a picnic, how angry he had been when she rebuffed his further sexual advances early in her pregnancy; how he had coldly suggested she pay a visit to the herbalist Thomas Patterson, whose potions and instruments could bring about a speedy miscarriage.

The matter had dragged on for weeks. The herbalist ended up being sentenced to seven years' hard labour and, in the only decent turn of events he had experienced this year, the Crown had decided not to pursue the charges against Yuill.

But now things have gone from bad to worse. Yuill is in a prison cell in New Caledonia, accused of trying to smuggle a French prisoner out of the country. Another two of his crew – the steward and another seaman – are also facing charges, meaning the 120-ton boat will not have enough manpower to sail back to Sydney to pick up its next cargo.

How fortuitous it is, then, that there just happens to be a man looking for a swift passage back to Australia with a formidable seagoing background?

By 13 December, as she sails out of Noumea with the help of former British naval officer George Scott, William Yuill has been tried and sentenced to 13 months' imprisonment. There's no keeping the man down for long, though. By February he will have disguised a dummy and left it sleeping on his prison cot, giving him enough time to escape the prison and catch the next ship for Australia.

But the *Sarah Pile* makes it back well before then, limping into Sydney on Christmas Eve, its canvas torn after encountering gales and stormy seas on the approach to the Australian coast. By the time Yuill manages to return to Sydney a few months later, there will be two men back in New Caledonia wondering where in the hell is George Scott.

—

Holworthy has urged Scott to work quickly in Sydney. 'I need not remind you that the safety of the firm depends on your being back by the first of February,' he tells him in a letter dispatched soon after the *Sarah Pile*'s departure from Noumea. '. . . independently of every consideration it will be much more jolly for me when you are back.'

But February and then March pass without news. Where is George Scott? By May, Hughan has organised the seizure of Scott's goods, including a rifle, to raise 36 pounds toward the debts he has left behind. His dewy-eyed view of the man has been replaced by the realisation he and Holworthy have, at best, been strung along and, at worst, duped.

Hughan writes a letter to Scott that is laden with desperation.

'No news! No money! No cotton seed! No fulfilment of engagements, no letter even but one, and that of such a character that when put before me to read even I had to admit . . . that it was most unsatisfactory. But one letter in four or five months and that written "in extreme haste" – you absolutely idly spending your time all the while and could not write a letter on the only business [that] you had to engage your attention.

'If you don't see the folly and the *shame*, yes I say shame italicised, as soon as possible of your proceedings you must be a perfect idiot . . . and I hope the scales fall from your eyes and be forever buried [or] you are going to the devil headlong.'

But even in his fury and frustration, Hughan cannot but help reveal his deep affection for Captain Moonlite. 'I would understand [your behaviour] in a mean, low-spirited mongrel – but in you?

Oh heavens! It is monstrous, a shameful paradox. Unless, my little heart's treasure, my joyous, innocent darling, I would rather see you than anyone on earth . . . but I would firmly close this letter tho' I knew it would prevent me ever seeing you again if by doing so I could wake you up to a proper sense of your position and duties.'

It's easy to feel for Hughan. In early February when Captain Yuill escapes from his prison cell, the French authorities raid every ship docked in Noumea. The *Pilot* suffers more damage than most, being 'turned upside down'. Four weeks later it takes on water after hitting a reef not far out of Noumea and has to be abandoned. Hughan has lost money on a cotton plantation that will never go ahead. He has lost his boat. Far worse, he – a married man with two children in the prudish Victorian era – has lost a man to whom he had surrendered not only his good sense, but his heart as well.

So he is understandably angry and bitter. But he is also wrong. George Scott has not been 'idly spending' his time in Sydney at all. He has been remarkably busy, actually. In fact, he has been having the time of his life.

11

BLACK SNAKES AND
BAD CHEQUES

That wild drop in the blood? It is more like a raging torrent by the time George Scott returns to Australia. If it has already punctuated his life with bursts of manic energy and extraordinary recklessness, it is about to surge out of control in 1870.

If Holworthy and Hughan are growing concerned about his whereabouts, even the man himself will find it difficult to recall his movements in the coming months. He will seem to be everywhere, in so many different guises, slipping in and out of reality, as always.

There he is – standing at the counter of the Union Bank just days after arriving from the Pacific Islands, depositing 503 pounds in a new account – the direct proceeds of the sale of a cake of gold to the Sydney Royal Mint.

Here he is – standing in the auction room of R. F. Stubbs and Co, a big smile across his face after splashing out 270 pounds to purchase a 53-foot ketch called *Comet*, well known for hauling cargo along the east coast and as far away as New Caledonia.

There he goes – skippering *Comet* up and down the east coast of Australia after forking out a couple of hundred pounds on repairs. He is taking a family of English settlers, the Hobbs, south to Wagonga Inlet, navigating the turbulent waters of the Heads and helping them unload 30 tons of supplies. 'The three weeks we were cooped up with him on the *Comet*, no one could have been more kind and considerate than him to our family,' the youngest son of the family will write. 'He was not a tall man . . . a rather pleasant good looking man . . . well spoken . . . very moderate in his language and altogether appeared to be a thorough gentleman. I could hardly credit that our Captain Scott could turn out to be such a bad character, and take on bushranging . . .'

But hang on, here comes a different Captain Scott – using his ketch to smuggle goods off the coast of northern Australia. 'I went [on] a long voyage around the islands,' he will later write to his father in New Zealand, 'and got a good deal of profitable trade. I acknowledge I did smuggle a good deal in Queensland . . .'

He is everywhere; living on the *Comet* down at Cowper's Wharf at Woolloomooloo, sleeping in a newly purchased bed with a fluffy pillow; wandering through city streets buying himself new shirts and fashionable collars to go with them; admiring several scarves in a store window and deciding he *must* have them; a new pair of boots would not go amiss, so he buys them, too.

There is plenty of hard drinking, too. He will openly admit that this year becomes a right old blur after a while. The unpaid bills at hotels will prove it. But every so often he disappears from view and others will be keen to fill in the gaps of this remarkable year.

There is the young man hired as a helping hand on the *Comet* who will one day emerge as a respectable businessman in Sydney. He will tell the astonishing story of how Scott, meeting Bully Hayes in Apia in Samoa, tries to form a partnership with the notorious pirate and blackbirder. But even Hayes shies away from a man whose erratic temper he believes will lead only to misfortune.

This same former crew member of *Comet* will also claim Scott becomes besotted with Eleanor Carey, a popular actress appearing in a string of pantomimes and burlesque shows at the Adelphi Theatre. Scott sits entranced one night by her depiction of the Italian peasant girl Columbine. He becomes her self-appointed agent in a bid to woo her. But repeatedly rebuffed, that erratic temper that supposedly even worried a man like Bully Hayes takes hold. One night at the theatre, Scott rises from a box and fires two shots into the air when she embraces a fellow actor. Scott escapes – and ticket sales for subsequent shows soar.

Where is that line between myth and reality?

Scott says he goes into partnership with a mysterious German called Count Geldern, who swindles him out of hundreds of pounds. It is one of the few stories he will tell with consistency down the years. In that letter to his father Scott will claim that 'Geldern was a most accomplished forger as I have found to my cost. [He] came from Auckland and forged me for nearly all I had.'

Almost a decade later Scott will sit in his death cell and repeat the same story. Geldern, if he does exist, is a far more ghostly figure than Scott will ever be. He leaves behind few traces. A 'Count Geldern' will be on board a ship that arrives in the colonies from London in the late 1860s; a couple of letters addressed to 'Count Geldern' will remain uncollected at the Sydney post office in 1870 and there will be a fleeting report in New Zealand of a 'Count R. Geldern' racing a six-year-old horse called Medusa.

Maybe he does fleece Scott for most of his money. But George Scott hardly requires assistance when it comes to losing money – by 14 November his bank account is empty and he closes it down.

He had already sold the *Comet* when funds were dwindling. Now the pressure is really building. Listen closely and you might even hear that wild drop of blood surging through him. With no cash he starts passing bad cheques and within a week he hears there are creditors chasing him all over town.

Here he is, on 28 November, climbing out of a horse-drawn cab in Hunter Street (surely that wasn't Nosey Bob in the driver's seat?) – and walking into an ironmonger's store. He hands over a four-quid cheque for a revolver and a deed box. The man behind the counter, William Foy, knows Scott. But he is taken aback by how quickly

Scott speaks. He seems agitated and in a rush. The cheque, of course, will bounce.

Scott has already tried to purchase a barque called *Celestia* for 200 pounds, but it was repossessed when the money failed to come through. On 30 November he hands over a soon-to-be-worthless cheque of 130 pounds for the yacht *Why Not*. There is a plan forming in Scott's mind. He has Charles Dillon with him, a former sailor on Allan Hughan's ill-fated *Pilot*. Dillon has agreed to help Scott sail *Why Not* to Fiji. Better to face the wrath of Holworthy and Hughan than remain a hunted man in Sydney.

The plan is simple. They will leave Sydney at 4am the following morning, slip unseen through the Heads and then sail carefree into the Pacific. Scott has met a woman he wants to take with him; that former *Comet* crew member will maintain it was that actress, Eleanor Carey. But Charles Dillon thinks it is a Burwood woman, Eliza Jane Horner.

But Eliza Horner has no plans to travel with Scott. He has already duped her for a paltry pound and when he turns up outside her house, she turns him away, telling him she already has one useless cheque of his. Horner will tell police later that Scott appeared to be 'wandering in his mind . . . Captain Scott was not in a fit state of mind to transact business . . . He appeared to be in trouble and was often saying "funny things".'

A diligent police officer, Detective Bowden, has been on Scott's trail for the past week as more and more recipients of Scott's bad cheques began to lodge complaints. At sunset on 30 November, Bowden arrives at the wharf and handcuffs Scott. It will be a long time before George Scott is a free man again.

—

This year of 1870 ends badly for both men destined to bring the bushranging era to such a climactic end.

By Christmas both are behind bars. In late December Scott pleads not guilty due to insanity to various charges of obtaining goods by means of false pretences. Given his manic behaviour in the previous months it seems a justifiable defence. It suggests a bipolar disorder of some kind – or it would if such a diagnosis existed in the 19th century. But Justice Simpson doesn't believe it and sentences him to 18 months' hard labour in Maitland Gaol.

In Victoria, a sullen Ned Kelly sits brooding in a stuffy granite cell in Beechworth Gaol. He has just turned 16 and is serving six months hard labour for violent assault and indecent behaviour.

It is not the first time he has been behind bars in recent months in what is already becoming a critical year for the bushranging fraternity. Back in May, Ned had left Harry Power, tired of the old man's abusive temper and his constant bowel complaints. He had ridden more than 180 miles to get home to Eleven Mile Creek, but days later the police had arrived at the old bark hut and arrested him on two charges of highway robbery.

Harry had been mightily aggrieved at the boy's departure but he would have been proud of the way the kid sauntered into the Benalla police court in handcuffs. Kelly had arrived in town in police custody the day before and put on a brave face. 'Power's cub has been taken,' reported the local paper. The cub had been clearly well-schooled in defiance. 'The entrance of the escort into Benalla was quite imposing, the prisoner being surrounded by his captors, and every now and then a smile passed over his face as he recognised someone he knew.' But it had been a different story once the boy had been thrown in the cells. There, he became 'very moody . . . and appeared quite exhausted with the life he had been leading. He is very pale and has learned to smoke while out at night with Power.'

A taste for tobacco, however, was the least of the lessons bestowed by Power on his protégé. He walked into court the following day 'quite indifferent to the danger of his position,' reported another newspaper. 'While casting eyes among the crowd, he smiled complacently and assumed a jaunty air. Previous to his appearance in court, and while confined in the lock-up, he sang like a bird and seemed quite proud. The misguided youth evidently considers himself a character to be admired.'

He sang like a bird. It is a sentence that will indelibly stain the Kelly character. While waiting on remand for his trial, Kelly had been interviewed by two police officers hunting for Harry Power. They found 'a flash, ill-looking young blackguard' who did his best to give vague and unspecific answers to their questions about Power's whereabouts. Indeed, it would not be Ned but his uncle and an old Pentridge mate of Power's, Jack Lloyd, who will lead police to the old bushranger's lair.

But the stain will remain. In the coming months Ned managed to get off a series of robbery charges. In a combination of police incompetence and suspicions of intimidation by Kelly supporters, key witnesses went missing while others struggled to provide positive identification. For a family haunted by bad luck and obsessed with the notion that the traps were constantly – and wrongly – persecuting them, they have little appreciation for good fortune when it makes a rare appearance. In the same week as the first two charges against Ned were being dismissed, Ellen Kelly had escaped charges of illegally operating a sly grog shop out of her dirt-floor hut when the main witness – an undercover officer – refused to swear on the Bible that it had been Ellen who had served the grog to him.

Still, word that Ned had ratted on Harry had quickly spread. *He sang like a bird.* The phrase took on a life of its own throughout the district. The local newspapers were in no hurry to dismiss it either, hinting Kelly '. . . was let off in consequence of giving information about Power. It is to be hoped that this young man will act with more prudence in future, and beware the fate of Power . . .'

You could call a man a horse thief and a highway robber. The Kellys had been called all that – and worse. But being labelled a snitch reeked of cowardice and dishonour. By late August young Ned had been mortified by his growing reputation for having dobbed in Power. He became so desperate he penned a short note to a trooper he had struck up a friendship with while on remand, asking if he might be able to help. 'Every one looks on me like a black snake,' he wrote.

Things soon grew worse. At the end of October a stallion belonging to a couple of former convicts from Tasmania, Jeremiah and Catherine McCormick, had been found close to the Kellys' property. The incensed McCormicks, who had set themselves up as hawkers in nearby Greta, came by to collect it and accused the Kelly clan of stealing it. Later that same day, Ned had been out in the yard castrating calves with his uncle Jack Lloyd, whose bank account had recently swelled after being paid for snitching on Harry Power, when an idea had struck. Ned was dispatched to Greta with a gift for Catherine. It contained a note and a pair of calf testicles, suggesting her barrenness might be improved if she took the balls and got Mr McCormick to 'tie them to his own cock [so] that he might shag her better the next time'.

The crude missive naturally led to a physical confrontation. Jeremiah McCormick would tell a court that Ned returned to confront the couple at sunset. 'He rode his horse past me, and then came back again. My wife and I were standing by the side of our covered cart ... he then said, "I will ride my horse over you and kill you bloody wretches." He then jumped the horse upon me and knocked me down ... he then rode about 10 yards further away and said, "Come on, you old bastard, and fight me!" He held a stirrup iron and leather in his hand.'

Ned, still a couple of months away from turning 16, provided a written statement of the encounter that contained all the hallmarks of a naive teenage excuse. Mrs McCormick, he wrote, had struck the flank of his horse with a bullock's shinbone, causing 'it to jump forward and my fist came in collision with [Mr] McCormick's nose and caused him to loose [sic] his equilibrium and fall prostrate . . .'

He was sentenced to three months for assaulting Jeremiah McCormick and received another three months for sending indecent letters and using obscene language.

And so the year ends. It has been a good one for the authorities trying to rid the colonies of the bushranging menace. Harry Power's creaking body occupies a cell in Melbourne's Pentridge prison and his apprentice is in chains in a granite cell in Beechworth.

12

MARTYRDOM AND THE LEGEND STRIPPED BARE

His body lies crumpled and slumped on the bank of a creek in northern New South Wales. The sun has just set and his soiled clothes, drenched in water, mud and blood, are turning stiff in the cold air. A gun blast has ripped apart his chest. For those who have pursued the celebrated Captain Thunderbolt through all these years, that seeping wound has become a punctuation mark, a full stop marking the end of the bushranging era.

Little do they know it is only a pause.

Here lies the man who, even as he bleeds to death, has become the epitome of the Australian bushranger, a striking example of how public desire and the bush telegraph, with the help of a decent sprinkling of history's magical mythic dust, can transform a small-time criminal into a lionheart.

In reality he is laden with the pedestrian name of Frederick Ward. A chronic horse thief and prison escapee who has slowly been dying of an incurable lung disease, he is a man who has shown how circumstance and timing can catapult the mundane into the extraordinary in an instant.

It had started when Ward bailed up the tollgate at Campbell's Hill near Maitland in 1863. He told a customs officer called Delaney that he was known as Thunderbolt – 'thunder' because of the noise he made and the 'bolt' a reference to his gun.

At least, that was one of the stories. According to another version, Ward woke Delaney from a deep sleep by banging loudly on the door. Startled by the noise, Delaney leapt from his slumber. 'By God, I thought it must have been a thunderbolt,' he would reportedly recall later.

It doesn't really matter where the truth lies. The seeds of a legend had been sown and would only grow when stories began circulating that Ward had crossed paths with Delaney not long after the hold-up. As the flustered Delaney made his way to a nearby drinking house, Captain Thunderbolt took pity on him and magnanimously returned some of the money he had stolen.

And then there was the time he bailed up a band of German musicians making their way along a track at Goonoo Goonoo, south of Tamworth. Thunderbolt took what few pounds they had earned between them and ordered them to play him a song, sitting back in his saddle and tapping his feet in the stirrups in time with their piano accordions. But it was not long before the hardened steel inside the man softened with remorse. The winning owner of that day's big race in Tamworth would soon be heading down the same track and Thunderbolt promised the musicians that if he successfully bailed him up, he would return their savings. Sure enough, when they finally arrived back in Brisbane, there was a post office order for 20 pounds waiting for them.

A good bushranger knew the worth of playing to his public. And it didn't hurt to sprinkle some of that mythic dust around the place by giving a nod to that ultimate outlaw, Robin Hood. Was it any wonder those salty types of the New England district of NSW – the horse-breakers and smithies and carpenters and toilers of the soil – began to celebrate him in song?

I'm Frederick Ward
I'm a native of this isle
I rob the rich to feed the poor
And make the children smile

For years Frederick Ward had been supported by Mary Anne Bugg, the daughter of a convict overseer and an Aboriginal woman. She had been married at 14 to a former policeman turned shepherd before starting an affair with Ward. She would give birth to two of Ward's children and, as a trained Aboriginal tracker, had often ensured he avoided the traps.

But it was never going to end well, not even for a gentleman bushranger who they said rarely fired a shot in anger. Well, he had shot three policemen over the years, but that was a minor detail easily overlooked if you were in the legend-making business.

In May 1870, after bailing up a group of travellers including an Italian hawker, Giovanni Cappisoti, near Split Rock, Thunderbolt takes his captives to an inn near Church Gully and demands drinks. Cappisoti asks if he can leave. Ward allows him to bid farewell on the proviso he does not approach the nearby town of Uralla.

Cappisoti heads south and then takes a U-turn into the bush before heading straight to Uralla and reporting to the police. Two troopers set out to capture Thunderbolt and one of them, Alex Walker, ends up chasing him for miles through steep gullies and rocky outcrops.

It becomes one of those classic hero-villain shootouts involving near-misses and dogged pursuits. It ends with the two men, now horse-less, wrestling in the middle of Kentucky Creek. Walker manages to fire the remaining bullet in his gun into Ward's chest, then drags the dying Thunderbolt to the bank of the creek. As darkness descends, Walker leaves the scene to sleep the night in a nearby inn. He will return early the next morning to collect one of the greatest prizes in policing history.

They take Thunderbolt's body back to Uralla and make sure a local photographer records the moment for posterity. The man has been so elusive down the years no-one will believe he has finally met his end unless proof is provided.

So they prop him up on a cot, his chest wound so crudely stitched it looks like the work of a sailor hastily repairing torn canvas during a storm. The legend is stripped back to its raw reality and Captain

Thunderbolt is reduced to plain old Frederick Ward, a slight, balding man who might pass for a meek bank teller. He is about 35 but looks twice that age.

But see what happens afterward. This is why men like Sir Alfred Stephen despair and grind their teeth over the adulation bestowed on the most wicked of the wicked. There will be tears shed at Frederick Ward's funeral. Stories will be told late into the night about his charity and good intent. Songs about his courage and honour will continue to be sung in the local taverns and pubs.

Soon that mythic dust will settle and harden into concrete and fact. More than a century later the town of Uralla will erect a bronze statue in his honour.

Beneath an enormous, endless sky, Thunderbolt will sit astride one of the hundreds of horses he was estimated to have stolen, pulling on the reins, a gun in his belt and with the look of a man who knows he has fooled them all once again.

—

Thunderbolt. The Darkie. Brave Ben Hall. This theme of the gentleman outlaw who looks after the poor by stealing from the rich is an old one. They have been telling stories about honourable highwaymen for hundreds of years in England's taverns and, more recently, celebrating the exploits of chivalrous gunslingers in the saloons of the lawless Wild West of the United States. It's as if there is a finishing school for criminals whose students graduate with degrees in charity and honour. It is a theme steeped in a desire for heroes and a need to soften their hard edges with a veneer of respectability.

The first of the proud line of gentlemen bushrangers in Australia had been Matthew Brady. He had been sentenced to seven years' transportation to Van Diemen's Land at the age of 21 in the 1820s for stealing butter, bacon and rice in Manchester. After escaping from the penal station at Macquarie Harbour, he and a gang of fellow convicts roamed across the island staging hold-ups and defying the increasingly frustrated authorities led by Lieutenant-Governor George Arthur.

Brady had been a horse groom in England and his riding skills were unmatched in the colony. His gang were also under strict orders. Women were to be treated with respect and violence to be avoided. Well-organised and always on the move, Brady's gang held up the town of Sorell and captured the local military garrison. Humiliated by the incident, Arthur posted a 25 pound reward for Brady's capture. Brady responded by posting a note on a tavern door announcing that: 'It has caused Matthew Brady much concern that such a person known as Sir George Arthur is still at large. Twenty gallons of rum will be given to any person that will deliver his person unto me . . .'

He was eventually captured and sentenced to hang. His cell was overflowing with cakes and flowers from the grief-stricken women of Hobart Town, who sent constant petitions to the government pleading for the verdict to be overturned. Many cried as he was led to the gallows. 'There was a hush, broken only by stifled sobs, as the bushranger knelt to receive the last consolations of his faith,' reported one newspaper. 'Then, standing erect, he bade adieu to the multitude and died more like a martyr than a convicted felon.'

This martyrdom. These star-struck crowds. It is why men like Sir Alfred Stephen so abhor the cult of the bushrangers. They know that deep in the psyche of the colony is a simmering defiance of authority, a kernel of resistance and disobedience sown by generations of convicts and more than a little Irish spite toward the Empire.

Look at the way they had revered Ben Hall, the son of English and Irish convicts. A friend of Frank Gardiner, Hall had taken to bushranging soon after his wife took their young son and went to live with a former police officer. He had been part of Gardiner's 10-man band that robbed the coach at Eugowra. When Gardiner escaped to Queensland, Hall assumed leadership of the gang. By 1865 they had staged dozens of robberies and stagecoach hold-ups and Hall was being hailed as a hero in the hills and valleys of central NSW. But just like Captain Thunderbolt, it was his death that gave new life to the legend.

In early May 1865 eight policemen found him sleeping beneath a tree outside the town of Forbes. He woke at dawn to find himself surrounded. As he ran to escape he was cut down by an assortment of double-barrelled shotguns and Colt rifles. Almost a dozen bullets pierced his back and head, and when his body was taken back to Forbes and put on display, more than 500 people filed past to take a final look. A long and solemn cortege followed the hearse to the cemetery a day later. By the time holy water had been sprinkled on the coffin and it was lowered into the ground, songs were already being sung about 'Brave Ben Hall'. And for more than half a century afterward a regular stream of visitors made their way to the spot where Hall was killed, a nearby tree still riddled with bullet holes.

13

CONVICT BLOOD AND A DROP OF MADNESS

George Scott has a plan, of course. A man of action always does in the face of adversity. Within weeks of his arrival at Maitland Gaol he is complaining to the authorities that his food is poisoned. He has found a lump of silver nitrate – commonly used to cauterise wounds and ulcers – in one of his meals. It has probably fallen in there by accident, but it is enough to give Scott cause to claim he is being drugged. He begins refusing all food unless it is potatoes. The guards believe him to be delusional and he does nothing to dissuade the prison doctor when he examines him.

By the middle of February 1871 a decision is made that Scott's 'insanity is delusionary and is reputed to be hereditary . . . his health is good and he is neither dangerous to himself or others.'

He is transferred to the Parramatta Lunatic Asylum, whose doctors quickly begin to suspect Scott is feigning his mental illness. One of them writes in the asylum's medical register that 'he does not refrain from any article of food in his ration or confine himself to potatoes here, and does not betray any evidence of his insanity besides his assertion that he was drugged in Gaol, which probably means no more than he was under medical treatment'.

Compared to Maitland's high security, Gothic surrounds and malevolent gangs, the asylum is everything Scott imagined it to be. The food – a pint of soup, half a pound of meat, vegetables and daily servings of tea – is more than adequate. Dinner is often served, weather permitting, in a large courtyard outside. Inmates are granted a fair degree of freedom during the day and most, despite many with violent records, seem to Scott to be sedate and impressionable – just the sort who could fall easily into line when guided by a shrewd and calculating voice such as his own.

But he is being watched closely by the asylum's supervisors and they do not like what they see. 'He is civil but an unprecedented fellow without a spark of honour or honesty in him,' one of them notes.

Within weeks these suspicions are confirmed. 'He is making attempts to get up an escape party,' notes the medical register on 15 April. 'His associates in the yard are the very lowest and hardened criminals in it and though he is of a very respectable family and education, he avoids the quiet and decorous among the criminals.'

Throughout April Scott rallies the inmates. Would they not like a taste of real freedom? To live like real men? He points out how simple it would be to rush the guards as a large group and simply storm through the front gates. He makes a half-hearted attempt to throw a sand-filled pillow attached to a rope over one of the walls. But then he makes a mistake. He approaches Henry Louis Bertrand.

Henry has had enough of scandal. He prefers to spend his time painting watercolours, carving objects out of bone and ensuring no-one is in any doubt about his insanity. He knows he is a lucky man to still be alive. Just a few years earlier Sir Alfred Stephen had sentenced him to hang for murder.

There had been no other case like it in the Victorian era. Its allegations of illicit sex, a cuckolded husband, murder and mesmerism had filled newspaper columns around the country and as far away as London and America. The juicy plot: a mild-mannered and seemingly happily married Sydney dentist (Bertrand) falls madly in love with a new patient (married woman Ellen Kinder). The pair conduct a passionate affair that is revealed in candid diaries presented to the court (Bertrand: 'She is my life – the very air I breathe. I shall go out of my mind with excess love'). Bertrand uses his powers as an amateur mesmerist to hypnotise his wife and draw her into the ploy. He and Ellen hatch a plan to kill Ellen's husband. Bertrand shoots the man in the head, using a gun he has purchased while disguised as a woman. But the bullet only tears off part of the face and ear of Ellen's husband. He lingers for days until Bertrand poisons him with a potion containing belladonna, the deadly herb the Renaissance women in Italy often took in small doses to enlarge the pupils of their eyes and make them more alluring.

The jury in a first trial could not reach a verdict and so, to the eternal gratitude of newspaper editors around the world, a second trial was staged. This time the jury took only two hours to deliver a guilty verdict, giving Sir Alfred another opportunity to fulminate from the bench.

'You were madly in love with this woman, with a passion eating into your vitals, and you would have committed any crime to have her as your own,' he scolded Henry. 'You are not a human being in feeling. I can speak of you with compassion, because I do not think you are fully possessed of the mind that God has been pleased to give to almost all of us.'

Henry, the appeals court later found, certainly did not possess a normal mind. It commuted the death sentence on the grounds of insanity, helped by erratic outbursts from Henry and a little impromptu rolling about on the floor of the court. Since then Henry Louis Bertrand has spent a quiet few years keeping to himself and pursuing his hobbies. When Scott suggests he join his plans for a mass escape, Bertrand declines.

The asylum register records an outburst of that fiery Scott temper: 'He has sounded Bertrand as to whether he would join him in a rush and on his declining called him the vilest and most blackguard names.'

The patience of the asylum's administration with Scott begins to wear thin. The doctors cannot 'see any satisfactory proofs of his insanity. He is not communicative and always appears on his guard. He is always agitating some plot . . . and I believe there would be no villainy he would scruple to commit. This talent and disposition to combine with others is uncommon in real insanity. He is certainly more fit for Gaol than a Lunatic Asylum . . .'

On 3 June an official overhears Scott boasting that there is now 'six to six' – that those planning to escape match the number of guards. The men are separated and not allowed to mingle in the yard. Scott holds a meeting with the supervisors to deny he has hatched any escape plot and blames Bertrand for being behind the allegations.

'He said it was all the invention of Bertrand, whom he designated as a Sodomite and everything that was filthy,' reads a note of the meeting. 'Told him that my information was not derived from Bertrand; upon which he said he had a right to know. Denied his right, upon the grounds that if I gave up my Informant, besides subjecting them to injury, I should never get any information at all . . .

'He thanked me, and went straight up to Bertrand on entering the yard and told him I had given him up . . . [Scott] appears to have an absolute disregard to truth, and from all I have heard of his previous career, I believe him to be a scoundrel to the core.'

Three days later Scott is transferred to Parramatta Gaol, where he will calm down and serve out the remainder of his sentence.

In Sydney, his trial and sentencing had received little publicity. The news he had been transferred to the asylum in Parramatta had been recorded in a simple sentence by *The Sydney Morning Herald*. But all the colonial newspapers were read avidly in newsrooms around the country. It had not taken long for word to spread in Victoria that George Scott had once again found himself in the midst of trouble.

The Bacchus Marsh Express had quickly told its readers back in December 1870 that 'Andrew George Scott, known in Bacchus Marsh, Ballan and Egerton districts as "Captain Moonlite", has been arrested in Sydney on various charges of swindling . . . it appears that he had purchased a yacht and was about to sail for Fiji when he was arrested.'

Julius Bruun and his wealthy father were among the first to hear the rumours. Bruun had walked out of that courtroom back in 1869 a free man after the charges against him of robbing the Mount Egerton bank had been dismissed. The crowd had cheered and the papers had been sympathetic toward him. 'Young Bruun is to all intents and purposes a fellow-townsman,' said the *Ballarat Courier*, 'whose mode of life and official conduct have been under the public eye ever since his adolescence. Before this robbery he bore an irreproachable character – he was beloved at home and fully trusted by the officers of the bank. Who, then, would not sympathise with his situation? Found guilty, he would have had to herd with atrocious villains, and when his term of sentence had expired, be compelled to begin life anew in another country . . .'

Guilty or innocent, small towns never forgot and some never completely forgave. With no hope of furthering his career with the London Chartered Bank, Bruun had accepted a role as an assistant master at a private boys' school in Geelong.

The Bruuns were naturally intrigued by the news that Scott had been splashing money around Sydney. The amounts he had reportedly spent were close to the value of the gold and cash stolen from the Egerton bank.

So they had engaged a prominent Sydney solicitor, George Sly, to run some background checks on Scott and what, exactly, he had been up to. Now that they had found out where that scoundrel was, they were happy to wait.

—

Scott has a letter in his pocket on the day he finally walks out of Parramatta Gaol in late March in 1872. He has not seen his father for five years and there is so much to tell.

'My dearest father,' he begins. 'I am thank God a free man once more, although I have been convicted of the crime of obtaining money under false pretences. I am innocent and I can prove such when we meet again.'

The handwriting is neat and orderly on the first page. There is plenty of space between each line. George Scott has a complicated tale to relate and it is clear he has prepared for this. He tells his father he 'was doing very well' at the time of his arrest. He had been sailing around the Pacific Islands, picking up trade and making money. He concedes he smuggled into Queensland. He tells his father how he was swindled by this Count Geldern.

But within a couple of pages Scott's disciplined handwriting begins to fall away. He is agitated. The lines begin to weave and slope, the words more hunched and difficult to read. This Count Geldern, this accomplished forger, was actually 'one of the highest freemasons'. Scott's father will know what he means by that. God-fearing Christians have always viewed the Freemasons – a fraternity that bases itself on medieval stonemasons who used secret words and symbols to recognise one another – with suspicion and hostility. At best they are a centuries-old global conspiracy whose members have infiltrated the highest levels of society, always promoting one another and looking after each other's interests. At worst, they are a cult that dabbles in mysticism and the occult.

Geldern was not just a forger and a Freemason, according to Scott. He was an expert liar as well. Scott tells his father the Count had even convinced him that Thomas Scott had become a gold commissioner in Thames, a small town near Coromandel where the elder Scott was now practising as an Anglican minister.

He had given Geldern money to pay bills while he had been at sea. He had sent him funds to send on to his father. All of it swindled. Fortunately, he writes, 'when I left Victoria I had left shares in a gold claim and had a share in a horse of . . . Crook's called Saladin, who won 300 pounds last week . . . I am not there-fore that badly off.'

It is true – Saladin had run a dead heat with Flying Dutchman in the Australian Cup on 8 March, and then won by a head in the deciding heat. The prize had been 300 sovereigns. The race had taken place on the same day that a former Irish sailor named Edward Feeney had been found guilty of the wilful murder of his suspected lover, Charles Marks, more of which later.

So Scott believes life is finally looking up. He tells his father he intends to sail to Melbourne immediately and then on to New Zealand 'as this Colony is no longer a safe place for me, a man once convicted. The police who are all professional perjurers would swear anything against me.

'The convict blood is in the population. Nothing will efface it. This colony is a fearful place for crime. Within the last few days (I will send you a paper) a series of most dreadful murders have been discovered in Sydney. Everyone is excited about the affair. It is believed that hundreds are missing and that there is a large gang of murderers yet at large.'

Scott can only be referring to – and exaggerating wildly about – the Parramatta River murders, an infamous case that just a few days before had climaxed with two men being sentenced to death for murdering two men they had lured to the river using job vacancy ads in the local paper.

But Scott has more pressing problems. 'A friendly detective advised me to leave . . . as the freemasons body were very strong and Geldern had poisoned them much against me.'

His writing is now even more slanted. Words run together and disappear off the edge of the page. He apologises for the mess: 'I am in great haste and there are people talking around me, so you must not expect this to be accurate in grammar or spelling.'

'Believe me, dearest father. I am a steady man now, although I feel a little odd at liberty after 16 months in gaol . . . I am in the greatest health . . . you cannot believe how anxious I am to see you all again. May God bless you and keep you all.'

He signs off 'Your ever affectionate son, who has been treated badly but now triumphs. God bless you, your ever affectionate son, a.g Scott.'

So many plans. So much optimism. He is in a rush. He has been told to report to Sydney's police office to collect his possessions. When he arrives he is arrested and charged with robbing the Mount Egerton bank. Within a few weeks he will be extradited to Victoria and the letter to his father will be seized and never sent.

14

THE GINGERBREAD GAOL

The engineer casts his blue eyes around his prison cell. So much for the claims by the Ballarat locals that this new gaol of theirs is escape proof. How proud they are of their prison. You would think they had built a cathedral given the way they prattle on about it. Barely 10 years old with high red brick and bluestone walls, its 58 secure cells and tunnel that leads to the adjoining courthouse are a constant source of wonder and smug satisfaction among the town's upstanding citizens.

But what do they know? It is only his second day in the Ballarat Gaol after his journey from Sydney, but already George Scott's trained eye can see shortcuts taken by builders on tight budgets. Look at the tin sheeting covering the cell door. It can easily be removed to expose a lock hidden behind a bar of pine secured to the door by a single nail.

Such shoddy workmanship. That lock is only held in place with a spring and a single catch. And then there is the red brick wall that separates his cell from that of another Irishman, James Plunkett. It would not take much effort to loosen the bricks and create a hole large enough for Plunkett to climb through and enter Scott's cell.

Plunkett is a chronic offender, a stout man with a sallow face and a head of unkempt black hair. He has been in and out of gaol for a string of offences and is lucky he is not dead already; he had been convicted of highway robbery years earlier and sentenced to hang, but this had quickly been commuted to a dozen years of hard labour. He may not have the sharpest of minds, but Scott doesn't need him for his brain. He needs the muscle and strength in Plunkett's squat frame.

On Sunday 9 June, the prisoners are locked in their cells for the rest of the day following church service. At 10pm, Warder William Irwin begins work and is happy to find all is quiet. But four hours later he hears a noise in Scott's cell. It sounds like a tub being dragged across the floor. Irwin wanders over and asks Scott if there is a problem.

Indeed there is. 'I'm very bad in my bowels,' Scott tells Irwin. 'Could you give me a drink of warm water?'

Irwin has no hot water, but fetches a pannikin of cold water and passes it to Scott. Not long after, Scott's cell door bursts open and Plunkett rushes out and grabs Irwin.

'Scott was behind me,' Irwin will tell a group of reporters the following morning, 'and caught hold of my legs and threw me down. We wrestled together, I should say, from 15 to 20 minutes and I got on my knees and tore Plunkett's shirt and things nearly off him.

'Plunkett had a black-handled knife, which he flourished, and said he would plunge into me if I wasn't quiet. I was shouting for help [by] then. They got a blanket and put it over my mouth, and one of them knelt on it with his knees. Look and see, all my front teeth are loosened.'

One of the reporters reaches over to see how loose those teeth are. 'No, don't touch, please,' Irwin will say. 'They are so sore.'

Scott and Plunkett tie Irwin's wrists with a leather belt and his feet with a cord of hemp and drag him roughly downstairs to the prison kitchen, where Plunkett grabs a large knife 'as long as my arm' and stands menacingly over him. He must be tempted to use it – during the struggle Irwin had bitten Plunkett so hard on the thumb he almost took it off.

Scott returns upstairs. Soon after, there is the unmistakeable sound of locks being smashed and other cell doors swinging open. Four other prisoners soon join them and turnkey Irwin is taken outside and tied to a table. The escapers take the warder's cape and an assortment of boots belonging to other guards. Irwin is worried they might steal his watch but Scott assures him they will leave it behind. 'He said I was the finest man that he ever saw, and he would not take anything from me.'

By 5am the six have gone over the wall using a water spout, wooden frames and ropes. Irwin eventually struggles free and sounds the alarm. Within an hour more than a dozen troopers are scouring the area around the prison. But even the gradual appearance of the sun on an early winter morning fails to shed any light on the prisoners' movements. They are long gone, their freedom won for them by a man with an engineer's eye for detail.

———

News of the escape quickly spreads. The *Ballarat Courier* will note the 'stamp of daring ingenuity . . . ascribed to the notorious Captain Moonlite . . . it is decidedly to be regretted that his genius did not find a more legitimate channel than it has done'.

Plunkett is the first to be recaptured a few days later. Others will soon follow. But Scott's whereabouts will remain a mystery until 10 days after the breakout when the police are told he is in a hut on a hill outside Bendigo, more than 70 miles to the north of Ballarat.

Scott is asleep at 2am when several officers crawl slowly toward the hut on their hands and knees. It is one of the few opportunities he has had to rest since the escape. He had originally planned to break the telegraph lines linking Ballarat to Geelong and Melbourne. After that, several small police stations would be held up, their weapons seized and, before the telegraph lines could be repaired for news of the escape to spread, Scott's band of escapees would make their way to Geelong, steal a boat in its harbour and make their way to Fiji.

But that plan had fallen apart almost from the moment the six men went over the wall. Some disliked the idea of holding up police stations; others just desperately wanted a drink. Scott had eventually ended up on the run with John Harris, also known as Jack Dermoody, a former butcher facing three robbery charges.

Scott had formed friendships with many people in the area during his time as a lay reader in Bacchus Marsh and Mount Egerton. He called on one for a favour and was given a gun and a revolver. But Scott and Dermoody soon quarrelled – Scott labelled him a cur and threatened to strike him for not wanting to hold up a nearby police station and being terrified of using a gun.

With his plan to escape to Fiji now scuppered, Scott had left Dermoody and moved north-east through thick bush in the Dead Horse ranges, using the sun as a guide and hoping to reach the Murray River and cross into New South Wales. He would later confide to the *Ballarat Courier* that sleep was a luxury and food a rarity. 'He was twice for forty eight hours without food, and he slept inside once . . . and that was when he turned into bed beside a drunken bushman.

'Once, after being two days without food, he came across a house where there was an Irish woman. He at once, he says, opened his heart by talking of Ireland and making her believe he knew her friends in New Zealand, and she then prepared a meal for him, the best he had since he left the gaol.'

Now he is resting in a small shack on Specimen Hill and four officers are creeping slowly toward it. They have a young boy with them who used to live in the hut and has been working night shift in a nearby mining gully. After giving them a confident description of Scott, he has reluctantly accompanied the police on their slow crawl toward Scott's hideout.

With the officers crouched next to the door, the boy calls out: 'Mate, give me the billy.'

'What billy?' comes the voice from inside.

'The black billy in the chimney.'

The door opens slightly and a man's arm extends clutching the billy. The police quickly rush the door. Scott moves toward a small cot to grab a loaded single-barrel gun but is overwhelmed by the four men, who pin him to the floor and then handcuff him.

'My intention was not to be taken alive,' Scott tells his captors. 'No man in the country could arrest me . . . if it were not that you took me so suddenly, I would have shot the first man that entered.

'If it was daylight when you came to arrest me I would have cautioned you to only come a certain distance and if you ventured to approach I would have shot you and then destroyed myself.'

The officers haul Scott off to the nearest police lock-up in Sandhurst. Despite the hunger and privations of the past 10 days, he has lost none of his eye for detail.

He looks around the cell, studies its thin tin walls, peers intensely at the cell door and then turns to the officers with a contemptuous look.

'Do you call this lining?' he asks.

—

The next morning Scott is brought before a Sandhurst magistrate and charged with escaping from gaol. Hundreds have gathered outside the town hall as he is led inside the small hearing room guarded by a large group of constables and troopers.

The police court sits for only a few minutes and Scott is remanded to appear in Ballarat the following week. He is soon back in the watchhouse, bustled by half a dozen officers through a crowd of more than a thousand spectators all trying to catch a glimpse of the man they know as Captain Moonlite.

A local barrister, Dublin-born James Martley, arrives and tells Scott he has been asked by some of the press men outside if he would mind posing for a photograph.

Scott, who has been chatting and joking with some of the police about his escape, looks up and loses his smile.

'What do you want my photograph for?'

'Oh, you have such a large number of friends who would like to see how you look,' Martley assures him.

'Well, I cannot understand why so many people can be found to neglect their business and gather round a lock-up to see a man in trouble.'

'You have made yourself quite famous by breaking out of that gingerbread gaol,' says Martley. 'They want to see a man of such celebrity.'

Martley pushes a little more. New clothes can be found. Besides, if Scott doesn't have a photograph taken there will be artist sketches circulated instead that might not be as flattering as an official portrait. 'I cannot see why you should object when you are not particularly a bad looking man.'

Scott is sullen now. 'People want me to do this merely for the gratification of morbid curiosity . . . I am quite notorious enough.'

He tells Martley that he has no time for the Victorian press. One of the papers had called him a ruffian; he had never committed an act of ruffianism. In breaking out of gaol he had merely 'followed the instincts of human nature, which had a repugnance to being deprived of liberty'.

So there will be no photograph. At first it seems an odd refusal because the man has always loved an audience. But he is also exhausted. Stress is always the detonator for that wild drop of blood circulating inside George Scott and the fallout is often unpredictable. Still, if he thinks he can control his newly won notoriety, the next 24 hours will teach him otherwise.

—

The crowd on the station platform has been growing since early morning, hours before the afternoon train to Ballarat is due. Now there are hundreds spilling everywhere – all of them craning and jostling for a better view of the newly captured Captain Moonlite.

He had seen faces like these at every stop on the train journey from Melbourne. They were all the same. They stared and peered into the windows as if he was some kind of exotic animal. A reporter travelling with the group of detectives guarding Scott would talk about how 'extremely dissatisfied' he was with the crowds: 'One of his remarks being that the faces he had seen lately were making him a believer in Darwin's theory.'

When he steps out of the carriage at Ballarat station, Scott is escorted toward a nearby police cart that will take him back to gaol. There are shouts and cries as the crowd presses forward to catch a glimpse of the man whose name now peppers every conversation in the colony. Some in the crowd, according to one newspaper, are disappointed 'at not seeing someone strong and fierce looking; for crowds generally picture a robber as someone powerful and savage'.

Instead they find themselves staring at a man with a gaunt and weary face. He is wearing a pepper-and-salt coat and trousers and has a large felt hat 'of an ancient and seedy appearance' pulled down over his eyes. He had exchanged his former clothes with an old swagman in the days before his capture and even though he musters a smile of acknowledgement for the crowd, he does not 'look anything like the ideal bushranger'.

But to many gathered at the Ballarat train station Scott is a hero of sorts, a man who not only staged a breakout from what was supposed to be an escape-proof prison, but had also avoided capture for 10 days despite the presence of dozens of troopers searching for him.

Many of the onlookers are murmuring and expressing sympathy for him. As the horse-drawn police cart pulls away with Scott inside, a large group of young boys begin to run alongside it. They break into a loud cheer – or a 'shrill, larrikin, wretched imitation of what a cheer is supposed to be'.

Older heads will shake in sorrow and wonder what the colonies have come to when a criminal like Scott is celebrated with such abandon. 'One could not help believing that the scene could not be read otherwise than as a bad omen for the future of many of those lads,' laments *The Ballarat Star*.

15

'I WOULD DO ANYTHING SHORT OF MURDER'

That sullen man who did not want to be photographed? That exhausted man who arrived at the train station in Ballarat resenting all the stares of the vultures and admirers? He is nowhere to be seen when the trial of Andrew George Scott for the robbery of the Mount Egerton bank gets underway in the final week of July 1872.

In his place is a confident, erudite man, despite having already been sentenced to 12 months in irons for escaping. Those irons shackled to his ankles may have 'opened honourable wounds . . . received in the service of my country and my Queen'. But Scott holds the crowded courtroom spellbound. He revels in the attention and thrives on the reaction his clever asides receive from the admiring throng. They will applaud him when he says his name has been 'disgraced by this horrible, deep-dyed villainous conspiracy'.

Even those who don't believe a word he is saying – the police, the prosecutor, the cynical reporters and even Sir Redmond Barry perched on the bench in his wig and gown – have to begrudgingly admit Scott knows how to put on a show.

It seems he was born to do this. He struts. He rolls his eyes in disbelief. He makes grand gestures with his arms to emphasise a point.

There was never any question it would come down to this. There had been tension between Scott and his lawyer soon after the jury was empanelled. Within hours – and with Julius Bruun on the stand – the lawyer had walked out, telling Sir Redmond his client had interfered with his conduct of the case by demanding he continue cross-examining Bruun.

So Scott, never one to miss an opportunity to entertain an audience – or to weave a story in his favour – has been more than happy to take over his own defence. He knows the odds are against him. He had confided in a detective just before the train journey to Ballarat that he did not think much of any evidence that would be given by Bruun, 'but the gold I sold in Sydney will be a strong point against me'.

The trial lasts seven days, its length mostly due to Scott's theatrics and his exhausting probing of witnesses. He has to work hard because the evidence – which paints an unflattering portrait of a man supposedly devoted to his God – is quite compelling.

John McDonnell, a wood splitter, will testify that at about nine o'clock on the night of the robbery he had seen Scott enter a public house with a poor reputation run by a Mrs Roberts on the outskirts of Mount Egerton. It was a dance night and he had watched Scott go behind the bar and pour himself a drink.

Richard Boyle, another local, will testify that Scott had told him he had been returning from Melbourne on the night of the robbery.

Dodson Harwood, an engineer, will tell the court how he had loaned money to Scott and in exchange received a cheque which had been dishonoured. After the robbery at Mount Egerton he had met Scott in Melbourne and asked him for the money; Scott returned from his hotel room with a wad of cash that looked like London Chartered Bank notes. He thought Scott was eccentric and had been forced to order him out of his home one day because he constantly carried a pistol in his pocket. He had heard Scott preach in such an impressive manner it would 'reflect credit upon any minister of the Gospel, and within an hour afterwards say, "If anyone were to say to me, you daren't, I would do anything short of murder."'

John Morgan, a local miner at whose home Scott had boarded for some time, testifies that he anxiously asked Scott where he had been for much of the previous week leading up to the robbery. 'Scott said he had been at East Ballan staying with a married woman. He would rather rot in gaol than say who she was.'

Two other witnesses – Henry and Hanna Heathorn – will claim Scott tried to bribe them with money and a horse if they would lie and say he had been at their house having dinner on the night of the robbery.

Julius Hammill, a handwriting expert, will say that whoever signed the note 'Captain Moonlite' was the same person who had written the letter to Scott's father in New Zealand that had been seized by police after his arrest in Sydney.

The Witherdens – Edward and Margaret – tell the court they had given money to Scott equal to the price of a harmonium – an expensive musical instrument similar to an organ. The money was supposed to have been kept in trust but Scott spent it 'for other purposes' and a later cheque to pay back the money owed was dishonoured. A couple of weeks after the bank robbery, Scott had appeared at their home 'and wanted her husband in order that he might give him a horse-whipping for something he had said about him'.

Thomas McKenna, a publican at Bacchus Marsh, will say Scott had no horse of his own kept in that town. But after the Egerton robbery he suddenly owned three horses and a buggy.

But none of this seems to perturb Scott that much. He cross-examines witnesses with forensic intensity. His main target will be Bruun, whose constantly shifting evidence is plagued with discrepancies, contradictions and uncertainty.

He will keep Bruun on the stand for almost a day, badgering him about all the flaws in his testimony and his 'strange ambiguity of language'.

Bruun told police he had never seen the robber before but now, says Scott, he is certain it was Scott.

The prosecutor interjects. 'Oh, of course,' says Scott. 'The Crown prosecutor does not like to hear the witness make two exactly contradictory statements.'

Scott turns back to Bruun. 'When were you most frightened: on the night you were stuck up or now whilst you are swearing gross and corrupt perjury?'

'On the night when I was stuck up.'

'Well, I'd rather be stuck up any time than commit perjury.'

Bruun admits he had been afraid of Scott because the Irishman was far stronger than he was.

'Oh then,' sighs Scott. 'Because I was suffering a gunshot wound in the chest, and a wound in the leg, you were afraid of me?'

'You carried a knife about with you and you were very determined in your manner . . . I thought you would have a down upon me for turning you out of the bank; that you would revenge yourself in some way.'

'In what way did you think that vengeance would fall on your devoted head? Were you in bodily fear?'

Bruun says he was not afraid of personal violence 'but I dreaded you'.

'You were afraid of a little corporal punishment – flogging – such as you give your boys?' Scott says, referring to Bruun's current job as a junior master at a boys' school.

'I did not anticipate anything but thought you would revenge yourself in any way whenever you got a chance.'

On it goes, Scott prodding and probing the nervous Bruun, who soon grows confused and uncertain. Sir Redmond warns Bruun to be careful and pay attention to Scott's questions.

'Oh, he can understand well enough, your Honour,' says Scott. 'As we say in Ireland, he's like Willy Weir – what he did not like he did not hear.'

The crowd titters and Sir Redmond calls for quiet. It goes on like this for hours, Scott threatening to keep Bruun on the stand for the next three days. But after more than six hours, including testimony about how Scott threatened to horsewhip him if he failed to apologise for accusing him of robbing the bank, a discredited Bruun is allowed to go.

The uncertain evidence given by the young man, coupled with his vague and nervous disposition, will always fail to erase suspicions that he may have played a role in the robbery, along with the alcoholic schoolteacher and former friend of Scott's, James Simpson.

Two days after Bruun's evidence Scott will refer to Simpson's love of alcohol while cross-examining a detective. 'Don't you think Simpson is half-drunk now? There he is – in the court. Isn't he half-drunk now?'

Simpson will be ordered out of the room by Sir Redmond – as a witness he is not allowed to listen to the testimony of other witnesses. But when he is summoned not long after, Scott questions him about his drinking. Simpson will deny he is a chronic drunk and claim that he is just as sober as George Scott. Why, before he arrived at court in the morning he had only had one glass of beer and a glass of brandy . . .

Scott will raise doubts about whether the cake of gold he sold in Sydney may not have been Egerton gold, but from some other place. He will embark on a long and often tortuous examination of William Birkmyre, a tall, grey-haired scientist at the Bank of Victoria with an expertise in analysing ores and minerals.

Scott will question Birkmyre tirelessly, trying to raise doubts that the gold sold in Sydney may not have been from Egerton. He will embark on a lengthy and detailed explanation about the different characteristics of gold in various parts of the world 'but his Honour failed in seeing the relevancy of the questions'.

Scott accuses Birkmyre several times of holding a strong bias against him and says he plans to keep him in the box for a week unless he gives a straight answer. Was the gold sold in Sydney from Egerton?

Birkmyre: 'It might or might not be.'

Scott: 'What countryman are you?'

'I belong to Scotland.'

Scott: 'Then you're no credit to it; but when Scot meets Scott, then comes the tug of war.'

'The gold might have come from Egerton or not.'

Scott: 'It might have come from the mountains in the moon.'

Sir Redmond: 'That is less probable.'

Scott is now on a roll. He begins lecturing Birkmyre on the qualities of gold found in various countries, from Africa and India to New Zealand and New Guinea. Did Birkmyre know that a vast amount of similar gold could be found in Algiers?

Scott 'was proceeding to explain the geological features of the various belts of mountains in the gold-producing countries, when his Honour interrupted him with the hint that the Court was not sitting for the purposes of being enlightened on the geological features of mountain ranges'.

Eventually Birkmyre concedes the gold Scott sold in Sydney could have originated from Maldon or Sandhurst.

'Why didn't you say that before?' asks Scott. 'Have I not been hammering at you for the last hour, and instead of giving me a straightforward answer, you gave me a multiplicity of verbiage when I didn't want it, and not a single sentence when I did want it. I may thank my stars you are not on the jury. I wouldn't like my life to be in your hands. You may stand down.'

The sombre Birkmyre returns to his seat, according to a reporter at the trial, 'with the downcast air of a truant schoolboy, who has just escaped flagellation'.

—

On the second last day of the trial Julius Bruun's father, Ludwig, is called to give evidence. He reminds Scott about the day he turned up at the Bruun home to demand an apology from his son.

'I believe you asked my son to accompany you to the police station and charge you with the robbery. You threatened to horsewhip or shoot my son if he did not go with you. I was not afraid of you. I advised my son not to go with you . . . I wished to obtain proper legal advice. Superintendent Hill told me that the police knew all about the guilty party, and the police would take steps to prosecute him at the proper time . . . my son was in ill health but whenever the police were ready to commence proceedings he would sacrifice health for honour.'

Ludwig Bruun details the showdown that had taken place between his son and Scott: 'I was between you and my son when you threatened to horsewhip him. You were standing before the pierglass [a mirror hanging from one of Bruun's walls] admiring yourself.'

Scott: 'What was I doing?'

'Admiring yourself before the pierglass and now the public knows it.'

'Do you think the public admired your son when he was in the dock?'

'No. They pitied him.'

But no matter how well Andrew George Scott – sailor, soldier, preacher and prisoner – acquits himself in the courtroom, his biggest problem remains his inability to explain how he obtained a cake of gold almost identical to the one stolen from Mount Egerton.

Not once does he say or even hint – as he will years later – that Bruun had given him the gold long after the robbery, and that he had travelled hundreds of miles trying to find Bruun to hand it back. If it is true there is nothing to stop him; his animosity toward Bruun is now widely known. He has had him in the witness box for six hours. Such a claim might cast enough doubt on the case against him to ensure a not guilty verdict.

But Scott never mentions it.

His address to the jury lasts more than two hours. Again, he struts and pontificates. The charge he was facing was nothing more than a 'deep and foul conspiracy'. Even now he would not trade places with Bruun, who had spent his time 'shivering in the dock'.

He also tells the jury some of what he did in the Pacific. After visiting Fiji he says he had gone on to New Zealand before arriving in New Caledonia. He had then left there as the 'duly authorised commander of the French schooner [*Sarah Pile*]' and in this capacity arrived in Sydney.

Claims he had been seen just an hour before the robbery entering Mrs Roberts' public house of ill repute on the outskirts of Mount Egerton had been raised by 'a horde of foul informers and perjurers'. He concedes he escaped from prison but does not say why. Years later, when he has again had time to add to the story, he will claim he went on the run to ask the woman whose house he had been staying at in the lead-up to the robbery if she would relinquish him from his vow to keep her identity secret.

But it is the cake of gold that might as well be sitting in front of the jury. Gold, that beggar's vice, changes everything. All Scott can offer is that he had had opportunities to buy a cake of gold in several countries he had visited before arriving in Sydney in late December 1869.

In his summary to the jury Sir Redmond certainly discusses the gold – and how Scott mysteriously went from pauper before the robbery to a man with wads of banknotes on him wherever he went. The jury agrees. It takes them just three hours to digest more than a week's worth of complicated and contradictory evidence.

Guilty.

Scott appears anxious but maintains his *honour* to the end.

'I have to say that I have been put on by my God and my country and that my country has found me guilty. But before God I solemnly declare that I am not guilty and that I will trust He will yet enable me to show that I am not guilty. Though I now walk into a living tomb, I would not change place with my accusers – though they have consigned me to worse than a grave. Your Honour, I solemnly declare that I am innocent.'

But Sir Redmond is having none of that. The trial had severely taxed the energies of all those involved, he says. He approves of the jury's verdict and sentences the prisoner to 10 years' hard labour.

That night no-one in Ballarat, Bacchus Marsh or Mount Egerton talks about anything else except the sentencing of the man they will forever call Captain Moonlite.

'Though Scott, through his bravado and daring escape, has awakened, it appears, some little sympathy in that peculiar class of

'He is a madman [with] strong homicidal impulses. Whenever he lectured he invariably carried firearms and was fond of levelling them at imaginary objects.' Captain Moonlite in 1879 before embarking on his series of public lectures. (The Victoria Police Museum)

'With his jug ears and full lips and honest stare, Nesbitt knew how to calm the man. If Scott was an unbroken stallion with more than a glint of madness in his eyes, Nesbitt was the patient, softly whispering horse-breaker.' Captain Moonlite's loyal partner, James Nesbitt. (The Victoria Police Museum)

'Prisoners are treated too kindly and kept too long. They get flabby. The muscles of the neck soften, and the neck gets as tender as a chicken.' Robert Rice Howard, the New South Wales hangman known as 'Nosey Bob', who presided over the execution of Captain Moonlite. (The Bulletin)

THE COMMON HANGMAN

'Most of them were young boys lost in oversized navy monkey jackets, staring ahead with the pale, unfilled faces of prepubescence.' Cadets and officers of the training ship HMS *Britannia* in 1861, where Andrew George Scott trained as a sailor. (*The Story of the Britannia*, E. P. Statham)

'Nosey Bob guided Queen Victoria's son through the rough streets of town, dropping off the "Dook" at the front door of the city's high-class brothels.' Prince Alfred, younger son of Queen Victoria and survivor of an assassination attempt in Sydney weeks before Captain Moonlite's arrival in Australia. (Official portrait, 1881)

'. . . and yet these bushrangers, the scum of the earth, the lowest of the low, the most wicked of the wicked, are occasionally held up for our admiration!' Sir Alfred Stephen, Chief Justice of NSW. (State Library of NSW)

'The hangman – broad shouldered, spider-legged, with arms like a gorilla, a flat face without a nose, and huge feet, presented a spectacle to be seen nowhere else out of Hades.' J. F. Archibald, co-founder of *The Bulletin* and long-time critic of executioner Nosey Bob. (State Library of NSW)

'The most bloodthirsty ruffian that ever took to the bush in Australia . . . propped on a country bed like a prized trophy, eyes kept open by a pair of toothpicks.' Bushranger Dan 'Mad Dog' Morgan after being killed in a shootout with police in north-east Victoria in 1865.

'I would understand your behaviour in a mean, low-spirited mongrel – but in you? My little heart's treasure, my joyous, innocent darling, I would rather see you than anyone on earth . . .' Allan Hughan, infatuated business partner of Captain Moonlite. (hughanhistory.blogspot.com)

'They prop him up on a cot, his chest wound so crudely stitched it looks like the work of a sailor hastily repairing torn canvas during a storm.' Legendary bushranger Captain Thunderbolt (Frederick Ward) after being shot dead by police in 1870. (NSW State Library)

'I am at war with society and the authorities. When I came here I saw I had either to submit to 10 years of insult and injury, or fight against it. And I have been fighting against it.' Prison photograph of Andrew George Scott after his arrival at the Pentridge stockade. (Public Record Office Victoria)

'Scott met James Nesbitt in Pentridge when the legend of Captain Moonlite was already growing and he was serving time for one of the most audacious bank robberies Australia had seen. From the start he had loved the man.' Scott's Pentridge file. (Public Record Office Victoria)

'A kid whose own father dispenses love with a leather strap and the back of his hand meets a man more than 10 years his senior who has travelled the world and burns with wisdom and experience.' Nesbitt's Pentridge file. (Public Record Office Victoria)

'Two years before their trial, both men posed for a photograph dressed in women's finery. Stella looks exhausted, her hands clasped around the waist of Fanny, her head resting on her friend's shoulder.' Frederick Park and Ernest Boulton before their arrest for 'conspiring to commit an unnatural offence'. (Essex Record Office)

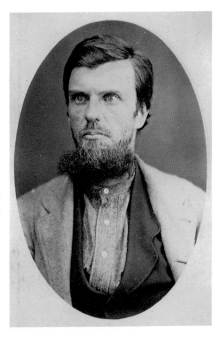

'I had one friend, my own dearest Jim (James P. Nesbitt). He comforted me and supported me in sickness and sorrow. We were one in heart and soul. He died in my arms and I long to join him where there shall be no more parting, no more injustice.' Captain Moonlite shortly after his arrest following the Wantabadgery siege. (NSW State Archives and Records)

'Poor old Rogan. He hadn't fired a single shot in anger. He had no idea how to use a gun and had spent 24 hours during the siege hiding beneath a bed, crying and praying to his God.' Thomas Rogan, executed alongside Captain Moonlite in 1880. (NSW State Archives and Records)

FROM A PHOTOGRAPH TAKEN TWO YEARS AGO.

'Based on a photograph taken in 1878, it shows a short, baby-faced 13-year-old, hair neatly combed, dressed in a pinstripe suit . . . his face a portrait of naivety and innocence.' Gus Wernicke, youngest member of the Moonlite gang. (*Australasian Sketcher*)

'Captain Moonlite and James Nesbitt are back outside and advancing on the police. Both are firing rapidly. "We fought, they retreated, we advanced, they ran," Scott will say later.' An artist's rendition of the Wantabadgery siege from *Australasian Sketcher*. (State Library of Victoria)

'What sort of dishonourable bastard is this Cassin? He is a big man with a full beard and dark eyes and Scott wants to pull him apart, limb by limb.' The police officers involved in the siege with Captain Moonlite (Sergeant Henry Cassin seated on floor). (NSW State Library)

'Bennett has just been shot in the arm and is crying out "surrender" and the young constable who fired at him has just belted him across the face with his revolver.'
Prison admission sheet of Graham Bennett after the Wantabadgery siege.
(NSW State Archives and Records)

'I was led astray by the oily tongue of a scoundrel. I was deceived. I have suffered, and am now suffering. The only desire of my heart is to sink in rest in death's oblivion.'
Moonlite gang member Thomas Williams – real name Frank Johns. (NSW State Archives and Records)

'No-one could doubt that you started with this band of young men, and apparently from a natural love of crime, commenced a course of plunder and violence in this country.' Justice William Windeyer, the judge who sentenced Captain Moonlite to death. (University of Sydney)

'Scott damaged his own cause wilfully at the trial, making his own guilt blacker that he might give his companions a chance at their lives.' The Reverend John Alexander Dowie, supporter of Captain Moonlite, in his robes as Elijah the Restorer, 1904.

...ould ask you to use your interest to obtain
a reprieve. Poor fellow I have known him for some
time and he has been to me a constant friend
When I was driven from shelter by police
persecution and was without a farthing he
has pledged his Coat and handed me the
money. I felt very much the fact that when he
was asked, had he anything to say why sentence
of death should not be passed on him. In fact
when asked to plead for his life, he forgot his
own danger, and only said a word or two in
my defence. I am aware it will be argued he
has been convicted before. But those who argue
thus. Know little of the merits of the case
For the crime for which he was so convicted
he suffered and paid the penalty the law
awarded, and should have had a chance to

to retrieve the past, this chance he never had
he was hunted down and could not get work.
In the name of justice how often is he to be
punished for the same offence? Is one false step
to lead him to death. If you have mad jury
men and prejudiced Judges let there be some
mercy to left with the representative of our
Queen. Rogan is but one year older than
Bennett. It is Known Rogan did not give
the fatal shot. he has been recommended to mercy
Why should he not have it? In this case
one Constable has fallen. two of my friends
are dead, if that does not appear enough to satiate
the love of blood. surely mine ought to pay
the price and fully satisfy so called justice.
a justice that can wink at the fact of a
mad juryman and tolerate a prejudiced

'If the law has been so broken that it must be avenged by a human life, then spare these youths – God created them for something nobler than the gallows.' One of Captain Moonlite's death cell letters pleading for a reprieve for Thomas Rogan. (Corrective Services NSW)

'I have now seen men expire under almost every variety of circumstance, and have learnt that death by the hands of the executioner is the most terrible of all spectacles.' J. F. Archibald's report on Moonlite's hanging in the first edition of *The Bulletin*, 31 January 1880. (National Library of Australia)

'The man wants to die bravely but Scott's stricken features – "a fixed appearance of utter helplessness and despair" – betray him.' The official decree confirming the date of Captain Moonlite's execution. (Corrective Services NSW)

'Scott and his men are taken through the front entrance where, overhead and in full view of the public, Alexander Green, the gaol's first hangman, carried out some of his best work.' The front gates of Darlinghurst Gaol, circa 1880. (National Art School, Darlinghurst)

'It was morally impossible for him to tell the truth or be honest . . . he was void of all moral courage, very secretive and would keep up to the last anything he once said.' The plaster cast of Captain Moonlite's skull after his execution. (Justice and Police Museum, Sydney)

ANDREW GEORGE SCOTT
CAPTAIN MOONLITE
BORN IRELAND 8-1-1845
DIED SYDNEY 20-1-1880

'A rough, unhewn rock, one that skilled hands could have made into something better. It will be like those it marks as kindness and charity could have shaped us to better ends.' The final resting place of Captain Moonlite at North Gundagai cemetery.

persons who make heroes of highwaymen,' opines *The Ballarat Star*, '. . . the conclusion of it all cannot but prove a salutary lesson . . . as the reply of outraged society to the maudlin admiration of the class [of] larrikins.'

A week later Scott is taken to Melbourne. He looks a different man when they remove his beard and shave his head. Without the whiskers and carefully combed hair, he cuts a stern and almost menacing figure. In a photograph taken when he is admitted to Pentridge, he stares past the camera and into the distance, mouth clenched, his hairline a dramatic V-shape on his forehead.

You can already see the defiance etched into his face. He is preparing himself for the hard years ahead in a harsh bluestone prison that is home to some of the most wicked and haunted men in the colony. Within days he might even cross paths with a young man who shares that same resistance to authority. He is now known as prisoner 10926. His real name is Ned Kelly.

16

MURDERERS AND MISFITS

The bloody traps and that wild Irish blood. At least George Scott and Ned Kelly have some things in common. You wouldn't think it at first. These two men who will bring the bushranging era to such a bloody end are together in Pentridge in the second half of 1872, separated by almost 10 years and an even greater gap in privilege and circumstance.

They will sleep on the same coconut mats, wrap themselves on cold nights in the same thin blankets and suffer the same agonies from the irons chafing their ankles. But surely that is where the similarities end.

George? His God blesses the Church of England, his father is a former magistrate and his family – well, the good Lord in all his wisdom may have taken it away from them now, but they have not forgotten what it was like to be on familiar terms with wealth and entitlement.

Ned? Let there be no doubts that his God is Catholic, that his father was a convict who now rots in the ground, or that his family has known only poverty and police persecution.

George? Hard to imagine the demand for it inside these bluestone walls, but if an inmate would like to hear a few verses from a popular Romantic poem, then Captain Moonlite will most assuredly oblige.

Ned? He's not what you would call classically educated. He's never known a comma or a semi-colon. But the man knows how to use words, all the same. And it is in their words that both men share much common ground.

Kelly is serving a three-year sentence for horse stealing. He'll be quick to tell you he never done it, that all he done was take a beautiful chestnut mare he thought belonged to Wild Wright for a gallop into Wangaratta. But as he neared Greta one of the traps had recognised the horse's striking white face and all sorts of bedlam had broken out. Turned out the horse had been stolen a month earlier. In the struggle that followed one of those loathsome coppers had tried to shoot Ned. But the gun had misfired and in the end it took seven of them to give him a beating and drag him off to the cells, a trail of fine Kelly blood staining the dirt track leading to the lock-up.

In just a couple of years Kelly will defeat Wild Wright in a 20-round bareknuckle fight in front of a roaring crowd that will further embellish his legend. But it will be Kelly's words that will echo far longer than the sound of the final bell during that epic encounter. Kelly will write how he and his family have had to 'put up with the brutal and cowardly conduct of a parcel of big ugly fat-necked wombat headed big bellied magpie legged narrow hipped splaw-footed sons of Irish bailiffs or English landlords which is better known as Officers of Justice or Victorian Police who some calls honest gentlemen but I would like to know what business an honest man would have in the Police as it is an old saying it takes a rogue to catch a rogue . . .'

Either ways a trap is a natural perjurer, says Ned, a disgrace to his Irish ancestors. He knows what lurks in such men's hearts. They are cowards who now serve 'under a flag and nation that has destroyed massacred and murdered their forefathers by the greatest of torture as rolling them down hill in spiked barrels pulling their toe and finger nails . . . and every torture imaginable'.

It will not be long before this seething resentment spills over and Kelly launches an open war on the traps – and all who support them. He will make sure they are 'pegged on an ant-bed with their bellies opened their fat taken out rendered and poured down their throat boiling hot . . .'

Scott's language might be more refined and will certainly be peppered with appropriate punctuation. But the sentiment will be the same. Both are men who sense enemies lurking everywhere. Their resentment of authority will end with them making their last stand against injustice amid a hail of police bullets.

But before they can do that, they must bide their time inside Pentridge. The following winter Kelly will be transferred to the prison hulks moored in Port Phillip Bay. Each morning he will be rowed ashore to work on the armoury fortifications that will protect the colony from any French invasion. He will then return to Pentridge before being released in February 1874.

Scott will remain in the prison for another five years. If what takes place three days after his arrival from Ballarat is any indication, it will be a long stint surrounded by constant violence and mayhem. Weeks earlier John Taylor, a chronic offender everyone knows as Weechurch, had begun spiralling out of control once more. Confined in his cell in A division for the past week on suspicion of having lit a fire that destroyed the shoemaking workshop, Weechurch is also suspected of having attempted to burn the private quarters of the Inspector-General of Penal Establishments, George Duncan.

When Duncan pays a visit to the stockade on a Sunday afternoon, Weechurch's name is placed on a list of prisoners wanting to see him. Allowing inmates an opportunity to voice their complaints to the most powerful man in the colony's penal system is a tradition Duncan has been keen to establish. But it bothers many others, who see it as another example of Duncan's deep desire to be loved by everyone – outside and inside the blue walls of Pentridge.

Duncan arrives at Weechurch's cell just before 4pm. Weechurch stands to attention with his cap in hand. When Duncan steps in, Weechurch drops the cap and lunges forward, stabbing Duncan in the left groin with a table knife he has sharpened to a fine point. Fortunately for Duncan it is not a deep wound. Weechurch knows it, too.

When a parade of prisoners is conducted near his cell soon after the stabbing – the newly arrived George Scott probably among them – Weechurch will shout 'at the top of his voice, at the same time using the foulest language, that he had stabbed the superintendent but he was afraid not deep enough'.

—

Just as he did in the Parramatta Asylum, Scott gravitates toward the meanest and hardest of inmates inside Pentridge. Much of his sentence will be served among the lifers who spend their days in a yard that sums up their existence. An adjacent yard is filled with flourishing vegetable gardens and chili plants used to season the prison soup. But the lifers' outdoor area is a grim, featureless block broken only by a large partitioned shed, where prisoners sit each day shelling husks off coconuts.

'A visitor would very likely see Captain Moonlite in all his glory laying down the law to his next door neighbours,' says one newspaper report of the time. 'The captain is put in the lifers' yard as he is considered a highly dangerous character. He takes things remarkably easy, and you will often see him having a rest – ceasing work altogether and leaning back on his seat in the most nonchalant manner.'

Scott soon forms a close friendship with Laurence Shanklin, an Irishman convicted of murder in 1861. Shanklin's original death sentence for stabbing a man to death in Geelong had been commuted to life imprisonment and sparked uproar throughout the colony. His mother had told the jury insanity ran deeply in the family and Shanklin had never been the same after suffering a knock to his head years earlier. Several witnesses reported Shanklin as having behaved strangely in the past, including one who one day found him 'lying on the ground on his face, tearing up the grass with his teeth and with his hands . . . he was one day deranged, and another day sensible'.

But despite lingering doubts about his state of mind, the jury had found him guilty. As he does with Weechurch, Scott quickly becomes a staunch defender of Shanklin. In the years they are together in Pentridge, Scott will watch Shanklin fall ill and become depressed. 'Disappointed hopes, and several causes of sorrow, assisted by a diseased liver, disordered his intellect and for some time he was insane,' Scott will write. '. . . it was said by the authorities that he was only acting and that I had advised him to such a course . . . I am perfectly sure he was really at the time insane and that he is totally incapable of falsehood or deceit. Among prisoners of every class he is respected and he is beloved by those who know him and we are honoured with his friendship.'

Everywhere Scott looks in Pentridge he finds justice being miscarried and good men going to waste. They are like him – all of them wrongly convicted on the word of perjurers, all of them hunted and pursued by the authorities. Even in prison they are given no rest from the petty scrutiny of the authorities. As the months pass his outrage will grow. The colony's rulers are mere hypocrites; they talk of the redemptive nature of prison, but there is no such thing – nor do they really want it. So he begins to take them under his wing, all those lost and hopeless causes, all those men who lack the confidence to speak up and the education to understand how the system has let them down.

The Captain befriends them all, including Thomas Rea, another inmate Scott is certain is innocent.

Rea is a trained gunsmith but his real passion is for entertaining. Born in Scotland, he had settled his family in Launceston in Van Diemen's Land in the early 1840s, advertising himself as 'the celebrated Ventriloquist, Performer of Mechanical Figures, Deceptions &c'. He claimed to have performed in front of Queen Victoria, his demonstration of articulated puppets 'honoured with unbounded applause'.

But the self-dubbed Professor Rae soon found the raucous crowds of ex-convicts and settlers unappreciative of his talents. In 1844 he had promised them the first manned balloon ascent in the colonies and asked that 'his friends will not be backward in patronising him upon the day'. An excited crowd of more than 500 made the 15-minute walk to the Cataract Gorge to watch history being made.

It did not take long for their anticipation to turn to anger. 'The affair turned out to be a complete hoax,' reported the *Launceston Examiner*. 'The curiosity of the multitude was greatly disappointed when the aeronaut, instead of performing his promised feat, inflated a small paper balloon. The indignation of the multitude was with difficulty restrained, and strong hints having been thrown out that the perpetrator of the hoax was to be well ducked, he quietly made his escape.'

A few months later Rea was at it again. This time more than 100 people paid admission, with another thousand gathered in the streets. Once again they were left disappointed. Rea had promised them that he would ascend in his 'Leviathan Balloon . . . and will not leave it, unless he is obliged to descend in his PATENT PARACHUTE!!!'

It never left the ground – Rea accusing one of his assistants of allowing the balloon to be torn by a roof shingle. Other failures followed and the public humiliation forced him to move across Bass Strait to Port Phillip. He settled in Geelong and announced he had invented a perpetual-motion machine that would replace the steam engine and that he 'only awaits an opportunity to get his invention patented before he makes it known to the world'. It never appeared and later attempts to set another balloon aloft also failed.

By the early 1870s Rea had settled in Sandhurst and returned to gunsmithing. A notorious publicity seeker, his name was soon associated with something far graver than swindling the public. He was found guilty of criminally assaulting two girls under the age of 12. On a day when his wife was absent, he was alleged to have 'tampered with the girls . . . the details of the case were of a very disgusting nature'. A sordid incident grew worse when the older brother of the two girls hanged himself after Rea's son issued death threats against the family.

In the years to come there will be suspicions that, after his release, Rea provides guns to Scott when he leaves Victoria. In his death cell at Darlinghurst Gaol, Scott will write to him and lament how his mission to bring about prison reform had failed.

'I hope the cause which was too much for me may meet a better advocate. Mr Rea, like myself you have suffered much. The death of your fine, clever, noble grandson was a sad blow; and then the cruel, false charge which sent you to Pentridge – I am perfectly sure [you] were innocent. I believe you are incapable of an unmanly, dishonourable or unchristian act and feel proud you were once my friend.'

Murderers, molesters and misfits. To Scott they are all innocent men whose honour and manliness remain intact. And one of them is about to win his heart.

17

HOUSES OF HATE

He's a right old bastard, this one. You might not know it at first because the neighbourhood is filled with bastards just like him – hard, flinty characters whose thin lips rarely break their stubble with a smile, who brawl down these dirty streets, bellies full of grog, bellowing and spitting and snarling at one another like leashed dogs.

But not one of these men in their shabby clothes stained with sweat and blood and desperation comes close to James Nesbitt Senior. Even on a warm night when all the squalid little houses in Bouverie Street in the Melbourne suburb of Carlton are being lashed by rain, when the thunder from a summer storm is beating a drum roll on their tin roofs, his threats and curses boom through the thin walls. No tempest can match his fury or frustration. Every beer fuels that furnace of bile, stoking the anger until it erupts and finds the nearest and easiest target: his family.

He is at it once more on this early February night in 1875, the old bastard drunk and mean and just itching for an argument.

Of course, there's no money left because he'd rather squander on himself what few shillings he makes from stealing. So that means his wife Catherine can't feed the kids and the three girls will have to go hungry.

Once again.

It's always once again in this house. It's not so much a home but a cramped, stuffy stage for James and Catherine to play out their nightly ritual of mutual hate and loathing. It wasn't even two years ago that the pair of them were dragged out by the police and taken to the Melbourne city watchhouse. He'd given her a taste of his knuckles and she had stood her ground and called him every low thing she could think of. When they fronted the judge the next day, the grog had worn off and a new morning had softened the memory of the previous night. The newspapers – regular chroniclers of the exploits of James P. Nesbitt Senior – noted that 'the prisoners had made up their disagreement and were allowed to go away in peace'.

Of course, in the House of Once Again, peace is a notion as thin as the soups Catherine dishes up when the old bastard hasn't pissed away all the money he's earned from pinching tradesmen's tools and reselling them. And on this night, when the rain is turning Bouverie Street into a river of sludge, there will be no détente reached, no sweet moment when differences are put aside for the sake of the children and the neighbourhood.

This time James Nesbitt Senior has it all figured out. His lousy life, his lousy home – the reasons for his entire second-rate lousy existence – have been in front of him all along. Even that skinny teenage son he named after himself turned out bad. Thank God the bugger no longer lives here, eating them out of house and home. Let the prison warders at the Pentridge stockade use their fists to teach him a lesson about where petty crime can lead you. Look at how such a life turned out for himself. God knows he pummelled the kid enough and no thrashing seemed hard enough to knock any sense into him.

It may have taken a few drinks for it to become apparent. But now he knows why he is left suffocating and gasping through every waking moment. It's that damned woman and those children she gave birth to after their drunken tumbles in the sack, back when they still felt something for one another before the hate took over.

Look at how that turned out, too. Three needy girls and a teenage son who doesn't even know how to pinch money from a bakery without being caught.

Yes, they are the reason for his daily torment and why the grog is the only thing that can erase it.

Well, now that he has enjoyed this moment of enlightenment, he knows what to do. He orders them out. Of course, there are more than just angry words involved in this eviction because everyone in Bouverie Street can hear the thuds and whacks coming from the House of Once Again and not even the rain can muffle the screams and cries of the children. There's the sound of a door slamming shut and through their foggy windows the neighbours can see Catherine and her daughters out there soaking in the street, thin woollen clothes already drenched and certain to stink for weeks.

Say what you like about the Nesbitts – but this Catherine, she's no shrinking violet. There are women all over town who live with violent drunken husbands and who quickly learn to shut up and hide their bruises and their constant fear for the sake of their children and their own lives. But Catherine is a fighter – maybe that's what drew her to James in the first place – and she is not going to let the old bastard get away with humiliating her like this. It might be one thing to raise a racket beneath their own roof – but hurling her out on the street like this, with all those damn nosey faces watching on?

She marches back to the front door and begins trying to open it. If she pounds on it just a little harder she might splinter it – which is not such a hard thing given that the doors around here are almost as thin as the walls. But James saves her the trouble. There he is, standing in the doorway wielding a butcher's steel. Its cold metal has known the squealing of knives as their blades slide across to create a sharp edge. But it has rarely been the cause of a woman's screams as it thumps into warm flesh.

Not long after, a police officer, perhaps summoned by a worried neighbour prepared to venture out in the wet and down to the nearby station, tries to intervene. He suffers a few blows for his trouble too before Nesbitt is finally wrestled to the ground, arrested and dragged away.

A day or so later the newspapers are eager to give their readers yet another sordid chapter in the ongoing saga of James P. Nesbitt.

Under the headline 'A Brute', one of the reporters writes that Nesbitt 'believes in starving his children and turning his wife and family out all night into the rain'. He is remanded and a few months later 'this old acquaintance of the City Bench' – described by police as a 'brutal husband, a bad father and a disorderly drunkard' – is gaoled for six months.

For Catherine and the girls, a brief respite. But the old bastard will be back. You can bet on it. In the House of Once Again, the fury and the hate never ends.

—

James Nesbitt Junior no longer lives in the House of Once Again. But his new lodgings just eight miles up the road from Bouverie Street are hardly an improvement. Pentridge's walls are thicker than those in Bouverie Street, made of impenetrable bluestone, but they serve only to swallow the cries and smother the hopes of those within. The entrance is guarded by double gates; the first fashioned from strong oak, the second made of iron bars.

Nesbitt enters these gates as a teenager barely needing to shave. He's also spent time in the old Melbourne Gaol in the city, a haunted dungeon filled with tortured souls and angry ghosts. His father might loathe him but that's probably because he has had as much luck as the old man when it comes to being a petty thief. Nesbitt Senior must stare into the mirror every morning and see Nesbitt Junior's reflection, but without all the hate. Junior has already had a couple of stints of hard labour for stealing from a baker and a grocer and now he faces four years for assault and robbery. If life has been hard on the streets of Carlton and inner Melbourne, and grew even worse when he walked through the door of that little house in Bouverie Street, Pentridge has elevated those daily horrors to a new level.

Here is finishing school for all those inner-city gangs of young toughs; a nightmarish stone tomb filled with twisted and broken men.

But even the most haunted and depraved bow before Michael Gately. The first time young James Nesbitt set eyes on him may have been when he heard shouts and laughter from a large group of men gathered in a circle in one of the prison yards. Here was the famous rat pit where Gately, originally transported from Ireland to Van Diemen's Land in 1841, took delight in showing off one of many macabre skills. He would collect half a dozen rats, set them on the ground and then get down on all fours and catch them with his yellow teeth, shaking them to death before placing them on a 'spit' and roasting them.

A journalist visiting the prison in 1877 finds Gately to be 'a frightful animal – the immense head, powerful protruding jaw, narrow receding forehead and deficient brain space, seemed fitly joined to tremendous shoulders and long, strong arms, like those of a gorilla, which he resembles more than a man. All the evil passions appeared to have their home behind that repellent, revolting countenance . . . a natural brute.'

When he is not serving time inside Pentridge – and those times are rare, for Gately's rap sheet reveals few crimes he has not attempted – he can sometimes be found living in a humpy in scrubland on the banks of the Yarra River with an infatuated 16-year-old girl.

But they say there is a role for every man in life and Gately's skills and passions have finally been recognised with his appointment as the prison's new scourger and hangman. Admirers – most of them guards – believe he has lifted the job of whipping fellow prisoners to an art form. Those gorilla-like arms turn a routine flogging with the cat-o'-nine-tails into a tawdry spectacle of blood and lacerated flesh. With his victims tied to a triangle in one of the courtyards – everyone calls it being 'married to the three sisters' – Gately sets to work with a gleam in his eye, almost salivating at the prospect of what is to come.

'All who saw him scourging knew that he would have taken on the job for nothing rather than have missed it,' one witness will recall.

He can be just as thorough and diligent on the scaffold. Old mates are dispatched with the tenderness of a doting mother, a perfectly positioned knot sending them into eternity before the sound of the trapdoor swinging open reaches their ears. But those he doesn't like can be assured the brute will ensure a messy end; a slow, twisting strangulation, their last earthly vision the beaming countenance of Michael Gately.

Every day at Pentridge begins at 5.45am when the prison bells toll, as they toll 16 times more throughout the day, tolling for the final time at 8pm for lights out. Sleep follows, then the bells again at 5.45 and another day of hard labour and survival, surrounded by men like Tommy the Nut and the chronically depressed Peter Stuart, always plotting another suicide attempt.

In the prison yards, the guards have been known to force the inmates to wear calico masks so they cannot identify one another. Punishment is meted out with stints on a treadmill crushing more of that bluestone rock, or sent to solitary confinement to dwell in stygian darkness on a diet of coarse white bread and water. It's a meal that might sate the hunger pains but after a week it can leave a man in pain from constipation. Nothing, though, compared to the anguish of all those days and nights in the silent blackness, an abyss that deadens the soul and sharpens every fear and dread.

But somehow, deep in the belly of this twisted fortress, embers of admiration and fondness and even love still manage to glow. James Nesbitt meets Andrew George Scott. He may not have realised he was even searching for a father figure, but in Scott he has found that and much more. A kid whose own father dispenses love with a leather strap and the back of his hand meets a man more than 10 years his senior who has travelled the world and burns with wisdom and experience.

It's a theme that has become a regular occurrence in Scott's life. He draws the broken and the wounded to him. He inspires them with tales of bravery and daring. He lifts them up with his fast Irish patter by telling them they, too, can do great things. He quotes the poets and philosophers and exhorts these young men like a preacher to reach for more, to have the courage to stare down the unfair world and make it submit to their wants and needs.

Scott may not be tall or physically imposing. He might drag that right foot when he walks. But it's his steel blue eyes and silver tongue that have drawn Nesbitt to him. There is no other man like him in this prison. Others might have similar fiery and unpredictable tempers. But few can match Scott's passion. The man they call Moonlite rails against injustice and unfairness and is prepared to stand against it, often recklessly and with no thought for his personal safety.

It started three years earlier on the first day he entered Pentridge. The warders ordered him into a bath. Scott was indignant. Three Europeans and a Chinaman had already dirtied its waters and he refused to bathe in their dirt and sweat. He was punished for that and his reputation as a troublemaker began. Not long after, he heard that one of the superintendents had been going around saying Scott was a problem and he would have him shot and draped over the gaol's wall as an example to others.

James Nesbitt has never met a man who stands by principles, so it was ironical that it has taken a stint in Pentridge for him to find one. He can listen to Scott all day. The man is a gifted storyteller and has a never-ending supply of riveting accounts about his adventures. There might be a streak of vanity running through him. Understandable, though. Who would have thought someone could squeeze so much into just three decades?

It amazes a young man like James, whose world was completely bound by the small streets of inner Melbourne. Scott has been a soldier, a civil engineer, a preacher, a smuggler, sailor and thief. He has wielded guns, ridden wild horses, bled from gunshot wounds and steered small boats through plunging seas. He has seen bodies broken by war and hollowed by famine.

If there is a common theme that underpins all these tales – apart from Scott featuring as the key heroic figure – it's that most of them end with the hero's downfall because of one injustice or another.

The lesson in all this for young James is unmistakeable, not that he hasn't been schooled enough in its truth. The world is a dark place – unforgiving, unfair and unwilling to hand a lucky break to the deserving few who aspire to greatness. Perhaps that is why James Nesbitt is in awe of the man. No matter how hard things get, no matter how many times he has been shot, imprisoned, humiliated and beaten, Captain Moonlite simply gets back up, dusts himself off and limps forward to fight another day.

'I am at war with society and the authorities,' Scott will soon tell a visitor to the prison. It's a sentiment Nesbitt will hear regularly in the next few years.

'From the first they have had a down on me. When I came here I saw I had either to submit to 10 years of insult and injury, or fight against it. And I have been fighting against it.'

Even in casual conversation this is how Scott often speaks. His life is filled with grand causes, his speech littered with grandiosity. His mission is to identify and weed out the cruelties inflicted by the powerful upon the weak. And there will be few better examples – apart from those having to do with himself – than the case of old Weechurch.

He had been a bookbinder in Nottingham before being transported to Van Diemen's Land for theft. He made his way to the colony of Victoria after serving his time, but life's usual miseries followed him. He has been in Pentridge for years, a small man with a formidable reputation for trouble. He has assaulted guards and inflicted severe injuries on several of them.

He has also spent more time in the black cave of solitary confinement than any other prisoner. There was that time he stabbed George Duncan, the Inspector-General of Penal Establishments. A more recent stint in the hole lasted weeks and Scott believes it finally sent him mad – crazed enough, anyway, to stab a guard in the face with the steel handle of a pail. Charged with attempted murder, Weechurch defends himself in Melbourne's Central Criminal Court and calls Andrew George Scott as one of his witnesses.

The crowded courtroom is filled with spectators and newspapermen. They have all heard about Captain Moonlite. Scott, wearing his grey prison clothes and with his legs in irons, looks at them approvingly and knows he has been granted a rare opportunity.

He nods and agrees with Weechurch when he claims he has been unfairly targeted by gaol officials and is yet another victim of that degrading and savage institution known as Pentridge.

'I have been aware to a certain extent that you have been subjected to brutal treatment all through,' Scott says.

'I can only judge of your treatment from that of every other man in Pentridge.

'I could give you information about the penal establishment and its tendency if you keep me long enough and ask me questions.'

Scott certainly has form when it comes to lengthy addresses to packed courtrooms. 'The regulations are a dead letter at Pentridge, except when they are used as a means of tyranny and oppression to a man. So far as the reformation of a prisoner is concerned they are a dead letter.'

Scott goes on to detail more of the prison's shortcomings and how complaints made by prisoners – usually to do with violence and mistreatment at the hands of the sadistic guards – end up going nowhere. Visiting magistrates will listen but never take any action, he says.

But just as he is warming to one of his favourite topics, he is cut short by the need to get to the next witness. Scott turns to the judge and asks: 'May I make a statement?'

'No, certainly not,' says his Honour.

You can see Scott bristle. His stage has been taken from him. As he is led from the courtroom he begins to yell.

'It will be necessary to bring me before the court on a charge [of attempted murder] like this,' he shouts. 'The injustice and brutality carried on at Pentridge is dreadful. It is the most immoral and disgusting place in the world. If that man [Weechurch] is found guilty and hanged, he will be murdered, and the inspector general will be his murderer.'

From the dock, Weechurch says: 'That man speaks from his heart.'

But Scott's passion fails to sway the jury. They only need an hour to find Weechurch guilty and the judge sentences him to hang.

Less than three weeks later the small frame of Weechurch is escorted onto the scaffold at the old Melbourne Gaol in the city. For years he has clung to a belief that he has been wrongly imprisoned. Like his friend Scott, he is a victim of a system heavily weighted against the oppressed. This certainty dampens his fears and keeps him in control, his nerves betrayed only by a slight tremble running through his body.

There are 30 people watching below as he says a few final words. Among them is a young man trying to make his way in the newspaper world. John Feltham Archibald, a reporter with Melbourne's *Daily Telegraph*, is a nervous, fidgety type. In later years many searching for an apt description of the man will politely settle on the word 'eccentric'. Archibald is a Francophile and in a few years' time will change his first names to Jules Francois. But right now he is doing his best to make an impression on his new bosses and carve out a career as a writer. He scribbles quietly in his notebook as Weechurch, 'a poor, mad, nervous, wild-eyed creature about 8 st. in weight' utters his final words.

'Kind friends – I cannot call you enemies, for I must try to forgive my enemies – I am a poor criminal about to be launched into eternity to appear before my God upon a charge of intending to commit murder,' Weechurch says.

'So far as that charge is concerned I am truly innocent before God.

'Before God I stand here today, an innocent man. The law in its literal sense does not demand my body but the law in its perverted sense does demand my body and Christ, I hope, will demand my soul.'

As Weechurch finishes speaking, Archibald looks up and watches as Gately 'seized his victim, and went through the hideous process of baring his neck, which was placed in the fatal halter . . .'

Then 'the hangman stole from his victim's side, and pushed the lever from its position, and the convict's light frame fell with a horrid creak some 6ft into the open trap. It slowly swung round, and then remained perfectly motionless, not a singular muscular contraction being visible.'

It is true what they say. Gately may be a brute and a sadist who thrives in the violent world of Pentridge. But he looks after his friends and has given John Weechurch the best gift he knows.

A sudden and instant death.

18

THIS TERRIBLE DARKNESS

Those inner streets of Melbourne and the nightly horrors of life in the House of Once Again have left their mark on James Nesbitt. There is a scar on the top of his head, a couple of nasty two-inch gashes running down the side, another to the right of his upper lip and one on his left jaw. But somehow those deep hazel eyes and that mass of brown hair conspire to hide the blemishes. When he entered Pentridge Prison a guard closely examined him and scribbled that Nesbitt had a 'fresh complexion'.

It's true. He may have run with rough gangs like the Bouverie Street Push and he has almost certainly never gone a week without being belted by that right old bastard of a father. But his prison photograph will show a handsome 18-year-old with slight jug ears and full lips and a soft dimple in his chin. He will look as if he is about to break into a sad smile; a young man who learned at the blunt end of the old man's knuckles not to expect anything from life.

Yet in Pentridge in the middle of 1875 he has met an older man with different lessons to teach, someone who encourages him to speak and say what he thinks, a man who is curious about where those scars came from, a man who extends a hand in friendship and even love, rather than anger.

In this claustrophobic prison with its bluestone walls and ever-watchful armed guards, Andrew George Scott is opening up a vast new world of possibilities to James Nesbitt.

It's extraordinary, the adventures Scott has managed to squeeze into his three decades. Just take the past seven years since he arrived in Australia from New Zealand. He has spent four of them behind bars. But the other three? He has a seemingly inexhaustible litany of exploits to keep Nesbitt spellbound.

Scott has sailed throughout the South Pacific and skippered a small ketch through heaving seas safely into harbour. He has worked as a smuggler off Queensland and even worked legitimately hauling coal and passengers up and down the east coast of Australia. He has pulled off one of the most audacious gaolbreaks in colonial history, purchased an island just north of Fiji, preached the Lord's word to packed congregations, toted guns and sat sullenly in an asylum for months claiming his food had been poisoned.

Little wonder James is quickly drawn into his world. The pair are always together in the prison yard and the mess hall. In fact, they grow so close gaol officials become concerned and will tell the newspapers: 'The two were great chums in Pentridge, and, in order to preserve discipline, had to be separated.'

Great *chums*. Intimate *friends*. Do the officials separate them 'to preserve discipline' – or because these two are clearly more than just close associates and have crossed the line when it comes to acceptable behaviour?

It will not just be historians peering back at this time with their modern lenses, sifting through the newspaper reports and the florid batches of Scott's letters declaring his love for James, who will search for evidence that the pair were lovers.

Their bond is clearly a talking point at the time as well.

In a few years, when Nesbitt is already buried in Gundagai and Scott is waiting for Nosey Bob to send him to the same grave of his young friend, a lengthy letter will appear in a Ballarat newspaper. The anonymous author clearly has a great deal of experience with the Australian prison system and has noted comments made by Scott that gaols are 'universities of crime'.

The writer urges readers to take Scott's words 'and lay them carefully up in their memories as words of truth, for that such they are, in a given sense, I am here to authenticate by years of experience in the knowledge of the habits of a large portion of the class from which this wretched being has recently sprung'.

The man penning the letter is a classic specimen of the 19th-century windbag. He will opt for a sentence rather than a word, a lengthy paragraph filled with tortuous, comma-filled musings instead of a straightforward declaration. But it's easy to understand his reluctance to get to the point. He wants to warn readers about an evil that exists in the prison system – a horror that no right-thinking civilised person could possibly even imagine. But how to say it? This darkness that is beyond the imagining of polite society flourishes when 'indulgences are granted under certain conditions, but most especially prisons and reformatories'.

'One phase of the inner life of prisoners and boys of the reformatory class is quite unknown to most of your casual readers of newspapers, and it is only to such as myself, and a comparatively few persons gifted with a desire to acquire positive knowledge of the dark side of human nature for the purpose of aiding in the amelioration of it, and to penetrate to the elements of cause . . . that the terrible knowledge weighs with the oppression of a nightmare.'

Burdened by the weight of this terrible darkness, the writer of the letter finally gets to his point: 'Some years ago a most extraordinary case of shooting took place in the Treasury Gardens in Melbourne. The facts as known must be fully alive in most men's recollections. The striking feature in the probable cause of the deed arose from the terms of intimacy in which the murderer and his "friend" lived.

'Scott, Nesbitt, and the rest of his companions have, it is said, their causes of interest in each other, and a close observer of the habits and tendencies of many such men may gather food for useful reflection ... there is no doubt that theft, burglary and even murder are each in turn the theme and burden of the hours of "association" in the cell and the dormitory, but the general public must be told that the limits of such "education" are not confined merely to the acquisition of other men's goods.'

—

That shooting in the Treasury Gardens? There will indeed be few men who can fail to recall the incident on 5 March 1872 that scandalised the city for weeks with its sordid details of unusual relationships and suggestions of unnatural crimes.

The austere Melbourne newspaper, *The Argus*, revealed many of the disturbing details to its readers the following day, telling them that the facts behind the incident 'form a narrative more resembling the weird stories of horror told by Edgar Allen Poe than a sober statement of facts.

'An extraordinary affair, with a tragical end, happened in the Treasury Gardens yesterday afternoon,' reported *The Argus*. 'About a quarter past 4 o'clock the loud report of a firearm was heard in the lower part of the grounds, and immediately afterwards two men were found reclining under a clump of willows. One was dying; the other, on his back, smoking.'

It turned out the man smoking a cigar was Edward Feeney, an Irishman who had arrived in Victoria 20 years earlier as a private in the 18th regiment. The dying man was Charles Marks. Both men were wardsmen at a local hospital and shared a room at the Great Britain Hotel in Flinders Street. They were described as inseparable, 'intimate friends' prone to squabbling and fits of jealousy.

The owner of a wine bar the pair regularly visited 'courteously informed' *The Argus* about the closeness of the two men: 'Feeney seemed to be completely under the control of Marks, who was the directing person in all transactions ... there was an unusual fondness on the part of Marks toward Feeney, more like that of a man for a woman or a woman for a man, than that which usually subsists between even intimate friends of the same sex. Marks used to put his arm round Feeney, and he often said that he could not live without Feeney.'

There would be suggestions Marks, who had frequently threatened to commit suicide, often lay his head in Feeney's lap. On the day of the shooting both men had dressed as bushrangers and had their photographs taken at a local studio with guns they had just bought at a local armoury. Both had been drinking – the photographer could smell wine on their breath and found it hard to capture them as they swayed in their costumes. In one photograph they are awkwardly shaking hands, Marks staring intently at his bearded friend. In another, they hold their guns pressed against each other's chests.

The pair went drinking again after being photographed, sitting quietly in the corner of a bar writing farewell letters to their mothers and friends, before heading to the Treasury Gardens with their guns intending to shoot one another in an apparent suicide pact.

But things went wrong; it was only Feeney's gun, overpacked with gunshot and powder, that fired. The shot pierced Marks' heart and the powder from the explosion burnt Feeney's hand, although not so badly as to prevent the Irishman from lighting a much-needed steadying cigar.

Feeney was arrested and anally examined by a doctor looking for evidence of the men's 'intimacy'. He was hanged a few months later for murder, the judge telling him '. . . if the statement you made is true, that both of you went out to die together, it was a cowardly act on your part that when you found that the deceased's life was gone you did not take the pistol and blow your own brains out . . . it was cowardly in you not to perform your part that you had agreed to do.'

The case had exposed a seam of Victorian life most preferred to pretend did not exist. Here, in this era of the beloved euphemism, an emotional and physical bond between two men is an 'unnatural crime'. The newspapers are littered with reports of crimes brought before the courts where women and children have been asked to leave when certain evidence is tendered. Some of these particulars are 'unfit for publication'.

Feeney, who will take two minutes to die at the end of the rope, reportedly spends the weeks before his hanging disparaging Marks 'who had often been troublesome to him owing to his expressions of fondness and endearment. Feeney further stated that Marks had continually boasted of an intimacy with Park and Boulton, of London notoriety.'

—

Park and Boulton were representative figures of the Victorian age. In the decades to come the 63-year reign of Queen Victoria will be lampooned as one of the most sexually repressed eras in history. It will conjure images of women standing erect in whalebone skirts so wide and round they instead appear to be sitting on giant cushions. Their heads will be adorned in laced hats, the tantalising flesh of their shoulders and necks hidden behind frills and tightly buttoned tunics. They are women who are taught that sex is not to be enjoyed, but to be clinically viewed as a mechanical act necessary only for procreation. When their husbands – far baser creatures driven by animal lust – climb on top of them, they will be instructed to simply 'lie back and close your eyes and think of England'.

It's a quote many will say comes from the Queen herself while advising her five daughters on how to navigate the marital bed on their wedding night. But history is often a liar. The Queen says no such thing. That Victoria is prim and staid when it comes to relationships is true. 'I think people really marry far too much,' she will say. 'It is such a lottery after all, and for a poor woman a very doubtful happiness.'

But Victoria is a successful gambler when she proposes marriage to her German cousin, Prince Albert. The pair will have nine children and a young Victoria will hint that lust and physical attraction play just as important a role as the sense of duty that brings them together.

'Albert really is quite charming, and so excessively handsome,' she raptures as a young woman. 'Such beautiful blue eyes, an exquisite nose, and such a pretty mouth with delicate moustachios and slight but very slight whiskers; a beautiful figure, broad in the shoulders and a fine waist.'

The Victorian era is not as frigidly repressive as it will be portrayed. More than 80,000 prostitutes will work on London's streets and in her brothels in the 1870s. It's just that in public, the act of sex, with all its grinding and pumping and primal moaning and sighing, is a distasteful, embarrassing and often tortuous subject. Preachers and other guardians of public morals will obsess over masturbation, the sin of 'self-love'. They will warn of the insanity awaiting any of its enthusiastic and regular practitioners. They will urge men, whose desires can never be fully trusted, to wear cumbersome metal devices similar to mediaeval chastity belts in order to prevent 'nocturnal emissions'.

Yet the real fear and loathing will be reserved for homosexuality, the ultimate betrayal of God and nature, the almost unimaginable act of one man or woman lying with another.

A year before Feeney and Marks' complicated relationship ended in a cloud of gunpowder and conjecture, and only four years before Scott and Nesbitt first exchange glances in Pentridge Prison, London had been titillated by the arrest and trial of Thomas Boulton and Frederick Park.

The pair, suspected homosexuals and cross-dressers who worked as prostitutes, regularly toured and performed as a stage act known as Stella and Fanny. They faced court charged with 'conspiring and inciting persons to commit an unnatural offence'.

They could consider themselves fortunate. For four centuries until 1861, 'the detestable and abominable vice of buggery with mankind or beast' had carried the death penalty in Britain. Boulton and Park had been arrested after being seen by a detective while dressed in women's clothing and meeting other men in a private box at the Strand Theatre. They, along with another man with them, were quickly subjected to an intense medical examination to discover if the trio engaged in anal sex.

The Strand was a notorious burlesque theatre that seated more than a thousand and had become a nightly outlet for all of London's repressed passion. Young men who desired sex with other men – known as 'So's' – regularly filled the auditorium. Male prostitutes would entertain their guests in private suites – either gullible clients convinced they were dating women, or men who didn't really mind a little 'back door work'.

The case attracted thousands of onlookers and garnered headlines for days. A trunk filled with Boulton and Park's dresses was presented as evidence and indictments were lodged against prominent politicians and aristocrats for being involved with the pair. One of them – Lord Arthur Clinton – collapsed and died a day after receiving his subpoena, although rumours would persist for more than a century that he had faked his death and escaped overseas through a network of wealthy and influential supporters. If he did, it was a waste of time and money. The prosecution was a shamble of unreliable witnesses and allegations of fabricated evidence.

Boulton and Park were quickly cleared by a jury and the zealous guardians of Victorian prurience left humiliated. Had they lived a century later they might have been celebrated as heroic figures bravely making a statement about the rights of individuals to pursue their own sexuality. But in 1871 they were nothing more than carnival attractions on a par with the bearded lady. Two years before the trial, both men had posed for a photograph, just like Marks and Feeney, dressed in women's finery of the era. In one of them, Stella (Thomas Boulton) looks exhausted, her hands clasped around the waist of Fanny (Frederick Park), her head resting on her friend's shoulder.

The image seemed to represent everything that sex had become in this era; an age filled with so many severe moral rules and expectations they left a suppressed and unfulfilled generation demoralised and bone weary.

—

'What will ensue when we have thousands of men cooped up in the colony without wives and unable to seek them elsewhere?'

The question is posed by the good Reverend James Brown in 1854, the prison chaplain to the Fremantle Convict Establishment. Like everyone else in these wicked colonies, he knows the terrible answer.

'Evil will be the result – too humiliating for the mind to dwell upon – too revolting to name . . . that moral evil of far greater magnitude, which has of old brought down the signal judgment of Heaven, will result.'

The reverend need only point out what happened at the Norfolk Island penal colony, a place so close to hell even those sitting in judgement in Heaven were forced to look away. For more than half a century this small speck of land way off the east coast of Australia had been a dumping ground for the most hardened and twisted convicts sent out to the colonies. Its brutality was unequalled across the Empire; at one stage so many men had been whipped for so long the island's stock of cat-o'-nine-tails began to fall apart. Other prisoners had ropes tied around their wrists and squeezed so hard until blood flowed from their fingernails.

More shocking to churchmen and officials, however, was how Norfolk Island quickly became a sweaty and heaving home for those debased creatures engaged in the unnatural crime of sodomy.

The penal colony's chaplain, Thomas Naylor, found the place a sordid and horrifying defiance of God's word. 'In the open day the weak are bullied and robbed by the stronger. At night the sleeping-wards are very cesspools of unheard-of vices. I cannot find sober words enough to express the enormity of this evil . . . I saw very boys seized upon and lost; I saw decent and respectable men, nay gentlemen . . . thrown among the vilest ruffians, to be tormented by their bestialities.'

But if buggery by force was a nightly occurrence, there was also a place for affection and tenderness. A convict department magistrate, Robert Stuart, at one time estimated there were about 150 convict couples on Norfolk Island in the 1840s who called themselves 'man and wife', along with others in more casual relationships. '. . . these parties manifest as much eager earnestness for the society of each other as members of the opposite sex,' he noted.

If sodomy is the unspeakable crime, they spend a great deal of time speaking about it throughout this 19th century. The idea of two men forming the closest of bonds is no different inside the bluestone walls of Pentridge Prison. While there will never be solid proof that James Nesbitt and Andrew George Scott become physical lovers, theirs is an unusually close and intense relationship, even by prison standards.

Nesbitt, with his dimpled chin and wide ears and faint worry lines on his forehead, has a gentle face that is betrayed by his prison record. He is serving four years for assaulting and robbing a man in the grounds of St James Cathedral, just near the Victoria Market.

Soon he will have a day added to his sentence for 'giving tea to prisoner Scott'. It's a small and affecting infraction; James is a well-behaved inmate compared to many of the others, particularly Scott. His worst offences during his incarceration will include wearing 'trousers improperly' and 'leaving his seat at Divine Service'.

Nesbitt has no need to sit through lengthy sermons. He has Captain Moonlite for that.

19

'A WAR TO THE KNIFE'

James Nesbitt has never seen anything like it. The sheer tenacity and persistence of the man is boundless. Once George Scott embarks on a crusade, he will never let it go.

The only doggedness Nesbitt's father has ever shown has been hunting down his next bottle of grog; the only commitment has been reserved for swinging those fists at his wife and children. Scott, on the other hand, is a force of nature. He is not just driven but *compelled* to right wrongs and correct injustices. It matters little whether they are real or imaginary; Captain Moonlite tackles them all with the zeal of the truest believer.

Scott need never look far in Pentridge for something to fuel his constant sense of indignation. There are campaigns to be waged everywhere. He will be charged 'with having written a document in his possession of a very objectional nature, which no doubt he intended to have passed out of the prison when any opportunity should offer'. He will write a lengthy letter claiming a guard named Bates had been rorting the prison using cheap materials and charging them for more expensive goods. An investigation will clear Bates, an overseer who just a few weeks before had observed Scott 'leave his place of labour and work at a piece of gas-pipe, which it was thought was intended for the barrel of a pistol'. Two weeks will be added to Scott's sentence for that infraction, one of many to come in the years ahead.

Nesbitt's old man might not think twice about hitting police when he is fully in his cups, but young James never sees such crudity in Scott. Instead he watches and admires a man who is willing to stand on his principles and debate even the most powerful men in the colony.

There will be no better example of this willingness to tackle authority than when Scott hears of a planned inspection of Pentridge by Sir Redmond Barry, his old courtroom sparring partner.

Sir Redmond's passion for married women and assiduous note-taking (*31 July: 'Mrs S twice.' 4 August: 'Mrs S 4 times'*) may have waned, but he has taken a liking to inspecting the institutions he fills with the miscreants of society. Indeed, he is about to embark on an overseas trip that will include tours of some of the toughest prisons in America. When he visits Pentridge in January 1876 – just months after Nesbitt meets Scott for the first time – he is pleasantly surprised by what he finds. The local officials have pulled out all stops and Sir Redmond is 'highly pleased' with the quality of the food, the bed linen and the industriousness of the prisoners, one of whom has requested to meet him – 'the notorious "Captain Moonlite"'.

It will be easy to imagine his Honour rolling his eyes when he is told of the potential meeting. There are few men in the colony unaware of Scott's capacity to challenge regulations and even fewer who do not know about his capacity to launch into lengthy monologues in that perpetually outraged Irish accent. But in Sir Redmond, a fellow Irishman from Cork, Scott has a worthy opponent.

When Scott walks into the interview room at Pentridge he tells the judge he desires 'to make some complaints about the regulations'.

Sir Redmond stops him there. Accompanying him is a reporter from *The Argus*, who dutifully notes the ensuing discussion, perhaps a little nervous at not having brought a large enough supply of pencils and paper to record this confrontation between two of the colony's most famous windbags.

'His Honour quickly remarked that he had nothing to say to the regulations,' the reporter will write. 'They were wisely formed, with the advice of the Governor in Council, and all the prisoner had to do was to comply with them.

'His Honour then, addressing Scott, said that if it was of any gratification for him to hear it, he would inform him that he had visited most of the principal prisons on the Continent . . . and it gave him the greatest pleasure to express the gratification and surprise he felt at the admirable arrangements and discipline of the establishment. He had inspected the food, which was of a most excellent quality, especially the bread, which was superior to that of any other prison in the world.'

Scott wants to interrupt but Sir Redmond isn't finished. He waxes in wondrous tones about the first-class bedding, the clean cells, the ample quantity of blankets available for the prisoners. Why, he was taken aback when he toured the prison's hospital to discover only 10 sick men being treated out of Pentridge's inmate population of more than 540, 'the clearest proof that the prisoners were well looked after . . .'

As far as his Honour can tell, most of the inmates are employed at useful trades. They look remarkably healthy. In fact, he tells Scott, he considers that the prisoners have 'no grounds of complaint whatever'.

Scott is overwhelmed. It is not often he is caught on the back foot. He begins to tell Sir Redmond that the regulations are the problem; they are biased and inconsistent. They do not allow prisoners to properly learn a trade and then find legitimate employment in the outside world upon their release.

His Honour shuts him down again, saying he has 'nothing to do with the management of the prison' and that he should make any complaints to visiting justices. When Scott asks if he could write a letter to his Honour outlining his concerns, Sir Redmond says he may not, for he is about to leave the country and will not return 'for some time'.

'Scott, who appeared to be quite surprised at the candid manner of his Honour, left the office with anything but a pleasant countenance, muttering some inaudible expressions as he returned to his place of labour.'

Bested again. By the very man who sent him to Pentridge in the first place.

—

But there will be others who will give Scott a lengthier hearing, including John Stanley James, a man who fully understands the value of a decent alias.

James is another of those quintessential 19th-century characters, a man forever striving to find his place in a rapidly changing world. Just look at what he crams into his first 30 years. Born in England, he runs away from boarding school to join a band of gypsies. He fathers a son to a domestic servant, who is sent to Australia to escape the shame and give birth. He serves a short and dull stint as a train stationmaster before moving to Dublin and sympathising with Ireland's Republican movement. He is imprisoned in France as a suspected spy for the Communards, a working-class socialist movement that temporarily seizes control of Paris in 1871. He then emigrates to the United States, picking up work as a freelance journalist specialising in migration and labour movements. He marries an American widow and becomes director of a bank. But after authorising a series of loans to friends with no security, he flees the growing scandal – and 'the only widow I ever loved' – and arrives in Australia 'broken in fortune'.

He is only 32 when he begins a new life as Julian Thomas. *The Argus* picks him up as a contributor who specialises in an early form of immersive journalism. Under the byline 'The Vagabond', Thomas infiltrates many of Melbourne's biggest institutions and highlights the lives of the poor, the sick and the downtrodden. His articles are long and detailed and cause a sensation, often leading to reforms in hospitals and lunatic asylums.

In 1877 he enters Pentridge under the guise of a medical dispenser, a job organised for him by a sympathetic prison guard. He will spend a month inside the prison. His role as The Vagabond will be suspected by many but it will take weeks before the authorities unmask him and order him out.

In that time he will come across many of Pentridge's most famous inmates. He will win admiration for the clinical way he removes a rotten tooth from the mouth of hangman Michael Gately. He will earn just as much respect for the way he later describes Gately as that 'frightful animal – the immense head, powerful protruding jaw, narrow receding forehead and deficient brain space . . .'

He will also spend time with George Scott and is inside the prison when Captain Moonlite delivers on the shouted threat he made as he was dragged from the courtroom during Weechurch's trial two years earlier: that 'It will be necessary to bring me before the court on a charge [of attempted murder] like this.'

—

'He is a dashing, smart, rather cunning-looking young man,' reports The Vagabond. 'His education gives him a superiority over the other prisoners, who also respect him for his crimes, and he has become a sort of leader amongst them.

'He is a regular "prison lawyer" and is full of quibbles and quirks and has proved himself to be . . . quite a terror and nuisance to Mr Gardiner, the superintendent. I don't think that Scott was quite judiciously treated at first. Petty punishments and annoyances appear to have been freely dealt out to him as to others. He has chafed against these, and has lately broken out into more dangerous breaches of discipline.'

That latest breach of discipline takes place in the middle of February, shortly before The Vagabond encounters Captain Moonlite for the first time.

It starts with Scott entering the office of Chief Prison Warder Kelly and standing over the man brandishing a blunt dinner knife.

'Give me your watch or I'll have your life,' says Scott, who then grabs the watch from Kelly and rushes into a nearby bathroom, locking the door behind him.

'The first thought of every one was that, like Shanklin, he was simulating madness,' writes The Vagabond. 'Dr Reed was sent for. That gentleman soon arrived and told Captain Moonlite that, having seen him lately, it was no use shamming mad, as he was perfectly sane. The festive robber in question muttered through the lattice-work: "I am armed, approach who dare!"'

Superintendent Gardiner is then summoned and, to the disgust of The Vagabond, refuses to order the guards to rush the small room and apprehend Scott.

'So Gardiner humoured the rebel, and begging him not to make a noise, had the door barricaded outside with a pair of steps for fear he should suddenly emerge on his quest for "blood". Moonlite, master of the situation, appears to have behaved well. He promised not to make a row but reiterated his threat, "I am armed and will have blood."

'And there, no doubt laughing in his sleeve all the while, Moonlite remained for two hours deaf to the coaxings of the superintendent to "give up that knife". Tired at last of his fun, he passed out the "weapon" and the door being undone allowed himself to be handcuffed and taken to a cell to await punishment for his crime.'

In all his short but very busy life, John Stanley James – aka Julian Thomas, aka The Vagabond – has never seen a greater farce. 'Here was a slight man, "armed" with a "weapon" a boy might laugh at, yet who kept the whole establishment at Pentridge at bay for two hours. I myself, and many a warder . . . could have broken open the door and secured and thrashed the man, which would have done him good.'

Scott is sentenced to a week in solitary confinement and has a month added to his sentence. It is not the first time he has visited the hole – a month earlier he had spent three days in solitary for 'idleness'.

It is not long after the incident with the knife that The Vagabond meets Scott for the first time.

'There is war to the knife between me and the authorities,' Scott tells him.

'You talk like an infernal idiot,' replies The Vagabond. 'You ought to know better than talk such nonsense about being at war with society and the authorities. If you will be foolish depend upon it – society and the authorities will get the best of you.'

'Will they? Don't you believe it. I have got friends. Wait till the next election, and I'll have [George] Duncan [head of prisons] turned out of his office. I've got influence and any of you I can get sacked. I told Duncan so the other day.'

James says if he had been George Duncan he would have placed Scott in solitary for seven days to punish him for his insolence.

'He daren't do it.'

Here, James says he saw the devil flash into Scott's eyes 'and he looked savagely into mine. Seeing there, perchance a spirit kindred in some things to his own, he turned on his heel and left.'

Now James might be exaggerating here, eager to plump up his own image as a man prepared to stare down the toughest of criminals. But there's also a wistful tone to his musings on Scott. It's as if he sees in Captain Moonlite the sort of attributes he would like to ascribe to himself.

Scott has, he says, one of those natures 'fond of adventure and of wild life, which revolt at the restraints of civilisation. He might have made a good sailor, and would have been a good comrade in a fili-bustering expedition . . . but at present there is no doubt he is a very dangerous man. He is essentially vain, and is fond of the admiration of the "lifers" and other hardened criminals.'

But Scott is not fond of every prisoner. In late 1877 he will challenge John Sullivan, known as the Yarra Track bushranger, to a knife fight in the lifers' yard. Sullivan contemptuously throws away one of the knives offered to him by Scott and begins throwing punches. In the ensuing struggle, Scott hits Sullivan on the head with the handle of his knife and stabs him in the shoulder. Moonlite ends the year in much the same way he began it – in solitary confinement and with a further month added to his sentence.

But he seems to calm down the following year. He has three months taken off his sentence when he goes to the aid of a guard being assaulted by another prisoner and, apart from some minor infractions such as 'receiving tea improperly' from the soon-to-be-released Nesbitt, comes the closest he has been to being a model prisoner.

But the anger and fury never subside. That wild drop of blood still simmers. Throughout 1878 Scott counts down the days until his release, hatching plans for a life with Nesbitt outside prison where both men might finally be able to settle down.

His parole is approved early the following year, not long after Nesbitt is released. But even then his final walk through Pentridge's gates is delayed. Scott has asked the gaol tailor to make him a suit with 'Yankee pockets' – small patches that can hold a pistol. When gaol officials see these 'holster-pistol pockets' they accuse him of wanting to join the Kelly gang.

Finally, on a cool and cloudy Tuesday morning, the 18th day of March 1879, he has the irons on his ankles removed and is handed a version of the suit he wanted.

He steps through the gates of Pentridge and back into the world, a free man for the first time in nine years – with the exception of 10 cold and miserable and hungry days on the run.

Waiting for him outside those grim bluestone walls, a big smile forming on that boyish face, arms wide open as always, is James Nesbitt.

PART II

Out of Ireland have we come.
Great hatred, little room,
Maimed us at the start.
I carry from my mother's womb
A fanatic heart.
W. B. Yeats

20

HATRED OF MANKIND
IN THEIR HEARTS

He is at work when he is interrupted by one of the most annoying sounds in the life of a writer. A man needs silence in the evening when he contemplates words, not an abrupt knocking on the front door.

And Marcus Clarke needs to concentrate. He may be the acclaimed author of *For the Term of His Natural Life* – a novel about the convict experience in early Australia – but his hopelessly extravagant bohemian lifestyle, with all its endless gambling and drinking and pontificating in crowded saloons, has already bankrupted him once. He needs every shilling he can muster.

Clarke opens the door and finds a respectably dressed man with a well-trimmed beard and light steel blue eyes staring back at him.

'Did you write *His Natural Life*?'

'I did,' says Clarke.

'My name is Scott and I wish to speak with you.'

'No relation to the great Sir Walter Scott?' Clarke asks.

For a man who prides himself on his wit, it is not one of his finest lines. But that wit has been the one tool that has helped distance him from that awful childhood; the mother who died when he was three, the anchylosed left arm he was born with – now shrunk to the point where it is next to useless – and the absent father who squandered the family fortune and died after a complete physical and mental breakdown.

Charm and a sharp wit have carried Clarke a long way. But they can never complete his escape from those sickly and troublesome early years in England. No matter how hard he tries, no matter how well he plays the role of extrovert, he still struggles to control a childhood stammer.

He will, of course, give no hint of that stutter when, months later, he recounts his meeting with George Scott. Clarke was sacked from his first job as a theatre critic for *The Argus* after reviewing a show he did not attend – a show which never went ahead because it was cancelled at the last minute. But apart from a few self-flattering references, much of Clarke's retelling of his encounter with Scott will ring true.

'You may know me better as Captain Moonlite,' says Scott, handing Clarke a business card belonging to the theatrical agent and journalist Richard Thatcher.

Clarke, of course, has heard of Moonlite and is well aware of Richard Thatcher. There are few people who move in the bohemian arts scene in Melbourne and Sydney who have not heard of the man. The brother of a renowned singer whose songs are celebrated throughout Australia and New Zealand, Thatcher has a stable of stars that includes popular stage actresses like Ada Ward and Mary Frances Scott-Siddons. Now the latest addition to his books is Andrew George Scott.

'I am but recently out of Pentridge and I am going to deliver a lecture on the evils of the present penal system,' says Scott. He has read Clarke's novel – an account of a convict's life based on research Clarke undertook in the Tasmanian penal archives – and tells him he is surprised at its accuracy. In fact, a man who fully comprehends the horrors of incarceration would be the perfect person to chair Scott's lecture series . . .

Clarke may be subject to flattery, but he knows immediately this is something to avoid.

'I am sorry that I can't oblige you, but you see . . . official duties etc . . .'

'I hardly expected any other reply,' says Scott. 'But I have some interesting particulars to relate.'

Sitting inside by the glow of a gas lamp, Clarke is drawn to Scott's blue eyes, 'which appeared without depth in the iris, and shifted a good deal, like the eyes of all men accustomed to being observed and accustomed to shun observation'.

Scott tells Clarke he was infamously treated in Pentridge.

'Of course, all prisoners are.'

Scott laughs and returns to what has become his obsession; the injustice of Pentridge and the falsehood that men are sent there to be rehabilitated. It is no such thing. The prison is little more than a training ground for the next generation of hardened criminals.

'Well, explain this to your audience and let the prison authorities defend themselves,' says Clarke. 'I think, however, that you had better try some other business than lecturing. It is not very profitable, and – you will excuse me, I'm sure – but I doubt if you come well recommended to the public.'

Scott laughs again. 'One must do something for a living. I vowed I'd expose the system, and I'll do it.'

Clarke will never make it to one of Scott's lectures. He will be too busy in the coming months unsuccessfully trying to stave off his second round of bankruptcy. In the years to come legendary literary figures like Mark Twain will hail Marcus Clarke as a genius, a man more appreciated around the world than in his adopted country. Clarke will never live to hear the plaudits. He will die early, just like his father, a bacterial infection killing him at the age of 35.

But Clarke's meeting with Scott leaves him with more than just a passing impression of Captain Moonlite. Despite the man's obsessiveness, perhaps Scott has a point about the futility of the prison system.

'Can it be said that our prisons are in any sense reformatories when they turn out such men as Moonlite and the Kellys?' Clarke will ask.

'Granted that the men were in the first instance prone to crime, it surely speaks but little . . . when the only result of the "discipline" is to send the released captives straight into the bush, with hatred of mankind in their hearts, raging to do deeds of violence and blood.'

—

It's a Thursday night in the big room at the Unicorn Hotel in Ballarat. Who knows how many are crammed into the place. Some figure it must be more than 500. Look over there – perched in the two-shilling seats. There are doctors and brokers and shopkeepers and, yes, even a woman. The one-shilling section is even more crowded, men and boys noisily jostling for space. At the back of the room – isn't that one of the warders from Ballarat Gaol? Word is he's already had a few too many beers and is making his opinions about this Captain Moonlite known to everyone.

Now there's a hush. A ripple goes through the crowd. Here he is – Andrew George Scott himself – striding to the podium. Look at the man. What sort of nerve must it take to return to Ballarat – the same bustling metropolis he shocked seven years earlier with his audacious prison escape? Surely there are some here tonight who remember how they crowded on to the train platform that chaotic afternoon just a day after he was recaptured. How they strained to catch a glimpse of that pale, worn face. Some of those boys who ran alongside the police cart taking him back to prison – hollering and cheering on good old Captain Moonlite – must be young men now. Why wouldn't they hand over a shilling to hear the man speak?

Take a close look at him. Tonight he is out to impress. His light brown hair has been combed perfectly with the part on the left. His black suit is beautifully tailored, a stainless white handkerchief adorning one pocket. His well-fitting leather boots shine from incessant polishing. Naturally, moustache and beard have been trimmed to ensure not a whisker is out of place.

He shows few signs of the setbacks he has suffered in the past week. This lecture had initially been scheduled for the large Alfred Hall.

When the booking was refused, the Academy of Music agreed to rent its premises for the night. But when its proprietor heard it was to be used by a scoundrel who had brought shame to Ballarat and the region, the performance was suddenly cancelled on the day of the event. Scott was handed 10 pounds in compensation.

He had already been suffering from a bronchial complaint and a friend had been forced to lend him money for medicine. More than a thousand people – some of them having travelled more than 50 miles for the event – had gathered in confusion outside, hoping Scott might deliver his lecture on the street. But the stress – *the wild drop* – quickly got to him. He was racked with anxiety and could not get out of bed.

Thank God for James Nesbitt. Always loyal, always doting on his soulmate like a mother with a sickly child. He had fussed over George, bringing him cups of tea, easing those powerful pangs of anxiety with his calming, soothing voice. Helping Nesbitt has been a 17-year-old boy Scott has just hired as an assistant. He calls himself Thomas Williams. Or sometimes Charlie Davidson. He has the same fair complexion and youthful features as Nesbitt. Even the police will later call him 'rather nice looking'. Williams is a good kid. Never made a big mistake in his life until a year ago when he put his left hand in the wrong place while working at a local biscuit factory and had it crushed between a series of rollers. But not even that moment of bad luck had managed to curb the kid's desire for adventure. People around here will always remember this son of a respectable miner as a bit starry-eyed – a polite boy spellbound by stories of American Indians and pirates.

Like so many young men, Williams had been smitten by the breathless daily reports of the Kelly gang and their brazen defiance of authority in the north of Victoria. So why wouldn't he answer an ad placed by Scott looking for an assistant? With those full brown eyes and fair hair, he was quickly given the job. But Tom knew his parents would not approve. It's why he is now using the name Thomas Williams. Or Charlie Davidson when he needs a back-up identity.

Much safer names, both of them. Better an alias than having his parents discover their beloved Frank Johns has gone off to work for the notorious Captain Moonlite.

With such two fine young men like Nesbitt and Williams by his side, Scott had quickly overcome his bout of anxiety, and the owner of the Unicorn, no doubt overcome at the prospect of such a large, thirsty crowd, had agreed to open up the hotel's big room. In the next few days, when this lecture and a couple of others in regional Victoria are over, Tom Williams will move to Melbourne with Scott and Nesbitt and live with them at Mrs McNabb's shabby boarding house in Fitzroy. They will soon be joined by others, too. Won't be long before Mrs McNabb begins wondering if Scott is recruiting a football team.

But first the lecture. It doesn't take long before Scott has his audience enthralled. Even the group of reporters with their pencils and notebooks are impressed. There is something about the man that is . . . *different*. They will have seen James Nesbitt attending him and noticed how the pair are inseparable. So they will do their best to drop hints to their readers. They watch him walking back and forth on the small platform hastily erected for the event, 'much using the spotless white handkerchief . . . for he is a swell and likes sensations and attitudes and the attentions of women – and men for that matter'.

They listen as he recounts a litany of misdeeds and outrages committed by the prison authorities: forcing men to bathe in water already dirtied by a dozen others; making them sleep on lice-infested blankets washed and disinfected just once a year; detaining prisoners in the notorious A division far longer than the law allows; a half-drunk warder belting young prisoners because they could not understand his slurred instructions; incarcerated youths placed next to hardened criminals who quickly induct them into a life of crime and infamy . . .

Scott tells the audience of his own troubles; the incident when he locks himself in Warder Kelly's bathroom, the occasional threats to his life. Of course, these being George Scott stories, he cannot help but show off that extraordinary brain of his. That time they found a piece of gas pipe on his work bench and he was charged with making a pistol? At the subsequent hearing he proved he was innocent by explaining to the visiting judge how 'the strain on a pistol when fired was 13 tons to the square inch, and that gas-pipe would break with a pressure of 600lb'.

When Scott raises the case of the martyr Weechurch and how the man was treated like a beast, the Ballarat Gaol guard at the back of the room, now well and truly in his cups, shouts out 'It's a lie!' and the crowd turns on him, shouting in unison: 'Turn him out!' There's a short scuffle and the man is ejected and Scott resumes.

He goes on like this for 90 minutes, dabbing his face with the handkerchief. There is a tear duct in his eye that sometimes weeps. But it also serves as a marvellous stage device.

He tells the crowd he is no angel but simply wants to see the system reformed. He finishes with a warning to all those young men listening in the room. Crime is a terrible mistake, he warns. 'Taking it merely as an affair of profit and loss, the criminal will suffer more, will work harder, will have less pleasure and less comfort than the hardest worked honest individual.'

It is a bright start to his campaign with an appreciative paying audience. But it will never get any better than this. Over the coming weeks there will be further lectures in other regional towns like Maryborough and Sandhurst and even – the gall of the man! – in Egerton. But the crowds will never be as large. Poor weather will affect attendances at two events, while others will suffer from dwindling interest as the novelty of Scott's campaign begins to wane.

On the day after the Ballarat lecture, a local businessman, Henry Glenny, shares the same train carriage to Sandhurst with Scott and Nesbitt and finds them 'both very chatty and agreeable'.

Glenny is a close observer of Scott. Seven years older than Captain Moonlite, he was born just 10 miles from Rathfriland. But their lives have taken vastly different directions. Glenny owns a chain of photographic studios and has amassed a fortune selling insurance, speculating, financing deals and dabbling part-time in journalism. In a few years he will place an enormous property portfolio on the market and return to County Down as one of its richest, most celebrated sons.

Glenny was at the Ballarat lecture and thinks Scott makes many good points. But he has reservations about 'this foolhardy, conceited, irritable fool'. He decides to attend the Sandhurst lecture 'and felt convinced from the remarks he there made, that a never-to-be-satisfied hankering after notoriety was the cankerworm of his life . . . I am inclined to believe he is not the hardened ruffian he is represented to be, but a foolishly-vain fellow that would run any risk in order to be talked freely about.'

Henry Glenny has made a fortune backing his judgement and following his instincts. But he has rarely been more certain of anything than his assessment of Andrew George Scott.

21

WRITTEN IN BLOOD

Come now. As George Scott's lecturing campaign begins to fall apart and his every move is closely watched by Victorian detectives, let us follow Nosey Bob on his way to work on this Friday evening in early June 1879.

Bob sits in his swaying carriage as quietly and anonymously as he can. Not that anyone chooses to go anywhere near him. He peers into the growing darkness outside. As his train belches and roars its way from Sydney to the Blue Mountains, he can surely feel the chill winter air settling over the hills and understand the threat it carries with it.

A decent executioner knows the rope cannot be trusted in cold weather. There will be no better example of this indisputable truth than in a couple of days' time when Joseph Mutter, a convicted murderer, goes to the gallows in Brisbane. This cold front sweeping through the eastern colonies will reach all the way to Queensland. An inexperienced hangman – and a rope hardened by a rare and heavy overnight frost – will conspire to completely decapitate Mutter when he falls through the trapdoor.

That gory fiasco will provide even more ammunition to the growing calls for an end to capital punishment for many serious crimes.

Bob has never seen such a thing. This year has already been the quietest he can remember for executions and now the world has been turned upside down. In the past few weeks Sydney's streets have been filled with noisy protestors calling on the government to do away with the death penalty – at least for lesser crimes than murder. Preachers have filled endless hours fulminating on the issue from their pulpits. Even those vultures in the press – always the first to obtain a pass to watch Bob go about his ghoulish work – have started singing from the same hymn sheet.

What has riled them are the very jobs Bob has been sent to perform in the next week. In Mudgee, Alfred, a young Aboriginal man found guilty of rape, has been sentenced to hang. After that Bob must travel to Bathurst to execute another two young men – 21-year-old Charles Wilkinson and 17-year-old Alexander Metcalfe – who have also been found guilty of rape.

A couple of weeks earlier 7000 signatures had been collected at a crowded meeting at Sydney Town Hall calling on the colony's Executive Council and its Chief Justice and acting Lieutenant-Governor, Sir Alfred Stephen, to commute the sentences of the three men. Well, that had been a waste of time. Bob has long had friends in high places – men like Sir Alfred and the Premier, Sir Henry Parkes, were often passengers in his Hansom cab back when he all but owned the rank in Darling Point. You might even say they were staunch supporters of Bob. He could have staked a year's salary – more than 150 quid – that a baying crowd would not sway the opinion of the most famous hanging judge in the country.

Just this morning the Executive Council had met and given Bob the all clear to go to Mudgee and hang Alfred. They have decided to postpone a decision on the Bathurst hangings for a few more days but it will not be enough to quell the rising movement. In the next 24 hours more than 10,000 people will march solemnly through the Domain, Handel's 'Dead March' sounding on muffled drums, some with lit candles cupped in their hands, others carrying oil lamps. The number of signatures on the petition will grow to 20,000. Already the editorial writers at *The Evening News* – the most passionate of the popular press – are putting together their Saturday edition and an editorial that will scream: 'Hang Him – He is Only a Black'.

The editorial, like its headline, will drip with sarcasm: 'Our merciful Acting-Governor has decided that he will at any rate hang the blackfellow. He has no friends and, therefore, may be executed with impunity, while his Excellency and his Council calmly consider whether they can venture upon a double judicial murder of white boys on Tuesday week. Such is the determination of the retired judge who, "dressed in a little brief authority", now wields the supreme power of the State, and dispenses life or death to the criminals who have been convicted of capital offences . . . eternal disgrace will rest upon them if they consent to launch the young aboriginal into eternity.'

No, Bob has never seen anything like this. He has had much to think about by the time the train pulls into its last stop at Wallerawang. From there he boards a Cobb & Co coach for the difficult trek to Mudgee. The past few weeks have seen several downpours. The track, which the locals have been complaining about for years, is a treacherous, rutted path that snakes its way through gullies and ravines before reaching the Crown Ridge, a sheer granite cliff that drops more than 1000 feet and scares the daylights out of passengers in the coach's box seat.

But the perilous path to Mudgee is easy compared to what confronts Nosey Bob the next morning. The governor of the local gaol, John Dick, is in a lather. Bob hadn't expected this. Everyone in the Prisons Department knows Dick is partial to a drink. But he also has a reputation for getting the job done. Yet here they are, just three days from the execution, and the gallows are a shambles and Dick is on to another bottle of whiskey. It's not the first he has downed in recent days from what Bob hears. The political pressure – will the execution go ahead or not? – and the mounting public dismay has left the man frozen and incapable of decisions. A man might even think this hanging will become a turning point in Governor Dick's life. He will never be the same. His love for grog will only deepen. In 10 years' time he will be exposed by another gaol warden embezzling money from the prison's private contractors. Dick will shoot the warden and be gaoled for 14 years after having his death sentence commuted.

So Bob, who doesn't mind a drink himself, will have to take on Governor Dick's responsibilities. He will have to show the carpenters where to place the trusses and beams. He might even have to help dig the bloody hole in the ground beneath the scaffolding so there is enough room for poor Alfred – a man convicted on thin evidence – to fall before the rope does its work.

It gets worse the following day when the assistant executioner arrives and sheepishly gives Bob the news that the rope the man had brought from Sydney has gone missing. Damn thing's disappearance is inexplicable. Now the pair of them will have to go into town and buy a new one and put up with all the stares and whispers of the good folk of Mudgee, who will know only too damn well what the two of them are up to.

Bob doesn't know it, but the rope vanished courtesy of a reporter from *The Evening News*. Why, it's none other than J. F. Archibald, the man who so ably – and critically – covered the hanging of John Weechurch back in Melbourne in 1875. Back then Archibald was trying to impress his new employers at the *Daily Telegraph*. Now he's doing the same for his new bosses at *The Evening News*.

Archibald and the assistant executioner had followed Bob's journey through the Blue Mountains and on to Mudgee the following day. When the coach had reached the bottom of a long hill, Archibald had climbed out, telling the driver to go ahead because he wanted to 'stretch his legs a bit'. He walked behind the coach for about a mile before reaching into its back compartment and grabbing unseen a bag containing the rope for the condemned man's neck, the bar of soap to grease it and the white hood to be fitted over Alfred's head. He then hurled it off the side of the hill and resumed his seat.

Yet despite all the obstacles, Bob manages to pull off the job without any further hitches. Well, there was that one moment when the reverend had finished blessing Alfred. Silence had fallen and Bob had looked across at the officials for permission to pull the lever that would spring open the trapdoor. One of those officials, thinking he had heard the ping of the telegraphic machine announcing a last-minute reprieve, said, 'Not yet – not yet!'

But Bob had pulled the bolt by then to send Alfred's body plummeting into that hole they had dug beneath the gallows.

It was a quick death. But even then Archibald found fault with Nosey Bob's work. The condemned man, he wrote 'struggled in a manner frightful to behold for several minutes, though, according to the doctors, he was out of pain in an instant. But the most revolting sight of all was when the hangman and his helper, a quarter of an hour afterwards, came and bore off to the coffin, as a butcher would carry a slaughtered sheep, the breathless body, on which the law's last indignity had been wreaked. That body had contained the soul of a man who had in him more good than evil . . .'

Bob is out of Mudgee that afternoon, bound for that double hanging in Bathurst. But by the time he gets there a telegram from Sydney has already arrived, commuting the sentences of the two rapists.

The Evening News was right all along. Sir Alfred and his Executive Council have been happy to hang a black man with few friends. But 20,000 signatures are more than enough to save the lives of two white boys.

It makes little difference to Nosey Bob. Work like this comes and goes. In a few months' time George Scott and his band of young men will keep him busy.

—

Nine years in prison and now that he is finally free they still won't leave him alone. Everywhere George Scott goes the police are watching. And if they're not in front of him, or just behind him eyeing off the crowd and taking notes, it's only because they have been held up interviewing old friends and associates as they prowl through his past and try to discover his future plans.

He sits in the office of Richard Thatcher and unburdens himself. It has become a regular haunt for Scott and his growing group of young admirers. They can often be found there, talking in that manner adopted by all former prisoners – voices low, eyes darting, always watching out for fear they might be overheard. Thatcher thinks Scott is making a mistake allowing these 'pals' of his to always be in his company. A theatrical agent like himself understands the importance of image. How is a man like Scott expected to change society's disdain for him when he insists on constantly befriending criminals and ex-prisoners?

But like most of the advice he gives Scott, Thatcher's counsel falls on deaf ears. It is a matter of *honour*, Scott tells him. He is mentoring and guiding these young men. If he abandons them they will have no option but to return to crime.

Thatcher has already told Scott that his lecture series is doomed to fail. 'I told him after the first lecture that the thing would not pay, but I continued to assist him,' he will later reminisce. 'Scott's vanity was hurt and he suffered more in consequence of that than he would have done otherwise.'

Thatcher's friends have been ridiculing him for his association with Captain Moonlite and even he struggles to explain why he continues to help. It's not as though he admires the man. He finds him to be a 'vain, pretentious man with a false high-falutin' notion of honour and a hatred of constituted authority – warranted in some respect by unnecessary harshness and disregard for his sensitiveness when in gaol'.

He also worries about his mental state and what he calls Scott's 'strong homicidal impulses . . . whenever he lectured he invariably carried firearms and was fond of levelling them at imaginary objects . . . he is a madman; that is, so far as all those who think deeply on one subject are so'.

But there is something about Scott that Thatcher must admire. Both are men with an adventurous spirit. Thatcher arrived in Fiji just a few months after Scott's brief visit to the island in 1869. He had walked into the office of the *Fiji Times* looking for a job and been told to knock out a paragraph about a five-legged pig on display at a local fair. Within a week he was appointed editor. But he soon tired of the role and ever since had drifted through the world of journalism and the theatre.

He also understands that while Scott may be unhinged, his paranoia is well-grounded. Thatcher knows how it works. The Victorian police are regular drinking buddies with the newspaper men and feed them a constant stream of lies and disinformation. It is why Scott is so frustrated now. Just months have passed since his release from Pentridge, and Scott and Nesbitt are being linked to every major unsolved crime in the colony.

When police uncover the body of one Frank Bates at the bottom of a steep embankment next to a major road, the word goes out.

Blame it on Captain Moonlite.

Bates, an American actor who had brought his wife with him to Melbourne in search of work, had gone off on one of his regular drinking binges. He had been seen drinking in a hotel where Scott had also been drinking. Or so the reporters said. Witnesses then claimed Bates, a flamboyant character known for wearing expensive watches, diamond rings and other 'massive jewellery', was followed down the street by a 'suspicious-looking' character.

One Melbourne newspaper – *The Age* – claims witnesses who had seen the 'suspicious-looking' individual following Bates were struck by how closely a prison photograph of Scott resembled the man.

Then, not long after, a Chinese market gardener at Merri Creek is found murdered. New rumours circulate.

Blame it on Captain Moonlite.

A few weeks later Scott and Nesbitt visit an old friend from Pentridge, William Johnson, who is now being held at a small remand centre known as the Williamstown Battery. According to Scott, he had gone to the area on business – presumably preparing for his next lecture – and dropped by to visit Johnson.

A week later he and Nesbitt are north of Ballarat collecting signatures for a petition demanding the government formally investigate abuses within the penal department when they hear they are wanted for breaking into the Battery. They hand themselves in to police and a preliminary hearing charges them with 'unlawfully convey into the gaol at Williamstown, where certain prisoners were confined, a certain weapon, to wit, a pistol, with a view to aid the escape of William Johnson, one of the prisoners so confined'.

Before the pair of them are taken to Melbourne for trial, Scott tells the court he has been targeted by the penal authorities who have 'sought to prevent him making further exposures in connection with Pentridge'. The extent of their lies and untruths is long – they have spread rumours that he murdered Frank Bates and intended to join the Kelly gang.

At the trial a week later the charges against Scott, Nesbitt and another man sharing a room with them in a Lonsdale Street boarding house are thrown out after a hearing punctuated by confusing and contradictory evidence. It is yet more clear evidence, says Scott, of a conspiracy and pattern of harassment designed to force him back into the silence of Pentridge.

So he does what he does best. He picks up a pen and begins composing a letter to *The Herald* that he hopes will set the record straight.

He addresses the rumours of his involvement in the death of Frank Bates. 'I pass over the kind speculations as to whether I was the man who followed, robbed and, perhaps, murdered Mr Bates, as unworthy of my consideration.

'[But] I ask you what sense of fair play can actuate the conductors of another Melbourne paper, who almost accused me by name of that base deed, who hazarded speculations about my being the man, and then, when the suspicion was found to be utterly groundless, refrained from saying one word to remove the foul stain they had labored to fix on an innocent man?'

And then Scott lets down his guard. For the only time in his life he will suggest he had a role in the Mount Egerton bank robbery.

'Were I a "respectable man" or a "respectable journalist" I might try to vindicate my character in a law court,' he writes, 'but being only one who has condoned an offence of which I may have been guilty, by spending seven long years in a dungeon, I must perforce put up with anything.'

It's a throwaway line – '*of which I may have been guilty*' – a small sentence easily overlooked in the many hundreds of words Scott pens to *The Herald*. But it is the closest he will ever come to admitting he stole that cake of gold.

The rest of his letter is a seething indictment on his favourite subject, the horrors of the penal system. Always mindful of ticket sales, he suggests readers should attend his lectures at Williamstown, Collingwood and Emerald Hill over the next four days to hear more about his version of events.

'How many men who have been confined in our gaols come out without being tenfold worse than when they entered them? I say your universities of crime are turning out some fine graduates. There is not one ounce of reformation to an ocean of punitive revenge.'

As always, once Scott gets going it is hard to stop him. 'I say your penal code breathes but vengeance, and is written in blood,' he writes. 'If by chance a man re-enters the world unscathed, he is dogged by the wonderful police, so powerful for oppression, so powerless for useful defence . . . he cannot move without gunpowder and arms in his track: and if he mounts the lecture platform, and appeals to the common-sense and justice of the community; if he tries to point out the injury done to the colony by ignorant and prejudiced Dogberrys [a Shakespearean character who led a bumbling group of police], he is treated as if letting the light of truth into an establishment where a good proportion of the community pass their lives . . . were a heinous crime.'

Scott says he has a number of friends – 'the truest and kindest of this colony' – who continue to encourage and assist him in exposing the ills of the justice system. 'I will speak the truth, fearless of perjury and corruption, till I convince the thinking portion of this community that it is better to make virtue easy and good conduct pleasant, than to make vice difficult and bad conduct unpleasant.'

Scott sounds like a man who is in it for the long haul, who plans to stay in town and see this thing through to the end. But there's a hint in his letter that perhaps he and Nesbitt's time in the colony has reached its end.

'Can you wonder that men suffering under a burning sense of wrong and injustice take to the bush, or in other ways war with society which tolerates and encourages such things?'

George Scott is close to making that decision himself. It will be the worst of many poor decisions in his life. But before he does the persecution continues.

—

Blame it on Captain Moonlite.

In the middle of August the bank in Lancefield, a small town 40 miles north of Melbourne, is stuck up by two armed men. At first there are fears the Kelly gang has struck again. But within hours these are discounted and replaced by an even stronger rumour that it is the work of Captain Moonlite and his offsider, Nesbitt. Photographs of Scott and Nesbitt are shown to two witnesses. One of them thinks Nesbitt looks a little like one of the robbers; the other witness can see no similarities at all.

Neither Scott nor Nesbitt are anywhere near Lancefield. Both are in Melbourne looking for work. In fact, Scott believes he is close to securing a job at a brewery in Collingwood. But when the Lancefield rumours hit the press, the brewery manager withdraws the offer. Scott and Nesbitt are also asked to leave their boarding house. It won't matter that within a fortnight a pair of well-known criminals will be arrested for the heist. The damage has been done and Scott has had enough.

He has spoken to Thatcher about leaving the colonies and returning to New Zealand to see his ageing parents. But such a journey is expensive and he has no money. Besides, what boat would willingly take him on board when Melbourne is swirling with rumours that the Moonlite gang plan to hijack a ship?

Those rumours have reached the ears of Marcus Clarke, who just a few weeks earlier had answered Scott's knock on his front door. The gossip is startling for its detail. Clarke will recall that: 'A friend of mine in Melbourne, who professes to be acquainted with many private matters, is accustomed to assert that the original intention of Scott was to capture a mail steamer, but that he could not get together a party sufficiently large.

'This was to be the plan: twelve confederates were to take passage and when the ship and passengers were at dinner, to seize the ship. Six armed men could hold the . . . crew, and three more could keep the deck. Moonlite and the remaining two would then "bail up" the cuddy and secure the captain and passengers. One officer would be kept to navigate the vessel and all the rest, together with the passengers, put into boats. The gold boxes would then be opened, the mails and bullion boxes ransacked, and sail made for a South American port, where a revolutionary government would not be too particular in inquiring as to the gift of a steamship.'

It's a fanciful idea because Scott and his party cannot even go to Sydney. In the months to come he will write that: 'We would have subjected ourselves to imprisonment had we publicly landed in another Colony, as we had not been many months free men and the merciful laws of these colonies will imprison an ex-convict who flies to their shores, even if he flies from dangers to his liberty and life.

'Numerous petty insults were given us by the police. I honestly felt I was unsafe in Victoria. I feared perjury and felt hunted down and maddened by injustice and slander.'

So he and Nesbitt decide it is time to head into the bush. Anything has to be better than struggling in a city where they are constantly watched and harassed.

By now their gang of 'pals' has grown. One afternoon Scott had been walking down Bourke Street – the main street in Melbourne – when he met a young 15-year-old boy called Gus Wernicke, who had been living in a brothel and was 'suffering from disease and [was] covered in vermin'.

Wernicke's father, Ernest, is a well-known publican who owns the County Court Hotel in Swanston Street. Gus' mother had died in 1876 when he was 11 and four years later his father had married his dead wife's younger sister, Isabella. Gus had left home soon after, following a series of disagreements with his new stepmother. He had found work in a plumbing shop, but when he lost a half crown in takings the boss had flogged him. Gus had been forced to go on the run again, finding refuge in a backstreet whorehouse also owned by his old man.

Scott had watched from a short distance as Wernicke signalled to a mate that he had spotted a drunk who would be worth following to rob. Scott stepped up, introduced himself to the wary boy, and bought him a meal. It will be hard to imagine the unwashed and unkempt Wernicke that Scott first meets compared to the only image of the kid that newspaper editors will plaster across their pages in the months to come. It is an illustration based on a photograph of Wernicke taken in 1878. It shows a short, baby-faced 13-year-old, hair neatly combed, dressed in a pinstripe suit and with his left arm resting on the back of a chair. It will be easy to see why he becomes the child of the Moonlite gang; his face a portrait of naivety and innocence.

Another new member of the Moonlite gang is his opposite. He was born Thomas Baker but everyone will know him as Tom Rogan. He is a 22-year-old bootmaker with a hard face and a shock of black hair who has been drifting in and out of trouble with the law for the past four years. He has served three months' hard labour for larceny and another two years for horse-stealing.

Under siege from the authorities and with no hope of earning a regular income, Scott and Nesbitt, along with Wernicke, Rogan and Tom Williams, quietly leave Melbourne one day carrying blankets, clothing and a set of guns Scott has been keeping in a safe box.

Scott is disgruntled and, in his own words, 'rabid . . . Though I knew I had committed no crime, bitter experience had taught me that innocence and safety from accusations were two different things.

'My life and liberty had been endangered by perjury and they would be endangered till I could secretly escape from those who seemed to hunger, if not for my blood, for my liberty and safety.'

So angry is Scott that he has decided he will resist any attempts to capture and return him to gaol. It is now, once again, about *honour*. But always, whispering to him and calming that wild drop of blood, is James Nesbitt. 'Even in that dark time the friendship of Nesbitt sustained and comforted me . . . he pointed to a brighter future and by his kindness saved me from being a hater of humanity, as like Job I was tempted to curse God and die.'

22

THE HARP OF DAVID

Five broken men. They have been walking for weeks, legs aching, hopes sinking, stomachs growling, tempers flaring. For George Scott it is a humiliating experience. He is the leader of four young men. His job is to inspire confidence. Yet here he is, just another number in a procession of the unemployed and destitute who have joined the swagmen and bushies wandering the country roads of Victoria seeking employment and food.

There is no honour to be found here on these dusty tracks, no dignity in knocking on farmhouse doors looking for work and pleading for food. Some Captain he has turned out to be. He had promised his men this trek north would bring an end to the police harassment and provide them with work and security.

But so far he has failed them. They were not many miles out of Melbourne when two plainclothes police officers arrived at their camp one morning, brandishing guns and giving them grief. They eventually left – 'they were cowards,' Scott will recall. But that experience was just a taste of things to come. 'We were wearied with impertinent and disagreeable interferences . . . they were out round the country asking for us, and in this way made us the objects of suspicion. I was very bitter . . .'

The suspicion sown by the police has been heightened by a false rumour spread by the officer in charge of hunting down the Kelly gang, Superintendent John Sadleir. Under pressure because of a series of clumsy failures, Sadleir has been putting it about that Scott has sent word to Kelly suggesting the pair should join forces. It is a fanciful notion. But it has stirred the pot and heightened anxiety about the bushranging threat throughout the colony.

Work is hard enough to find anywhere without the police soiling the path ahead. Back in Melbourne the building industry has paid for a fake newspaper advertisement seeking 30 carpenters as a way of gauging how deeply this economic recession is biting. Within hours a long queue forms outside the address given, despite the ad declaring that only three shillings will be paid for every 10-hour working day.

They are calling it Berry's Blight after the Victorian Premier, Graham Berry, who has been at war with the colony's powerful upper house, the Legislative Council. Berry sees the council as protectors of the wealthy landed gentry. He may not be wrong. With a little over 800 men in control of the colony's majority of farming and grazing land – many of them with seats in the council – he has threatened to impose a severe tax on their properties. When the council rejected several financial bills put to it by the lower house, Berry began to dismiss hundreds of public servants, police and judges among them. That move a year earlier has only aggravated the fallout from what will become known as the Long Depression.

Scott and his men are irritable, hungry and despondent. 'We sold some clothes and bedding and were content with bread and tea, sometimes bread without tea, and sometimes without either,' he will say a few months later. Some nights they sit around the campfire chewing on the oily, tough flesh of koala. Occasionally Scott shoots a sheep – 'only when we were starving and could get nothing else'.

The nights are cold because there are never enough blankets and the lack of sleep compounds their irritability. That wild drop of blood begins to simmer and, as always, there is only one thing that can stop it from spilling over. Nesbitt's voice continues to reassure Scott that everything will work out alright.

'His kindness ever smoothed me and as he softly spoke words of comfort they were like the harp of David which dispelled the evil spirit from Saul. We earnestly tried to obtain work and failed, and we met numbers who were equally unfortunate.'

They continue walking. Disillusioned with their leader, the two youngest members of the gang, Tom Williams and Gus Wernicke, take off on their own. Scott will say later that he had urged Wernicke several times not to accompany them because the conditions would be too tough. With the exception of Rogan, who spent a short stint on a sheep station, all of them are city lads with little idea of surviving in the bush. But Scott is not prepared to lose anyone anymore; within a day he has tracked them down and given Wernicke a 'thrashing'.

By late October they reach the Murray River just a few miles from Albury. A boatman, seeing them carrying revolvers and assuming they are a gang of bushrangers, rows them across the river for nothing. But he decides not to raise any alarms. If these men truly are outlaws, who knows what reprisals they might visit on him and his family.

It will be two weeks before he reports the encounter to the police. By then it will be too late.

A week or so later the bedraggled party are eight miles or so out of Gundagai. They find shelter in a traveller's hut on one of the many large sheep stations in the area. There, slumped on a makeshift cot, they meet Graham Bennett, a young sailor from Yorkshire. He jumped ship in Melbourne a couple of years earlier and has been earning a few pounds picking up work on rural farms and playing piano at some of the pubs in the district.

'He was alone and told us he was on the tramp looking for work,' Tom Williams will recall several years later. 'In the course of conversation the Kelly gang was mentioned. He [Bennett] said that rather than do as they had done, or act dishonestly for a living, he would starve.

'Scott asked him what he thought of Moonlite – that is, himself. He said he heard but very little of him, but that little was enough to convince him that Scott was a villain.'

The next morning Bennett joins Scott's band as they continue their search for work.

Williams: 'In the course of the day Bennett happened to catch sight of Scott's revolver under his coat in a pouch. He asked him what it was. Scott told him a telescope. But Bennett seemed suspicious of us after this; and I heard Scott remark to Nesbitt that Bennett knew we were armed and he thought it advisable to keep him with us.'

They stop at a small store on the way and tell the owner David Weir they are looking for food and jobs. Weir has no work for them. But he has sympathy for their plight, motivated perhaps by the sight of the men's guns. With the last shillings left in his pocket, Scott buys eight pounds of flour for his hungry horde. Weir throws in an additional three pounds of flour for nothing.

They thank Weir and leave. The flour will not last long. And the weather is turning bad. At least Wantabadgery Station, the largest farm in the district and famous for providing work and shelter to itinerant travellers, is not far away.

'We had walked I think about twelve miles,' Scott will recall about that final day on the road. 'We expected work – at least food and shelter. We were refused all, were insulted and ordered off. We slept that night in the hills, it rained heavily, we were hungry and thirsty and had nothing with the exception of too much water. In the morning we were unable to carry away our bedding. We were all wet, cold and hungry and there we did, in one wild hour, the deed that resulted in our present situation.'

The *deed*. The newspapers will say it was a premeditated raid, a well-planned and strategic assault on a vulnerable country station. At its height almost 40 hostages will be taken and three men will lose their life.

But Scott will always disagree. 'We had no intention of being bushrangers. Every fact supports me. Everything speaks to the broad truth that misery and hunger produced despair and in one wild hour we proved how much the wretched dared. It must be seen that Wantabadgery was the place where the voice of hunger drowned the voice of reason and we became criminals.'

—

William Baynes is one of those men who dislikes being interrupted. If a man spends his day on the land, always on call, always attending to every small detail and problem, then surely he should be entitled to eat his dinner in peace. But the interruptions never cease. Here he is, the manager of the Wantabadgery Station, hunched over his long-awaited plate on the evening of Thursday 13 November, and now one of the servant girls is demanding his attention.

There is a group of men outside, she tells him. They are asking if there is any work to be had.

Baynes is dismissive. 'Oh, let them wait,' he says.

He continues eating. A day barely passes when someone is not knocking on the back door looking for a job, a feed and a place to spend the night. It was a problem created by the former owner of this sprawling 100,000-acre station, Walter Windeyer. He might have turned the stone farmhouse into a grand estate overlooking the Murrumbidgee River, but he had also allowed it to gain a reputation as a guesthouse for any bone-weary traveller wandering the countryside.

Word had spread over the years that 'loafer or no loafer, sundowner, bushwhack, or whoever it might be, the traveller who called at Wantabadgery was never sent empty away'.

There was a sound logic behind this. Many of the drifters who roamed the hills and followed the winding path of the Murrumbidgee had plenty of time on their hands to devise acts of revenge if they were turned away and refused the hospitality that was such a part of bush culture.

Windeyer was one of those men who firmly believed that 'a few rations and the shelter of a hut are not missed, whilst on the other hand it is astonishing what mischief a wax match can cause at your homestead . . . or a butcher's knife amongst your stud sheep'.

But Windeyer had recently sold the station to two brothers – Claude and Falconer McDonald – and his charitable manner had left with him. Baynes, the McDonalds' gruff and pragmatic manager, is in no mood to deal with the latest batch of drifters. In fact, he has forgotten all about them. After dinner he is in the drawing room when one of the McDonald brothers walks in and says: 'Those men are still there.'

Baynes mutters under his breath and goes outside to confront them.

George Scott is one of those men who despises rudeness. He also dislikes being humiliated in front of his band of weary young men.

'We have been waiting two hours and a half for you, to see if we could get any work,' he tells Baynes.

'Have you?' replies the station manager. 'Then there is no work for you, and you can clear out.'

That wild drop of blood begins to simmer. Scott, of course, would prefer to stand and argue. But the hour is late and Baynes is clearly not a man in a mood to debate the issue. So Scott and his group retreat to the nearby hills to spend another night in the open and share the last of their rations.

Scott returns the next day only to hear much the same reply from one of the McDonald brothers. There is no work, no shelter, no food. They might as well move on.

The reputation of Wantabadgery is a lie. And now dark clouds are gathering. Scott leads his gang back to the hills where heavy rain soon begins to fall on this Friday night. Their blankets are sodden. There is no chance of a warming fire. Worse, they have run out of food and patience. For a man who cherishes honour and dignity, it is one of the most humiliating events in George Scott's life. He has known people to laugh at him – to point fingers and snigger. He has had judges lording it over him. He has walked in heavy irons and been treated with utter contempt. But this? In front of five young men? Even Nesbitt is beyond dispensing soothing words.

But as the rain tumbles and the night grows cold, there is hope. Captain George has a plan. Always does.

23

THE SIEGE

Say what you like about William Baynes. The man might be gruff, rude and overbearing. But you can never say he shirks from his responsibilities and shies away from hard work. As the sun sets the following evening, Baynes arrives on horseback at the back gate of the homestead. He has been overseeing fencers completing the wiring in one of Wantabadgery's huge paddocks, before shifting a flock of sheep into it.

Lindon the groom is always near the back gate at this time, waiting for Baynes to return. But he is nowhere to be seen. Baynes, clearly irritated, yells into the growing darkness, only to hear the voice of one of the station hands, a man whose wife is also employed as a cook.

The hand says Lindon is down in one of the paddocks. Baynes angrily throws the reins of his horse over the fence, opens the back gate and strides toward the homestead. Dinner is waiting. Will he eat that first, or wait for Lindon to return so he can give the young man a decent dressing down?

But before he can get to the door Baynes is confronted by four men armed with guns. One of them – he looks like the man who stood sulking at the back door two nights earlier – orders him to put his hands in the air. Before he can comply, George Scott rushes forward and kicks Baynes before dragging him into the house. Then he orders the station manager to his knees.

Scott is feeling better. He is now in command. Captain George's plan is working beautifully. They had arrived at Wantabadgery in the middle of the afternoon, a reluctant Graham Bennett in tow, and bailed up the station hand and his wife along with Lindon the groom. They ordered them to hand over all the firearms on the homestead. A sledgehammer had been used to open the locked pantry and after more than a day without food, the group had treated themselves to a decent slap-up meal.

Not long after, David Weir, the store owner who a few days earlier had given the band of hungry men extra flour free of charge, had arrived at the station on horseback with the local schoolmaster. The adrenaline had been surging among Scott's gang and one of them had fired a shot when the elderly teacher refused to dismount. Scott, telling the man he was a fool to resist, had dragged him from his horse and marched him into the dining room. Weir, meanwhile, had made a run for it but as he neared the entrance to the kitchen felt the muzzle of a gun at his ear. 'Bail up,' said a voice and within moments he, too, had joined the other three prisoners.

Throughout all this Scott issued orders and referred to each member by a number. Nesbitt, of course, was number two.

Soon after, the two men who had been fencing that new sheep paddock for Baynes had arrived at the homestead and also been ordered into the dining room.

And now Baynes is on his knees. Scott must be sorely tempted to carry through his threats. This is the man who has embarrassed him in front of his five young men, who has robbed him of his dignity. Making it worse is Baynes' defiance. Not only is he rude but the man shows little concern that his life is hanging so precariously. Scott needs him to grovel, to beg for forgiveness, to show Nesbitt and Rogan and the others the respect that Captain Moonlite deserves.

'You turned us out and would not allow me to stay in an empty hut,' Scott tells him. 'I and my mates had . . . to sleep over a cold and rainy night in the ranges. You told us to come back for work, and we did so at the time appointed, but you again ordered us away as if we were dogs.

'Now, however, I am master here and you will have to do as I direct.'

Baynes remains defiant. 'Take what you want and go away.'

The wild drop of blood ignites. Scott is apoplectic and screams at the station manager, asking him to choose the instrument of his death. Knife or pistol? Scott shows him an array of weapons including revolvers, bowie knives with blades almost a foot long and a selection of rifles. The two men will fight it out.

When Baynes indicates he cares for neither, Scott leans over and pricks him with the knife. This, he tells Baynes, is what happens when you are rude and treat good men in such a shabby fashion.

But there will be no more violence. Not yet, anyway. There is more noise outside. The two McDonald brothers – Claude and Falconer – have just returned from an inspection of the property. As they pull their horses up a voice in the darkness calls out, 'Bail up. Come now, boys, it's no good, the game is up. Get off and ship in with your mates.'

Claude, the younger of the pair, can see the shine of a pistol not far from his forehead. He has only just arrived from England and has heard about bushrangers. But here? He is amused by the absurdity of the whole thing and refuses to dismount until the order is given to 'pot him' if he refuses to get down.

Scott asks if any more visitors are expected.

'None.'

'If any more do come I will shoot them.'

The night ends in silence. Scott and his boys, now in new clothing snatched from the McDonalds' wardrobes, patrol the homestead with candles, checking on their captives. The McDonald brothers sleep restlessly in one of the bedrooms.

Baynes is given the hard floor.

—

Captain Moonlite must be obeyed. He is in control here and all his soldiers must follow his instructions. He has told his men to keep a close eye on Bennett in case the young Yorkshireman entertains any thoughts of treachery. Prisoners are not to be harmed or insulted. If any dare touch or abuse a woman they will be shot on the spot. Water and food must be given to the captives. 'Swagman's rations,' Scott calls them – meat and damper. He also makes it clear that watches and jewellery seized by his men must be returned to their owners.

By early Sunday morning Scott has taken a shine to Claude McDonald. He asks him if anything he values has been stolen.

'There is a cigarette case given to me by some particular friends,' Claude tells him.

'I am afraid I am the culprit, then,' says Scott. He pulls it from his pocket and hands it to Claude with an exaggerated bow.

But all this civility and calm vanishes when Baynes once again gets under Scott's skin. After being released from a stint in the laundry, the station manager has been given a meal. As he eats, he taunts. He has noticed the closeness between Scott and Nesbitt. When James walks past him, Baynes sneers and calls him a 'puff – a fashionably derogative word for a homosexual.

Scott ignores the slight. He knows he is being provoked and needs to remain calm and in control. But Baynes pushes his luck too far. Later, as Baynes watches Gus Wernicke eating a meal, he shakes his head and mutters, 'This is bad work, my boy. Bad work.'

Scott rushes over, grabs Baynes by the throat and threatens to kill him. David Weir and the McDonald brothers watch on as Scott roars and rails like a 'lunatic'.

Eventually calm is restored. Scott goes outside and shoots two turkeys and invites Claude to eat with him. The birds are roasted and the meat offered to all the hostages with the exception of Baynes.

'Don't say I haven't paid you for the dinner I am giving you,' he tells McDonald, handing over a shilling, a sixpence and a threepenny bit. Claude will carry those coins – attached to a ring – in his pocket for the rest of his life.

Their conversation flows. Scott is drawn to the 21-year-old Englishman. It might be the good breeding and manners instilled by an education at the 300-year-old Harrow public school.

Or the swimming holidays at Lake Geneva and life as the son of a prominent army major.

Or the fact that he is a good listener.

McDonald sits patiently as Scott explains the inadequacies of the prison system and the cruelties he has seen. He is impressed by the man's knowledge of engineering, history and literature. But even more fascinating to McDonald are the dual personalities he observes in Captain Moonlite. It is as if the man is at war with himself. Even Scott concedes to his new friend that his 'infirmity of temper' has often derailed 'his career' over the years.

It will not be long before it rears again.

———

Wantabadgery is a hub for the district. Workers, travellers and local businessmen are always dropping by and soon the number of hostages swells. Scott needs more weapons. He has posted his men on the roof and at the edge of the homestead as lookouts, but if the number of prisoners continues to grow he is not sure if enough guns will be on hand to combat an insurrection from within, or an attack by approaching police.

The pressure builds. Six more visitors arrive and are taken prisoner. One of them is a Chinese contractor, Ah Goon, who has come to discuss work with Falconer McDonald. Nesbitt bails him up and takes an American silver lever watch, a chain and two pounds in cash and hands the haul to Scott. It is one of the few thefts Scott will allow. 'I consider that the Chinamen here are taking the bread out of a labouring man's mouth and I assented to his being robbed, and I am not ashamed of it,' he will say later.

And then George Seymour, a station stockman, rides up to the farmhouse. He has been out all day breaking horses and sits astride Vanity, a young, feisty mare. He has taken a shine to the horse.

He found her in a mob of wild horses and after separating her from the herd, found himself with the sort of filly he knew came to a man just once in a lifetime. It's her spirit he admires most. Today is only the third time he has managed to mount her and keep her under control. If she is skittish and prone to straining at the bridle and lashing out with her rear hooves, he loves the way she gallops at full pace. She's full of life, Seymour will tell others. But not for long.

'Bail up,' he is told. Seymour thinks it is a joke until he sees a second man with a rifle on his shoulder pointed straight at him. He follows them into the dining room, which is now crowded with prisoners.

Scott asks him if his horse is 'a good one'. Seymour tells him she is, but he is still breaking her in properly and she doesn't like being tied up.

'I'll show you how to tie her up,' says Scott. They walk out into a nearby yard where up to 20 other horses seized by the gang are tethered to a rail. Scott hitches her to a post but Vanity rears in protest. Now Captain Moonlite finds himself in a difficult spot. He has boasted of his horsemanship in front of everyone and the damned mare is making a fool of him. She is also unsettling the other horses. All Scott needs is a complete stampede and he will never live it down.

He pulls a pistol from his holster, holds it against Vanity's head and shoots her.

Those watching are stunned. As the dead mare crashes to the ground, blood pooling beneath her, Seymour's face turns an angry red.

Scott looks across and sees the fury growing inside the man.

'Well, I'm sorry I did that,' he says.

24

THE RETREAT OF THE TROOPERS

This plan of Captain Moonlite's. What is it exactly? What is the end game? It started as an attempt to end their hunger, find some dry clothes and exact retribution for being treated so harshly. Now it is spiralling out of control.

Scott has told some of his prisoners that he plans to rob the Gundagai bank, others that he intends to go to Wagga. It is a ploy favoured by the Kellys; take the locals captive, lure the police away and then ride into town unopposed. But there seems to be little logic behind the whole thing. The dining room of the Wantabadgery homestead is looking more like a crowded hotel foyer with each passing hour. Visitors keep arriving and in turn are taken hostage.

Scott orders the young groom Lindon to draw up a horse and buggy. By late Sunday afternoon Captain George is behind the reins and making his way to the home of the station's superintendent a few miles away. Once there he seizes a Whitworth rifle and ammunition and orders the man and his wife into the buggy.

And then he makes a mistake. With Falconer McDonald alongside him as a hostage, Scott decides to travel a mile further down the road to the nearest hotel, the Australian Arms. Jack Patterson, the publican, isn't home. Scott warns his wife, Isabella, that when her husband returns they should make their way to Wantabadgery. To make sure his orders are followed, Scott takes the Pattersons' two young sons with him.

'If you or your husband stir, or warn the police, we will shoot the two kids,' he tells her.

He returns to the homestead with another 10 prisoners in tow, most of them drinkers taken captive from the hotel. There are now close to 40 hostages and, as night nears, the Pattersons soon arrive to be with their sons.

William Baynes has been keeping up his banter and Scott has had enough. He is convinced the man is trying to incite a mutiny among his men. This time he is determined to hang him. A length of rope is found and a horse buggy is summoned so it can be placed beneath a nearby tree. Chaos follows. The prisoners – led by the McDonald brothers and several women who are crying and screaming – plead with Moonlite to spare Baynes' life.

Scott screams back and says Baynes must die. 'I have never hanged a man in New South Wales and I am going to make an example of you.'

It is David Weir, the shopkeeper, who buys a reprieve for the station manager. He whispers to Baynes that perhaps now might be the time to show some contrition.

Baynes swallows his pride. He looks at Scott. 'Might I ask your pardon?' he asks.

Scott calms. Baynes has given him a way out. But the clash has heightened tension and guaranteed that few will sleep well. Weeks later Scott will still be fuming over the encounter.

'His insult was the last drop in the cup of bitterness,' he will write. 'He insulted me; he would not fight me. I was told he was trying to raise some sort of mutiny among our prisoners, and Warnicky told me he was trying to make him a traitor. I feared that if the prisoners mutinied life would have been lost and I brought out Baynes and told him he had only five minutes to live. I brought him out to the front of where the women prisoners were, knowing they would beg him off. They did so and I let him go.'

—

In the gloom, the growling of a dog. It's a little after four in the morning on Monday. Scott is instantly on his feet and out the front door. Shots ring out, followed by a voice.

'Surrender, in the Queen's name.'

'That be damned!' shouts Scott. He shoots in the direction of the voice and suddenly the early morning is filled with streaks of light and smoke from rapid gunfire. He runs back inside and summons his men and shouts the order once more.

'Fire!'

The police are outside. That visit to the Australian Arms the previous afternoon was bound to cause a stir. Not long after Scott had left with his latest batch of hostages, a young man had arrived and been told by a distraught Isabella Patterson that bushrangers had taken her boys and were holed up at Wantabadgery. The man had exhausted his horse riding more than 20 miles to Wagga Wagga to summon the police. At first they hadn't quite believed his story. But four officers had set out just after 9pm and now, after almost seven hours of hard riding, have discovered the truth.

They had dismounted at the back of the house, tied their horses to a post and were advancing cautiously toward the homestead when the dog barked. There had been that quick exchange of shots and one of the bushrangers, according to one of the officers, threatened to burn down a nearby stable if they failed to leave. Now, with Scott back inside and gathering his men, the police have remounted and ridden around the property to the front entrance.

Scott has sent Baynes and the McDonald brothers to the roof to act as lookouts. In the growing light they soon report that four or five police are grouped together near a gardener's hut.

And now Captain Moonlite and his number two, James Nesbitt, are back outside and advancing on the police. Scott has swapped his pistol for a Whitworth rifle; Nesbitt wields a double-barrel gun. Both are firing rapidly at the police. They use a small bank of thistles as cover before emerging into the open. Moonlite advances in a manner straight from the military manual. He crawls forward, props himself on his elbows and fires. Now he's standing, crouching, always advancing, falling to one knee and taking aim.

The man is almost single-handedly forcing the police to retreat. The four officers have pulled back to a grove of trees. Constable George Rowe takes cover behind a sapling and Scott splinters it with three bullets in rapid succession.

'We fought, they retreated, we advanced, they ran,' Scott will say later. Within minutes the police have been pushed more than 400 yards to a swamp. And then, still under sustained fire, they make a run for it. They hurtle across a paddock and plunge into a shallow swamp before reaching the main road. They will keep running for almost 10 miles until they reach the home of a grazier in Eurongilly, John Beveridge.

Within a couple of days reporters will flock to the homestead. One of them, looking out over a field strewn with spent cartridges, will report that 'the paddock across which Moonlite came to fire upon the police, and where he was followed by Nesbitt was, for some distance, free from any cover; and looking at the ground, one is struck as much by the impudence of the scoundrel as by the risk he must have run if any well-directed shots had been fired at him'.

In their chaotic retreat the troopers have left behind their horses. Scott and Nesbitt return triumphantly to the homestead with the four mounts. It is time for breakfast.

———

George Scott, of course, feels compelled to make a speech before leaving Wantabadgery. He tells the crowd of prisoners in the homestead that he is, indeed, Captain Moonlite and he will show no mercy to the police or any volunteers assisting them.

The hostages watch as Scott and his group depart. Several of them look away to hide their smiles. Others cannot help but smirk.

Some bushrangers they turned out to be. Few of the Moonlite gang seem comfortable in the saddle. Little Gus Wernicke, it seems, has never been on a horse before. His mount jumps and tries to throw him and he is forced to exchange his steed for a more sedate one.

Scott will later say this comical departure from the homestead will prove how he and his men had fallen into bushranging by accident. There had never been any intention to stage such a siege or draw the attention of the police.

'Had I wished to select a gang to go to commit robberies I knew a number of criminals from whom I could have selected determined men accustomed to the bush and good horsemen,' he will write. 'It is a matter of fact that my poor friend Nesbitt was brought up in the town and he was no horseman. Williams and Warnicky never had been on horses before the fatal day. Rogan was a very inferior horseman [but] could ride a little. They were all ignorant of the use of firearms, did not know how to properly load their guns. Their attempts at horsemanship created much half-suppressed laughter which, but for fear, would have caused unlimited merriment.'

Scott leads his uncomfortable band to the Australian Arms hotel. By mid-afternoon David Weir is returning home to his store and is passing the pub when Scott appears and invites him in for a drink. Weir declines and Scott says the man might as well join his party because they are heading in the same direction.

Off they go, Weir and Scott riding side by side, when they see three horsemen approaching. One of them is John Beveridge, the man who provided shelter to the Wagga troopers a few hours earlier. The other two are locals, including a battling sheep and wheat farmer, Edmund McGlede, who has volunteered to help the police. Weir suggests to Beveridge that he and his men are outgunned and outmanned and a quick surrender might be in order. Just as Beveridge agrees, seven of his shearers ride up unarmed and are also ordered to bail up.

What to do? Scott is under pressure again. People keep coming from everywhere.

He orders all the men to kneel on the road before him. They will be court-martialed, he announces. First, a jury needs to be formed. Scott remembers McGlede. On their way to Wantabadgery they had stopped by his hut and McGlede's wife had been kind to them, giving them something to eat and all the fresh milk they wanted. So he decides that the two men who had shown such charity to his group – Weir and McGlede – will sit in judgement alongside some of his men.

Scott, of course, will be prosecutor and judge. He is soon addressing his makeshift jury.

'He argued that the accused had come out with the intention of shooting him, and that he would therefore be justified in shooting them,' Weir will recall.

Scott then turns to the men kneeling before him. 'The accused can make any statement they like but remember that what you say will be used as evidence for the prosecution.'

In the middle of a Monday afternoon on a lonely country road the men plead for their lives. Several say they are only there because they felt they had to assist their friends.

The jury gathers. Weir thinks the only way to end this farcical but dangerous encounter is to play up to Scott's vanity by returning a guilty plea and asking Scott for mercy. But Rogan insists his boss is demanding a not guilty verdict.

Later, Scott will say the entire mock trial was designed to frighten other locals contemplating assisting the police. 'Had I been a cruel murderer I would have shot them . . .'

But even with a not guilty verdict there are lessons to be dispensed. Scott orders Beveridge to bring him his horse. It will need to be shot. Beveridge pleads for the animal's life. It is a favourite of his. He has another three he is willing to allow Scott to kill if he would only spare this one.

Weir: 'Moonlite replied that he would shoot every horse Beveridge had got, and at once put a bullet through his favourite's head. This did not kill the animal so he made Beveridge shoot him dead. He then made all the prisoners go down on their knees and beg his pardon. They did so and as they rose he kicked them. Beveridge evaded the kick and Moonlite thereupon drew a knife and threatened to cut off a piece of his nose but did not carry out the threat. The gang then collected all the spare guns, broke them into pieces and burned them at the roadside.'

25

THE DISPENSER OF DEATH

Edward Webb-Bowen is astride his horse, urging it on through the fields and along the rutted track that passes for the main road out of Gundagai. There is no time to be lost. Webb-Bowen's dreams have come true. The bushrangers have arrived.

He looks every inch the man he has always wanted to become. The straps of his police helmet cannot hide that chiselled face or disguise the square jaw. His fashionably wide moustache, waxed to fine points at each end, barely moves in the wind. But it is those expressive hazel eyes – the ones now staring into the distance looking for signs of the outlaws – that his friends find most compelling. They seem permanently tinged with sadness.

Perhaps they have already seen too much slaughter. If so, Senior Constable Edward Webb-Bowen is not the man to openly talk about it. Friends have to pry and push to get him to open up about the things he has seen and done in his 28 years. Many have no idea just what an expert at cheating and dispensing death the man has become.

It started when the ship helping him escape the drudgery of a clerk's life in London caught on fire several times on its way to

Australia, which left quite a few of the passengers concerned about the 20 tons of gunpowder it was carrying in its hold.

Not long after a hurricane in the notorious waters just off the Cape of Good Hope caused the *Marietta* to spring a leak. Webb-Bowen and the rest of the passengers spent more than a month below deck with the crew, pumping seawater to keep the ship afloat.

Still, the man could hardly complain. This was the sort of adventurous life he had dreamed about during those four dull years wrestling with forms and account books for a London wine and spirits company. In many ways Webb-Bowen is like George Scott. He is the son of a gentle Welsh vicar and a graduate of the finishing school at Eton. He is a character the second half of the 19th century specialises in producing; men who want to explore the world because they sense it is already shrinking and that soon there will be no parts unknown left.

He had joined the fledgling Queensland Native Police not long after the *Marietta* finally limped into Brisbane's port in the middle of 1873. Sent north, he found himself in the heat and humidity of the squalid goldfields on Palmer River. By the time he arrived he had already earned a reputation as a man of pluck and daring. The steamer ferrying him and his fellow rookie officers and their horses had encountered thick mangroves near Cooktown. Unable to reach dry land, it had been Webb-Bowen who dived into the crocodile-infested waters and guided the horses through deep water to the shore.

The goldfields were sprawling fields of misery. Food was scarce, the miners always brawling and the local Aboriginal tribes in a perpetual state of fury over their stolen land and a series of atrocities committed against their women. Whenever the Aboriginals attacked, the police were sent out on frequent hunting parties to exact retribution. Webb-Bowen would become an enthusiastic participant. Over the following two decades thousands of Aboriginals would be slaughtered by police and settlers in a series of massacres whose ferocity and scale was unmatched anywhere else in the colonies.

A year before Webb-Bowen arrived in Australia more than 200 Aboriginal people had been massacred at Skull Hole near Winton in central Queensland. 'The blacks infested the district of Palmer, occasioning great trouble,' an old friend of Webb-Bowen's will recall. '. . . day after day Bowen was scouring the country in search of them, and many a cannibal met death at his hands for taking the lives of his countrymen.'

But on one of those hunting forays Webb-Bowen was speared deeply in the groin during a hand-to-hand battle with an indigenous warrior. Local doctors, unable to fully extract the weapon and with Bowen gripped by fever, sent him back to Cooktown and then on to Brisbane. But to get him to the port and on to a ship, the police cavalcade caring for him had several narrow escapes as they battled heavily swollen rivers and more hostile Aboriginal clans.

In Brisbane, the doctors managed to extract the spear but could not cure his frequent recurrent bouts of fever. So he was sent to the milder climate of Sydney and had soon signed up to become a police trooper stationed in Tenterfield in the colony's far north.

The man was now an expert at facing death. If some suspected he was more than a little gung-ho, they could hardly complain about what happened next. When a well-known local criminal, Charlie Plummer, stole three pounds from a fellow drinker at the town pub, Webb-Bowen set out late at night on horseback to capture him. He caught up with Plummer several miles out of town just after midnight. Plummer repeatedly refused to accompany the officer back to Tenterfield. At one stage Webb-Bowen offered to dismount and engage Plummer in a fist fight. Eventually Webb-Bowen shot Plummer's horse from under him. Plummer continued to refuse to surrender. With the last bullet in his revolver, Webb-Bowen shot Plummer in the stomach. He died a day later.

The resulting inquest found Webb-Bowen justified in his actions. Not only that, it recommended him for a promotion and it came quickly when he was sent to run the station at Bendemeer. Now married and with a young son, Webb-Bowen's growing reputation was further enhanced when he confronted two bushrangers who had bailed up a local hotel. One of them – Fred Crawley – took aim at him twice. One shot went between Webb-Bowen's legs, the next misfired. He had cheated death once more, and now it was time to dispense it. He shot Crawley in the chest and Crawley's mate immediately surrendered.

The following year Webb-Bowen quit the force and moved to Sydney. A second son had arrived and required urgent medical treatment. But days after arriving in the colony's capital with his wife, Marion, the nine-month-old boy died. His passing triggered a rare run of bad luck for the Webb-Bowens. A decision to pursue a career in business quickly led to an appearance in the insolvency court. That bankruptcy hearing was told the Webb-Bowens were living at the Zeplins Commercial Hotel and had only five pounds in assets and almost 200 pounds in liabilities.

He had no choice but to rejoin the police force and by April 1879 he was sent to Gundagai, a small town 230 miles south-west of Sydney and almost three days' hard riding from the Victorian border. The posting had largely been at his urging. He had told his superiors he wanted nothing more than a chance to tackle the Kelly gang. Several reports had suggested the Kellys were planning to bail up Gundagai and Webb-Bowen arrived to find the town on edge. Townspeople had armed themselves in anticipation of a raid by the gang, the banks had increased security and the newspapers were filled with speculation about an imminent attack.

The rains in recent days had only increased the nervousness. There were many who had never forgotten the awful flood of 1852. It had started with the sort of relentless downpour that turns cemeteries into swamps and raises the bones of the dead. It ended when the Murrumbidgee River burst its banks and swept away the old part of town, taking with it almost 100 people – a third of Gundagai's population.

But on this Monday morning all that was momentarily forgotten. Word had reached the Gundagai police station of a bail-up at Wantabadgery Station the night before. The reports were rushed and confusing. But an hour or so earlier Gundagai's commanding officer, Senior Sergeant John Carroll, had finally confirmed them and ordered his men to mount up.

Edward Webb-Bowen, the expert at cheating and dispensing death, did not need to be asked twice.

—

Edmund McGlede and his wife Hannah are strugglers. Locals might even call them a little rough around the edges. Their hut, a few miles down the road from Wantabadgery Station, is a small bark slab with four tiny rooms and an iron roof. At the rear of the house, about 20 feet away, sits a separate kitchen with a bark roof.

The McGledes came here a year ago to take up a 120-acre selection and try to put the past behind them. Edmund was once the landlord of the Australian Arms hotel and trouble had always dogged himself and his wife. They had been dragged into court on charges of running a sly grog shop and Hannah and her son, Henry, had once been charged with assaulting a man at the pub when a heated argument turned physical.

So they have decided to make a go of it with a flock of sheep and a large wheat paddock. But the place reeks of despair. The brush fences are ragged and the yard out front is overrun with weeds, logs and tree stumps.

After that mock roadside trial, Scott has come to the McGledes with prisoners in tow. According to Edmund McGlede, 'Moonlite . . . asked me if I had any milk at my place and asked me if the Missis would be frightened. I said no, she has seen bushrangers before, they behaved honourably to her. I hope you will do the same.'

Hosting a group of rough men is something Hannah has grown used to over the years. She gives the gang milk and brandy and then, to everyone's relief, Scott and his men mount up and move on. But just as they reach the·road they spot a group of troopers galloping toward them.

There is nowhere else to go but back to the McGledes' for the final showdown.

26

THE FINAL SHOOTOUT

In the days and months to come all the statements and testimonies will make it sound so clinical.

They will tell how the police – now a combined force of troopers from Gundagai, those Wagga constables who fled, horseless, from the first battle and an array of local farmers and workers armed with a motley collection of weapons – arrive at the McGlede homestead in the middle of the afternoon.

They will detail how the bushrangers, quickly surrounded, retreat to the shack and its separate kitchen at the rear.

They will estimate the shootout lasts no more than 30 minutes.

They will report how more than a hundred spectators – some will claim 300 – line the nearby hills, cheering and hollering for the police to do their best.

And when the whole bloody mess is over, they will try to explain how three young men lie dead or dying.

But in all the millions of words of evidence and reports, nothing will tell you what it will really be like; how the air will fill with the stench of sulphur from all that burnt gunpowder; how the walls of the hut will shudder and splinter with every bullet; how it will sound when hot metal pierces the flesh and bone of young men and sends them crashing to the ground, or how it will feel to be trapped in the centre of all this carnage with nowhere to go.

If only they had not stayed for so long at the hut filling their bellies with milk and brandy; they could have put some distance between themselves and the police and perhaps even escaped. If only Scott had not spent so much time conducting his bizarre roadside court hearing; the six of them might have pushed on into those undulating hills and toward the horizon, still free men with nothing to complain about but saddle soreness and little Gus Wernicke's inability to control his horse.

But there is no time to ponder what might have been. Later, but not now. There is a raging torrent of that wild blood coursing through Scott and not even James Nesbitt can find the right words to calm it. Moonlite has issued orders and they must be followed. So they have tied their horses and taken up positions in a gully behind a garden fence not far from the McGlede hut.

Seconds later they hear one of the constables a few hundred yards away calling for them to give themselves up.

If only Nesbitt can find more calming words. Scott might emerge from his fog of fury and see how the police have them outnumbered and outgunned. He might step outside with his arms raised to make sure no blood is shed. Isn't that what he always says he cares most about? But Nesbitt has nothing left and the only words to be issued come from Scott.

'Come on and fight, you bastards, come on and fight. No surrender!'

There is no turning back now. Under the orders of Gundagai's Senior Sergeant John Carroll, the police are fanning out, 20 or 30 yards between them. His plan is a simple pincer movement. Their right wing will close in a half circle on the hut, while the left will move in and tighten the cordon.

The shooting starts. Carroll rides behind a large tree for shelter. A bullet just misses his neck and grazes the tree, sending up a shower of bark. Still holding the reins with one hand, he fires back at a figure crouched in the corner where the garden and wheat paddock meet. Bullets fly. Small clouds of smoke drift across the weed-filled yard. And somewhere in the distance is the sound of cheering.

Word has been spreading for hours about a possible showdown and now a large crowd of local workers and neighbours is gathering in the hills above the McGlede property to watch the police take on the bushrangers. The area is a natural amphitheatre and there are figures – the McGlede children and most of the other prisoners seized during that roadside trial – escaping from the rear of the hut and racing up the banks of one of the hills to join the growing audience.

David Weir is not one of them. Too many bullets are flying for his liking. He has taken cover behind a tree stump. But Nesbitt pushes him away, telling him there is no room for both of them. So Weir creeps along the fence line, metal slugs ripping the air above him, and squeezes between two logs lying about 15 paces from the hut.

So many bullets. Senior Sergeant Carroll is growing concerned his men might run out of ammunition. There is a group of volunteers on their way with supplies, but they might get here too late. Carroll leaves his horse near the tree and races across open ground to find safety behind one of the fences. He looks ahead and is greeted by the sight of Scott ordering his men to push back to the hut and the rear kitchen.

Carroll can see some of them already inside the McGledes' shack. He wants to take a shot. But there are two more women running up the hill behind the house and he is afraid there might be more inside.

He pushes forward, crouching and running through the garden. He clambers over another rail fence and now he is up against the chimney wall of the hut. He glances around its corner and there, just 15 yards away, is the man they call Moonlite. He is raising his gun and taking aim, but it is as if he doesn't see Carroll at all. His target is another officer in the distance. Carroll takes aim but his gun misfires. He reloads. The damn thing fails him again.

Scott turns and goes back inside for more ammunition.

Carroll motions to his men to continue moving forward. The trap is set.

—

Hannah McGlede has wanted to leave her small kitchen and run to the hills with everyone else. But now it is too late. She should have shrugged off the protective arm of James Nesbitt and charged through that door and sprinted as hard as her legs could carry her so she could be with her children. But Nesbitt had stopped her. It was too dangerous, he said. Too many bullets.

Now she wonders if the young man knows what he is talking about. A bullet has just passed through the slab walls and punched a hole in a tin plate next to her. The noise shocks her. She looks down to see if she has been shot.

Nesbitt is growing increasingly concerned about their predicament. Scott has sent Rogan and young Wernicke to take up positions in the main house and stop the police from entering it while he and the rest – Nesbitt, Bennett and Williams – hold the kitchen.

But the numbers are clearly against them. Through the window they catch glimpses of the police moving forward and every few moments Scott steps outside and fires on them.

Please George, says Nesbitt. We have to surrender. People are going to die. We'll all be shot.

'I'm not frightened of 20 bloody traps,' says Scott. 'I will never surrender.'

But Nesbitt persists. Bullets continue slamming into the kitchen, showering them in shards of bark. The room is filled with dust. Nesbitt grabs Scott by the shoulders. He has seen his friend like this before; jaw clamped, fury blazing in his eyes, the blood surging through him so loudly he can hear nothing else. Nesbitt needs to stop this madness before they all die.

He stares into Scott's eyes.

'George,' he says, 'for my sake, shed no more blood. Promise me not to.'

Scott stares back. Then he nods and makes the promise. Nesbitt grabs Scott's rifle and removes his coat and a belt carrying two small guns. Bullets continue punching the slab walls. Scott peers out of one of the windows and can see three, maybe four, troopers together and assumes they are planning to rush the kitchen.

Tom Williams is standing near Bennett, holding a police carbine rifle they had taken earlier. The kid has not fired a shot because he doesn't know how to load it. Some bushrangers they are turning out to be. Can't ride. Can't even shoot. Scott grabs the rifle and steps outside. The police are firing at him. He gets off a shot and goes back inside.

'I've shot a horse,' he tells Nesbitt. It's as if Scott is unaware of the maelstrom of noise and chaos around him. The kitchen is under siege. It groans and sways. The impact of every bullet sends a wave of more dust and smoke through the room. And all Scott wants James Nesbitt to know is that he has kept his honour. The only blood shed belongs to a bloody horse.

One of the gang is clutching a small revolver – no-one will remember who it is when it is all over but it is probably Bennett – and it accidentally goes off. The bullet grazes Scott on the foot and lower leg. The adrenaline conceals the pain. He steps outside and fires again in the direction of the police. A few yards away he sees a trooper fall to the ground.

When he comes back inside to reload again he has news. 'One of the traps is shot,' he announces.

Hannah McGlede thinks the news seems to lift Nesbitt's spirits. She watches him turn and move toward one of the windows as if he plans to take a shot. But Scott will remember it differently. Nesbitt moves toward one of the windows but only to yell 'Surrender!'

In the growing chaos Hannah seizes the moment. She flings open the door and makes a run for it.

—

Where is Tom Rogan? No-one has seen him since his gun became wedged in a fence and Scott told him to go and hold the main house. As for little Gus Wernicke, does he ever follow orders?

He was told to stay with Rogan. But the kid has moved out front of the shack and is sheltering behind the large wooden wheels of an old cart. Every few seconds he stands up and fires. The ring of troopers is closing in. One of them is Constable Alexander Barry, whose horse has just been shot dead from under him by Scott. It is still early afternoon and the milk Wernicke scoffed down from Mrs McGlede less than an hour earlier is still warm in his belly. He decides to make a run for a tree stump that might provide better shelter. Barry stoops and takes aim and hits little Gus twice.

Lying on the ground, Wernicke sees another constable approaching the cart. Edward Webb-Bowen, the dispenser of death, can't believe his luck. Finally, after all these years, one of his greatest dreams has been realised. A fight to the death with a gang of bushrangers. He leaps over a fence rail and marches forward. But something seems wrong with his gun. He stops and bends over slightly. It looks like he is trying to remove a jammed cartridge when a bullet travelling at 130 miles an hour penetrates his neck.

It is a small piece of lead, not even half an inch wide. It pierces the skin and crashes through the seventh cervical vertebrae, splintering bone and severing veins, before lodging in a muscle and narrowly missing a main artery.

Webb-Bowen slumps and gasps. A fellow constable, Patrick Gorman, hears Webb-Bowen cry out, 'My God, I'm shot.'

Gorman has already had a narrow escape. Moments earlier he had jumped into the field about 80 yards from the main house. Scott had been outside unleashing one of his frequent attacks when he had seen Gorman moving across his line of sight. 'There's a bloody trap down here,' Scott had yelled. Gorman had thrown himself behind a tree stump and Scott had swiftly put three bullets into it. Gorman had fired back and his shots had hit the ground just in front of Scott's feet.

Now Scott has rushed back into the kitchen to reload and pass on the news that a trooper – Webb-Bowen – is down. Gorman and another constable sprint for the main hut. He opens the front door, expecting to confront one of the outlaws. But the place seems empty. He moves forward and into one of the small rooms. There is a window that looks directly on to one of the windows of the separate kitchen. When he pulls open the blind he sees one of the bushrangers holed up in the kitchen taking aim. Gorman jumps back and a bullet whizzes past his shoulder and thuds into one of the wall slabs.

He returns to the window and fires. His shot strikes the man just behind the right eye.

—

Nesbitt falls backward and slumps to a sitting position. There is blood spilling from his temple from Gorman's bullet. Scott cradles him in one arm. Nesbitt is grasping his other hand. Scott can feel him pressing on it, as if to let him know he still recognises him. He is trying to say something. It sounds like a prayer, a dimly remembered verse or refrain the Christian Brothers must have drilled into him so many years earlier. But Scott can't be sure because the young man is breathing too hard and his voice is too soft and there is too much noise outside. One of the troopers has stormed the room. Bennett has just been shot in the arm and is crying out 'surrender' and the young constable who fired at him has just belted him across the face with his revolver and suddenly, here on this shabby floor inside this bullet-ridden kitchen shack, Andrew George Scott can hear everything; every damn bullet, every forlorn cry, every heaving sob. Including his own.

Who knows how long Scott holds Nesbitt. It can only be a minute or two. There is too much blood, too many small pieces of bone and not enough time to say what needs to be said.

Scott feels Nesbitt slump and at the same time he hears little Gus crying out in pain somewhere outside.

He gently lays the unconscious body of James Nesbitt on the floor and looks outside the window. A trooper is belting little Gus with the butt of a rifle.

Scott rushes outside.

'Captain – Captain George,' says Wernicke.

The officer moves off and Scott sees the boy has been shot twice – once through the wrist and another through the body. He will never forget this sight. 'He had all the marks of death and was in great pain,' he will recall later. 'He said, "I have done my best, George, don't blame yourself . . . lift me up. I'm in great pain."'

Captain George raises him with his right arm and allows Wernicke to rest his head on his chest. His men are dying around him. This one is still only a kid. Stubborn, scrappy little Gus. He should have left him in Melbourne in that flea-ridden whorehouse, preying on drunks and stealing just enough food to keep the hunger at bay. He should never have hunted him down that day when he and Thomas Williams had taken off on their own.

One of the troopers – Sergeant Henry Cassin – is coming toward them. Wernicke winces and tells Scott he is the officer who has been assaulting him.

Scott wishes he were still armed because at this moment he would be happy to break his promise to Nesbitt and shed as much blood as possible. What sort of dishonourable bastard is this Cassin? He is a big man with a full beard and dark eyes and Scott wants to pull him apart, limb by limb.

'Surrender,' says Cassin.

He is joined by another constable. They wrench Wernicke roughly away and handcuff Scott. 'I have no arms, damn you,' Scott tells them. He looks across the yard and can see Williams on the ground, three constables standing over him, one of them with his foot on Williams' neck, 'ill-using him most savagely'.

Scott and Wernicke are dragged back to the kitchen. Nesbitt is lying where Scott left him. He is still breathing. Scott falls to his knees and cradles his head in his handcuffed hands. He looks up and asks for a priest to be sent. Some of the constables snigger. No-one is taking any more orders from Captain George now.

Scott clings to Nesbitt, willing him to hang on. But not long after Gus Wernicke dies, Nesbitt slips away.

Scott cries out. He crouches over the body of the best man he has ever known and passionately, desperately, begins to kiss his face.

Moments ago this small hut had been filled with frightened shouts and acrid smoke and ricocheting bullets. Now the police watch on silently, surrounded by the bodies of broken men and the endless grief of Captain Moonlite.

27

MY FRIENDS WHO SLEEP IN YOUR CEMETERY

Just what is this Webb-Bowen made out of? He is paralysed and in enormous pain. The 26-mile journey back to Gundagai lying semi-conscious in the rear of a horse-drawn cart, plodding along that rutted track, was torturous enough. Now, lying on a cot in a small cottage, he drifts in and out of consciousness. The doctors have examined the wound, prodding it with their unwashed fingers, poking it with their unsterilised instruments, and then dressed it. They are not sure what else to do and fear the worst. A gently worded telegram has been sent to Marion Webb-Bowen, who is in Sydney with their young son. Without divulging their concerns, the doctors suggest she catch a train as soon as she can so she can join her husband.

Webb-Bowen should already be dead. But somehow the man clings to life. Those who know him understand how close he had come to death a few years earlier when that spear had lodged in his groin and not been removed for days. The resulting infection from that wound had persisted for months. But he had overcome it. Perhaps he might do so again.

Either way, the man is now a hero. The telegraph system has been overloaded with news of the siege. The newspapers are filled with wildly exaggerated reports of a band of merciless bushrangers who stuck up one of the country's biggest stations before embarking on a crazed shootout with a courageous band of troopers. To top it off, the leader of this gang of outlaws is none other than Captain Moonlite. All the old stories of the Mount Egerton bank robbery and his long stint in Pentridge are dredged up, recycled, enlarged.

But worse, much worse, is what it all means. Hadn't the government assured everyone that the era of bushrangers was finally over? The Kellys might still be a law to themselves but that was a Victorian thing. Lawlessness was not tolerated north of the Murray River. When *The Evening News* breaks the story of the siege to Sydneysiders, it is in no doubt as to the significance of Moonlite's outrage for the colony of New South Wales.

'Six men acting together under a voluntary and yet severe discipline might have become a nucleus for the whole criminal class of the colony, and have caused infinite trouble to the Government and all orderly citizens,' it thunders.

Reports that a group of Wagga policemen had fled Wantabadgery in such a panic after being outgunned by two men that they left their horses behind have not yet made it to the big cities. Even their hometown is choosing to ignore the embarrassing retreat, preferring to dwell on the bravery of the men who shot it out with the bushrangers.

'The men who were shot or captured yesterday appear to have been as dangerous as the Victorian outlaws,' reports the *Wagga Wagga Express*. 'The signal success which attended the efforts of the police will not tend to remove the suspicion which prevails, that the Kellys might have been hunted down had there been a stronger determination to do so. It is not, however, so much our present purpose to reflect upon the Victorian police as to congratulate those of this colony, and the entire force has to be congratulated on the conduct of the few brave men who fought it out with the bushrangers yesterday . . .'

But here in Gundagai everyone has heard the stories. Those wallopers from Wagga lost their nerve and had to wait for the good men of Gundagai to set things right. As Webb-Bowen drifts in and out of consciousness, a handful of prominent local citizens hold a meeting in the courthouse one evening to raise funds to be distributed to those brave officers of Gundagai who did the town proud.

The meeting hears the Wagga police had a splendid opportunity for thoroughly distinguishing themselves but 'that opportunity they allowed to pass by without any good results ... the retreat, even to the matter of the police leaving the horses in the hands of the bushrangers, was unfavourably commented upon both by the speaker and others. There was no second question that if the Gundagai police contingent had not arrived on the scene when they did Moonlite's gang would have had matters all their own way.'

—

They spent a restless night after the shootout in the McGledes' kitchen shack, a morose Scott, the injured Bennett and the heavily bruised Williams shackled together, trying to sleep on the floor, listening to the police discuss the firefight and everyone wondering about the whereabouts of Rogan. He had not been sighted since shortly after the battle began. A man had been seen riding away on a grey horse as it all ended. Perhaps it was Rogan. The troopers were confident he would be found by morning.

He was. But Rogan had not travelled far. He had been hiding beneath a bed in one of the small rooms of the main hut. He had lost his gun when the fighting started. Weaponless and riven with fear, he had taken shelter when Scott ordered him to hold the house with Wernicke.

Late that afternoon the four of them, along with the bodies of Nesbitt and Wernicke, had been taken to Gundagai on the back of a dray cart. They arrived in the late afternoon and pulled up outside the brick gaol where a large crowd had gathered, cheering the police and jeering the bushrangers. The bodies of Nesbitt and Wernicke were then examined by a doctor before being identified by a newly arrived detective from Melbourne. He then interviewed Scott in his cell and

'Moonlite . . . burst out crying about Nesbitt, to whom he was much attached'. Nesbitt, the detective told reporters, had informed him back in March that he and Scott had plans to leave Victoria.

The next morning Nesbitt and Wernicke are quickly lowered into unmarked graves in the local cemetery as a coronial inquiry is held into their deaths. A jury of 12 'good and lawful men of Gundagai' are sworn in and throughout the day they listen to a parade of police and other witnesses detailing the events at Wantabadgery and McGledes' hut.

But it is the evidence of a local doctor, Robert McKillop, that surely makes Scott wince. McKillop had reached the McGledes' hut after the battle was over and examined the body of Nesbitt. He had found, he says, a young man with brown eyes, 'a little hair on upper lip, light brown hair . . . I noticed a wound externally on the right side, the ninth rib was fractured, I could put my finger into the wound on the right temple to the posterior lobe of the brain on the opposite side. I found pieces of bone embedded in the brain along the track of the wound and also a portion of a lead bullet which I now produce.'

By 6.30pm the jury is clear: the two bushrangers died as a result of justifiable homicide 'whilst resisting capture by the police who were within lawful execution of their duty'.

—

The next morning more reporters from the Sydney newspapers arrive as the four bushrangers are charged with robbery under arms and wounding with intent to murder Constable Webb-Bowen. The four prisoners, still wearing the clothes they took from Wantabadgery, are led into the crowded courtroom. Scott is handcuffed to Rogan. Williams, his face bruised and beginning to scab, is handcuffed to Bennett, whose wounded arm rests in a sling made with a knotted towel.

If they are expecting to find brawny men with large chapped hands and cold mean eyes, the reporters are sadly disappointed. But they do their best. Rogan, writes one, 'is a tall, dark young man with something of the Negro in his appearance, and there is some indication of cruelty about his features'.

Cruelty? Now, that would be the 'little moustache and beard which meet around his mouth'. The two younger members of the gang – Williams and Bennett – are 'wholly destitute of hair . . . mere boys'.

But it is Scott they have come to see and even he 'shows but little of what one would expect to find about such a desperate scoundrel'. Everyone is an amateur phrenologist. They note his thin, pointed features. His small beard. The shaved area around his cheeks and lips. The small forehead.

But what catches them by surprise is the man's passion and eloquence. The prisoners are not provided with a lawyer, and Scott, more than familiar with courtroom proceedings, is quick to take on the role. It is only three days since he held the dying Nesbitt in his arms and every time James is mentioned tears well in his eyes and his voice chokes.

He is angry, bitter, depressed and certain that a conspiracy is afoot. The police are once again proving themselves to be perjurers, willing to say anything to cast himself and the others in the worst possible light. And the magistrate, William Love, is clearly complicit in their little game. Love is a former member of the New South Wales Legislative Assembly. He is 70 years old and knows what is expected from him – a quick verdict before packing the bushrangers off to the big city for a showy Supreme Court trial.

Scott sits at a small table behind the dock, scribbling with a pencil, underlining key points. He already has a plan. He will assume all responsibility for the shooting of Webb-Bowen and the events leading up to it. It is the only honourable thing to do. The young men with him were simply following orders.

But there is also the not insignificant matter of who shot Webb-Bowen. Scott is adamant it was not himself. He will spend hours in the next few days and coming weeks forensically examining witnesses about the characteristics of various guns. Was Scott firing a double-barrelled gun or a breech-loading Snider rifle? Or was it the police carbine he had taken from a lone constable taken hostage at about the same time he was conducting that mock roadside trial? What about the three Colt revolvers – and the rest of the weapons now piled on display in the courtroom?

It all comes down to the guns. One of the officers cross-examined by Scott will say he found Rogan hiding under the McGledes' bed on his hands and knees, holding a loaded revolver in his right hand.

'Are you sure that's loaded?' asks Scott. 'Will you let me examine it?'

'No thank you,' the trooper responds quickly as laughter ripples through the crowd. 'No, you are too good a shot.'

—

If Scott is unable to hide his disdain for Magistrate Love, he will show respect for some in the law. Senior Sergeant John Carroll is one of them, says Scott, a brave and honourable man who took the fight right up to Scott's men with little regard for his own personal safety. But Scott senses weakness in others. He takes an instant dislike to Constable Henry Headley, who had been one of the first Wagga Wagga troopers to retreat at Wantabadgery and sprint to that nearby swamp when Scott and Nesbitt had advanced on them.

It is Headley who is adamant Scott shot Webb-Bowen. 'The prisoner Scott was standing outside the kitchen door. I saw him aim his gun at Bowen and fire. Bowen fell, saying "Oh Cassin . . . My God . . . I am shot . . ." I am sure Scott aimed at Bowen. I was not 10 yards from Bowen at the time and was watching the prisoner Scott at the time.'

Scott cross-examines Headley. He cannot disguise his contempt for the man. When Headley says he is certain the rifle Scott used to shoot Webb-Bowen was the same one Scott used during his attack on the troopers at Wantabadgery, Scott sneers and mentions how Headley was so scared he had run at the first sign of danger.

'I did not run away at Wantabadgery as fast as my legs could carry me.'

The magistrate warns Scott not to bully or denigrate witnesses.

'I did not call the witness a coward, nor did I call your Worship a bully,' says Scott. 'But I can think what I like.'

Love begins to ask Headley a few questions of his own, queries that Scott suspects are attempts by the magistrate to provide the trooper with excuses for his actions at Wantabadgery.

Scott is already in a surly mood and Love's intervention has ignited that wild drop.

'You don't know how to conduct yourself on the bench, Sir,' announces Scott.

An astonished silence descends on the court. 'You are putting leading questions to the witness. Don't sit there as a prosecutor and not as a judge or I will disgrace you through the length and breadth of the land.'

It's certain that Love has never been spoken to like this before, not even on the raucous floor of parliament. Before he can splutter and interrupt, Scott continues to scold him.

'Keep yourself quiet. Conduct yourself with proper decency as a justice of the peace. Don't dare to interfere with my witness, Sir. Do you think I fear you? You have no brains or anything else.'

Love finally responds to the diatribe. Many are expecting him to order Scott to stand down. Instead he warns him that, if he continues with this abuse, 'I shall stop you from cross-examining and not suffer you to put a question to the witness at all. I will not suffer this to continue.'

'Your Worship, I know the law.'

'I will have none of your bravado,' says Love.

'It's going to be exchanged for a little of your bravado, your worship . . . conduct yourself properly, Sir. Just conduct yourself properly.'

The magistrate, unused to such impudence, says if Scott does not conduct himself properly he will not permit any further cross-examination of the witness.

Now his blood is up again. Scott suggests the magistrate should conduct himself 'like a gentleman and a justice of the peace, not as a special inquisitor'.

Love orders the witness to stand down.

—

When court resumes the next morning Scott is contrite. He turns to Love and says: 'I apologise for the unseemly remarks I made yesterday. My temper was ruffled by the fact of my best friend Nesbitt lying in a dishonoured grave, and my having lost my liberty, all within the last three days. I will endeavour to conduct my case temperately.'

And he does his best, even when he is allowed to recall Headley and the constable sticks to his story that Scott shot Webb-Bowen. In fact, Headley has even more detail to provide. He identifies the breech-loading Snider rifle as the weapon wielded by Scott during the shootout. 'I heard Constable Bowen say that you shot him. Bowen said: "Moonlite shot me with a rifle." I cannot swear to seeing either of the other three prisoners firing that day.'

On the strength of Headley's evidence the four are committed to Darlinghurst Gaol in Sydney to stand trial for shooting with intent to murder Webb-Bowen. But other charges are also pending. There is the indictment of robbery under arms. One of the first witnesses called is the Chinese contractor Ah Goon, whose silver watch and two pounds, five shillings in cash had been taken from him by Nesbitt at Wantabadgery. Ah Goon is sworn in by being asked to blow out a match, a common practice believed by colonial courts to reflect Chinese customs. In some Australian courts Chinese witnesses are also allowed to swear an oath by shattering plates or beheading chickens.

The McDonald brothers also testify. Much of it is complimentary about the manner in which Scott treated his hostages. Claude identifies the clothing taken by the bushrangers and agrees the man had shown a great deal of chivalry. 'Scott asked my brother for five pounds and said if he was not given it, it would not be forced from him.

My brother gave the five pounds. If refused I do not believe it would have been taken by force.' Scott, he says, had treated him with politeness 'all the time you were sticking up the station'.

When Falconer's deposition is read to the court, Scott wants to make it clear the women hostages were at all times treated with respect. 'I should not be surprised if when I am dead and gone it is said I insulted women.'

Throughout the three days Scott does his best to entertain the crowd. But whenever Nesbitt's name is mentioned, Captain George loses his composure. Sometimes he pauses and swallows deeply. Other times he openly weeps. No-one is left in any doubt the pair had an unusually close and intimate attachment.

When the four are committed for trial on the charge of robbery under arms, Scott asks Love for a short adjournment in order to prepare his defence on a host of other charges. Love denies the request. Scott mutters something under his breath and the magistrate tells him he has already been given more latitude than any barrister could normally expect. In fact, he says, if any lawyer in his court used the sort of language he had been hearing from Scott, he would be turned out of court.

'Well, your Worship,' says Scott. 'I wish you would turn me out of it – and if I thought you would I would use much stronger language.'

The court erupts in laughter.

Scott is weary and looks haggard. But such a warm reaction reinvigorates him. Now he has their attention it is time for one of his sweeping monologues. 'This is a case of importance to me, but more to the prisoners who are here with me,' he says. 'I do not stand here to defend these prisoners; I only wish to speak the truth.

'I am aware that vague, uncertain and false rumours are afloat, and it is a matter of great importance to me that the public furore should not be directed towards me or towards the prisoners in the dock with me.

'The way to prevent that feeling from arising and from influencing our fate is to allow the public to know the truth, as the public mind will be influenced, and the influence brought to bear on the public mind must to a certain extent affect my fate.'

Off he goes. Another chance to place on the record the shameful treatment he and others have suffered within the corrupt penal system. The constant harassment by police. The absurd charges that proved to be false. The inability of innocent men to be free of pro-secution. The days of hunger and misery. Their appalling treatment at the hands of the sneering William Baynes at Wantabadgery. The poor decision born out of frustration and empty stomachs to hold up the station. The comical shootout with the retreating Wagga troopers where 'I courted death, hoping that a stray shot might end my life and that the prisoners, my friends, might give themselves up to the Crown.

'At Wantabadgery they had run to a certain extent, but I blame the man who ran first [Headley] and I could and will afterwards point out those that deserve credit and those who deserve everlasting disgrace. The man deserves to be handed down to infamy who is a coward in the field and a hero in the witness box, who cannot use his carbine and who swears a lie with his hand on the Book.'

Magistrate Love has heard enough. He will not allow the prisoner to speak about any witness in this manner. Scott barely draws breath.

'I am only saying that a man under such circumstances deserves disgrace . . . at the fight at Wantabadgery I courted death. I was not so important as my friends are – one as good a friend as ever lived, with as soft a heart and as kind . . . .'

The crowd watches Scott become emotional again. 'He prevented bloodshed by taking that duck-shot gun from me when I could have fired from it. If a victim has to suffer I should like to do so and hold these lads innocent. I alone commanded, and these boys did as I bid them.

'But though not guilty of the blood of anybody I am ready to suffer for their sake and answer for breaking the laws of this country. I wish the country to know this, and when I fill a dishonoured grave with my friends who sleep in your cemetery, I wish that their names shall not be handed down with ignominy. No fate shall draw a tear from my eye, for I fear no fate. I had kind friends, and they are gone, and I wish to follow them. But before I go let those who stand beside me go free.'

It's a speech verging on the Shakespearean, a merging of all his favourite themes. Honour. Dignity. Death. Some of the reporters can see sympathetic faces in the courtroom nodding in agreement with Scott. One of them will write that it was easy to see 'in the crowd behind the dock quite a number of sympathisers with every point made by Moonlite against the constituted authorities'.

'The facts of this case shall appear from north to south; from Tasmania to New Guinea the truth will ring,' says Scott. 'I will speak the truth faithfully and I will tell you, as a man who has not long to live, that the responsibility of this should rest on me. These men are guiltless. I have said all, your Worship.'

Love must be relieved. The prisoners will be transported to Sydney in the next day or two. But before they leave the case takes a dramatic twist.

Webb-Bowen dies just before dawn on Sunday morning, almost a week after being shot. He had been drifting in and out of consciousness for several days, still in pain and unable to move as the infection from the lead bullet took hold.

A police officer is dead. The charge against the bushrangers is now one of murder. This whole bloody mess began when six men ran out of hope. Now it is certain to end with a length of rope.

On one of his last nights inside Gundagai Gaol, Scott is told he has a visitor. It is Webb-Bowen's widow, Marion.

'I have come to forgive you,' she says.

'What for?'

'They say you shot my husband.'

'I did not,' says Scott. 'But I am perhaps morally responsible for his death. It is, however, very kind and noble of you to say that you forgive me, and I shall always feel indebted to you.'

28

EVIL BE TO HIM

There is time for some true gallows humour as the Moonlite gang begin their journey to Sydney for the trial that will determine their fate.

As the Cobb & Co coach sways and jolts on the first leg of the trip – the 35-mile road trip from Gundagai to Cootamundra – Scott keeps his heavily ironed men amused by speculating about what sort of drop the hangman will require to finish them off.

The formula is not hard for a man used to doing complicated calculations in his head. Do the men know they have an Irishman to thank for such information? It seems only fitting that a man from an island so cursed by death and torture would dwell on the physics of hanging a man.

It had only been a decade earlier when a Dublin scientific writer and prominent philanthropist, the Reverend Samuel Haughton, published his revolutionary paper 'On hanging considered from a Mechanical and Physiological point of view'. Haughton had long been dismayed by the often sloppy and unscientific approach taken by executioners. For centuries they had been putting a rope around their victims' necks and letting gravity do its work. But any scientist knew gravity was the weakest of nature's forces. It was why so many botched executions ended with relatives or even the hangman pulling down on the victim's legs to try and end a slow and ugly strangulation.

Why not improve the downward energy necessary to break the neck between the second and fifth vertebrae by simply creating a longer drop? Haughton's equation was simple if you could do the math. The drop needed? Divide 1260 pounds – the 'striking force' needed to dislocate the neck – by the body weight of the prisoner in pounds.

The coach rocks and tilts. Scott does the sums. He will need a drop of about five and a half feet. He does the same exercise for Bennett, who also finds humour in the grim calculations.

'I'm going to perform some gymnastic exercises,' he announces. He will foil the hangman by flipping himself over at the last moment.

'I shall have the pleasure of supporting my body with my head.'

—

The telegraph wires have been humming. The Moonlite gang is on its way to Sydney.

The first crowd appears outside the Cootamundra lock-up. More gather when they are taken to the railway station to be placed in the prison carriage 'which resembles a lion's cage, having strong iron bars all round inside . . .'

A man in the throng of spectators on the platform calls out that Scott should be hauled away and lynched. A reporter watches Scott's blue eyes flash 'defiance upon the utterer'.

Scott snarls and calls the man a coward. Would he dare say such a thing if Scott was not so heavily ironed? Constable Gorman – the man who shot Nesbitt – is one of the police guarding the prisoners. Scott has an obvious distaste for the trooper. But he asks him to punch the man in the eye on his behalf.

The crowds continue to grow at each station as the train chugs its way over the hills and across the plains. It might be late at night but they have come from their farms and small shacks to catch a glimpse of 'these bloodthirsty wretches' and 'notorious desperadoes'.

When they stop at Murrumburrah, Scott hears a voice on the crowded platform call out in the darkness for the bushrangers to be lynched.

'Give me a rifle,' he says. 'I would like to see who would lynch me then.'

Not long after sunrise the following morning the train pulls in to Sydney at Redfern station. There are people everywhere – hundreds of them pushing and jostling and craning for a glimpse. They line the overhead bridge. They cling to iron gates. Some have climbed on top of neighbouring carriages for a better view. Those who cannot see have to be satisfied with the sound of clanking chains as the manacled men, capable only of small steps, hobble from the prison carriage to their Black Maria – the horse-drawn van that will take them to Darlinghurst Gaol.

Few fail to notice the black hearse parked nearby as the bushrangers are helped into the van. Its driver has risen early in order to cast an eye on the outlaws before heading off for another day's work hauling the dead.

—

Less than an hour later the horse-drawn prison van pulls up outside the entrance of Darlinghurst Gaol in Forbes Street.

For two years in the early 1820s gangs of chained convicts carved and hauled more than 30,000 tons of sandstone from nearby quarries to the top of Woolloomooloo Hill. Sydney was a prison town and a new grand gaol would sit on one of its highest points. Every block stained with the sweat of those convicts would tell a story; to keep tally of their work, the men scratched a 'darg' or mark into each stone that would remain for centuries.

Behind these etched, weathered walls lies a prison unequalled anywhere in the colony for brutality and cruelty. The Latin inscription above the main gate translates to 'Evil be to him who evil thinks'. But the horrors are not just restricted to within this sandstone crypt. They begin at the front door. Scott and his men will be taken through the front entrance where, overhead and in full view of the public, Alexander Green, the gaol's first hangman, carried out some of his best work.

Green was a Dutchman, the son of a circus performer, and had been transported for life in 1824 for stealing a 'piece of brown stuff from a shop'. He was a short man with enormous strength. His work as a flogger at the first Sydney gaol down by The Rocks had so impressed officials that within a few years they appointed him public executioner and awarded him the grand sum of 15 pounds a year to rid the colony of its offenders.

The work was constant. During one three-year stint under the tyrannical governorship of Ralph Darling, Green hanged 170 victims. He rarely complained. It was bloody work but 'The Finisher' revelled in his reputation for efficiency. He was an expert with the rope and a good judge of his victim's weight. Of course, a man could never be perfect. Some twisted and jerked and died painfully and slowly. But a busy man could be forgiven for the odd miscalculation. Green was prolific – one of the hardest working executioners in the western world. Best estimates had his tally of victims at close to 500, including 10 bushrangers in Bathurst in 1830 and the seven stockmen responsible for the Myall Creek massacre of up to 50 Aboriginal people in 1838.

When the new gaol at Darlinghurst was finally opened in 1841, Green had become a free man. But there was no escaping his line of work. Outside and above those front gates, where the public could gather and holler and approve of the law's ultimate penalty, Green continued to dispatch his victims with brutal efficiency. The first had been John Knatchbull, a naval captain convicted of murdering a woman for her purse. Green had not been at his best that day. Perhaps the crowd of more than 10,000 people had made him nervous. 'After ascending the gallows it took but little time on the part of the hangman to adjust the rope which, having been done, the bolt was drawn and the wretched culprit launched into eternity. He seemed to suffer a great deal, as he shook violently from head to foot, particularly in the lower extremities, which trembled . . .'

Everyone knew Green by sight. His skin was pocked, his teeth worn down to small, discoloured stubs. But it was the angry red scar running down the side of the executioner's face that no-one ever forgot, a constant reminder of how he had only just survived an axe attack by a fellow prisoner.

But for all of Green's apparent confidence – he was known to strut and swagger as he went about his work on the gallows – the grisly business began to wear him down. The cumulative effect of all that death and sorrow ran deep. Not even frequent bouts of drinking could drown out the hundreds of strangled voices that echoed inside his head.

He had been given a small whitewashed hut to live in just outside the gaol's eastern walls. But executioners were always doomed to be pariahs when not on the gallows and he was forced to take a room inside the prison when a group of larrikins burned his shack down.

He slowly turned insane and by the middle of the 1850s had been committed to an asylum. Alexander Green's ultimate sentence was to endure a long life tortured by his work. He never spoke again and would often be found in his room hanging toy dolls.

'He is . . . robust and very active,' a visitor to the asylum in 1877 will say about the old man with the livid scar. 'He always carries a piece of cord and at every visit he indicates by gesture that he would like to hang one of the officers. He produces his noose and points to the left ear, at the same time giving a click with his tongue and a final quiver of the feet, and plays many absurd tricks.'

—

George Scott has now seen the inside of several prisons and knows how easily they can break a man's spirit. Hadn't Weechurch been worn down by Pentridge and all those weeks in the black hole of solitary confinement?

But this place seems darker, more menacing. He and his men are guided through the entrance beneath the very place where the body of Knatchbull had quivered almost four decades earlier. Their chains clank as they are led down a dozen stone steps into a darkened tunnel. At the end of it they find themselves in a room where they are washed, deloused and then locked in their cells.

But Scott, worn and haggard after more than a week of court hearings and travelling, will not be able to rest. There will be a preliminary court hearing the next morning and a trial date is to be set for the following week on 3 December. It is an absurdly short amount of time to prepare for a murder trial. The government is moving quickly. Not only must it assure the good citizens that it has this bushranging menace under control, but it needs to be *seen* to be moving swiftly.

Scott will only have four days to prepare for a hearing that will decide whether he lives or dies. And he must do it within the haunted walls of Darlinghurst Gaol, where the spirit of James Nesbitt dwells.

—

Richard Thatcher barely recognises George Scott. It has only been six months since he last saw him but everything has changed. The man who was always so well-groomed and immaculately dressed, who always had a handkerchief at the ready to dab his eye, is still wearing the clothes he was arrested in at McGledes'. The heavy moustache has been shaved and is only just beginning to grow back. He is certainly thinner, gaunt even.

But all the old bravado remains. Inside the walls of Darlinghurst Gaol, two days before the trial, Scott is cheerful and grateful to discover a little support.

He holds out a hand to Thatcher. 'This is indeed an unexpected pleasure,' he says.

Thatcher shakes Scott's hand almost mechanically. There is no warmth to the clasp because Thatcher has 'not the slightest sympathy for him as a criminal'. Besides, he has a point to make.

'Well, this is a nice game to get up to,' Thatcher says. 'Did I not warn you that you would get into some such scrape?'

Of course he did. How many times had Thatcher warned Scott about his entourage of suspicious-looking young men? How many times had he told him that giving speeches berating the penal system would give him nothing but grief and more attention from the police?

Still, he feels bound to show some support for the man he considered such an impressive figure when he first met him. So he has come to Sydney to speak up and Scott, of course, is quick to acknowledge such an act of gallantry.

'I'm delighted to see you,' he tells Thatcher. 'You are the only man who befriended me.'

It is Monday afternoon, 1 December, and Thatcher's prison visit has been organised by Robert Burdett Smith, Moonlite's solicitor. Smith has vouched for Thatcher's credentials. But what he has not told the prison authorities is that another man accompanying Thatcher, who claims to have known Scott in Victoria, is actually a reporter for *The Evening News*.

The reporter watches as Scott introduces Thatcher to Smith. The solicitor is a large moustachioed man with fleshy jowls who persists in parting his wiry, wavy hair straight down the middle. He is a man comfortable in the presence of prisoners. His father had been one of them – a horse-stealer sentenced to seven years in the colonies in the early 1830s. The son has worked hard to erase the family's convict past and now is one of the most prominent men in a town of men vying for prominence. A month earlier Smith, an independent member of the NSW Legislative Assembly, had sat on a podium in Hyde Park and proudly watched the unveiling of a statue of Captain James Cook, a monument he had spent years campaigning to have erected.

'Mr Thatcher gave me a helping hand and took me round with my lectures . . .' Scott tells Smith, before conceding '. . . which I am sure was a losing game.'

The reporter moves off. Bennett, Williams and Rogan are sitting on a bed, legs dangling over the side, immersed in newspaper articles about their exploits and laughing and chiding one another about the various illustrations depicting their likenesses.

'Their appearance is anything but repulsive and ferocious,' the reporter will write the following day. 'In fact, they have the appearance of well-bred boys, belonging to good families.'

Williams tells the journalist how Scott had advertised for an amanuensis – an assistant to take dictation and transcribe some of his written speeches.

'Did Scott pay you for your work?'

'Not much, if any,' says Williams.

'Then it was a labour of love with you?'

Smith interrupts the conversation. 'I am trying to save the necks of these three boys,' he tells the reporter. 'This boy, Williams, belongs to a respectable family in Ballarat . . . .' Smith says he has already summonsed the mayor of Ballarat and the superintendent of Williams' Sunday School to speak for him.

The journalist asks Bennett if he was wounded and the young man pulls up his shirt sleeve to show his bandaged arm – along with a tattoo. He tells the reporter how he used to be a sailor who arrived in Melbourne two years earlier and jumped ship.

Then it is Rogan's turn to be quizzed. He says he is a bootmaker. The reporter is puzzled.

'Allow me to look at your hand. It is too soft and white for a bootmaker's.'

'I am nevertheless one,' says Rogan.

Scott has been talking quietly with Thatcher. He has been telling him about the trek that led to Wantabadgery, how hungry they had been and how Baynes' arrogance was the last straw that led to the siege. But he also has something else to confide.

He has been seeing something strange. Nesbitt's ghost has been frequently appearing in his cell.

Thatcher is sceptical. He knows how shrewd Scott can be. The judge listed to sit on the case is Justice William Charles Windeyer – the brother of Walter, the previous owner of the Wantabadgery Station who had given his homestead such a wide reputation for looking after itinerant travellers. Thatcher has heard that Windeyer is a man of his times, a committed spiritualist with a strong belief in the dead's ability to communicate with the living. Might this be a ploy by Scott to win the sympathy of the judge?

Scott is insistent. Nesbitt's ghostly visage has been standing there, right in front of him. Scott asks Thatcher for a few favours. He would like paper collars supplied so he and his men can at least look partly respectable when they appear in court. He also wants his boys to have an increased food allowance because they will need their strength.

And one more thing. Could Thatcher obtain the bloodied clothes James Nesbitt was wearing when he died? He wants them for his own cerecloth.

After they hang him, they can bury Andrew George Scott in the clothing of the man he loved so much.

—

The Evening News interview with the Moonlite gang is the talk of the town. Honourable members of parliament rise to their feet and denounce its publication as a means of stirring public sympathy for the bushrangers. The other newspapers also attack the publication for more selfish reasons.

There is a serious game being played here and the old boys club that dominates Sydney politics and cultural life is horrified. They have been outmanoeuvred just when it seemed they had put everything in place to secure a speedy trial.

With the appointment of Justice William Windeyer, they have a belligerent and combative man well known for sympathising with the victims of crime. Those who suggest the man might be conflicted, simply because his brother once owned the very sheep station at the heart of the case, can be damned. They have appointed Robert Wisdom to lead the prosecution. Wisdom is the current Attorney-General for the colony. Windeyer previously held that position and both men – favourites of Sir Henry Parkes – know each other well. It's a cosy little set-up and Smith's little effort at improving the image of the bushrangers has not gone down well.

Questions are asked. Inquiries are made. A flurry of correspondence is forwarded to the parliament. The Principal Gaoler, John Read, lays the blame on Smith, 'who said it was absolutely necessary for the defence that these gentlemen should see the prisoners'.

What has galled those in power most, however, are surely the comments of Captain Moonlite himself. Scott has already signalled he will defend himself and that Smith will work on behalf of his three young supporters. *The Evening News* report had carried a quote of Scott's admiring the diligence of Smith and how 'if I had the pick of the whole legal profession in Sydney I would take you if I required anyone to act for me'.

It's a quote that is a shameless show of gratitude by the reporter toward Smith for securing the interview. By the standards and practices of Sydney's ruling class, it is also understandable and forgivable.

But the quote that followed it is not.

The reporter had allowed Scott to question the entire process. The man had the temerity to suggest the fix was in.

'I am not prepared with my defence,' Scott had said. 'I have not even received the depositions. Undue haste is being shown in my case and if they hang me now, it will be judicial murder.'

29

THE TRIAL

Look at how hard they have worked to remove those stubborn convict stains. Is there any city in the world so committed to erasing its past?

For months they cleaned the streets, hung flags and built rostrums. They brought in world-class engineers to install a new-fangled steam-powered tram network. They hauled more than two million bricks and four million feet of timber down to the Royal Botanic Gardens, where teams of architects and tradesmen worked night and day for eight months to construct the majestic Garden Palace.

A visitor could be excused for thinking they had stumbled on to an ancient cathedral in the heart of Rome. Look at those soaring towers. That enormous white domed roof.

And not a stone carved by a sweating convict to be seen.

No-one can call Sydney a prison town any more. She's a lady now, a cultured and iridescent member of the world community. Yes, there have been the usual cynics sneering at the reasons for this transformation. Nothing but bread and circuses, they say. This staging of the Sydney International Exhibition, which has drawn 23 countries to display their latest advances in technology and the arts, is little more than an attempt by a troubled government to distract the public from its problems.

And well it might be. It has been pulled together in haste in part to beat Melbourne's attempt at a World Fair the following year. But who can argue with these crowds? They have come to see rare Italian statues and watch war dances staged by Fijian natives said to have only recently renounced their cannibalistic ways. They can drink exotic Teutonic beer in the Austro-Hungarian hall, nibble on the finest European cheeses and gaze upon newly designed bicycles known as velocipedes and wonder how on earth anyone could manage to ride such a machine through the hills of Sydney.

It has all been going swimmingly well these past eight weeks. Damn fine show, actually. Until those bushrangers turned up to remind all these distinguished international visitors that the colony's true past was rooted in crime and desperation.

Now there is a new spectacle in town. On Wednesday the 3rd of December, thousands gather outside the Central Criminal Court, all hankering for admission, all trying to talk their way through the doors so they can take a seat for the trial of the Wantabadgery outlaws.

But unless they have a ticket they will have to remain outside under the careful eye of a group of mounted troopers. The Sheriff's department has printed 1300 passes and those who know how things work in this city have secured for themselves the best seats.

Behind a railing in the courtroom close to the bench sit the distinguished visitors. Wedged among the various members of parliament and curious magistrates, all eager to see how William Windeyer will handle the difficult and often explosive Scott, are several visiting international dignitaries.

All of them, drawn to this crowded courtroom to gain a glimpse of, and listen to, this Captain Moonlite they have heard so much about.

—

Robert Wisdom, the colony's Attorney-General and chief prosecutor for the trial, is a large man, his thick, jowly face supported by a wide neck, wider shoulders, a broad chest and a stout belly. He shares Sir Henry Parkes' passion for verse. He has been penning sonnets since childhood and offers them regularly under a pseudonym to the Sydney newspapers. But Wisdom is admired far more for his political abilities than his literary skills.

'Like the great man [Parkes], he was a lover of poetry but a writer of doggerel,' one historian will unkindly note.

When Wisdom gets to his feet at the start of the trial perhaps there is a part of him, given the large captive audience in the courtroom, that would love to regale the crowd with one of his original poems:

Come fly with me my love to some quiet shady grove
Where the gay wild flowers are springing love

But it is not the spectators who are here to be punished. Wisdom has a far weightier – but just as tortuous – collection of words to read to the jury. It is the law that lies at the heart of the trial of these Wantabadgery bushrangers: 'Where several persons are together for the purpose of committing a breach of the peace, assaulting persons who pass and, while acting together in that common object, a fatal blow is given, it is immaterial which struck the blow, for the blow given under such circumstances is in point of law the blow of all, and it is unnecessary to prove which struck the blow.'

The bar has been set and it is a low one. Scott will spend these next four long days prosecuting witnesses and forensically examining bullet calibres and guns. But it will matter little who fired the weapon that killed Webb-Bowen. The Crown need prove only that it could not have been police crossfire for all four bushrangers to be found guilty of murder.

If the trial has been staged with almost unprecedented haste, it will proceed at much the same pace. Justice Windeyer is on a mission to get the required verdict as quickly as possible. Scott and the defence team for his men put forward an extensive case for an adjournment until February, claiming the overwhelmingly hostile press coverage means it is impossible to assemble a jury that will not have heard of the siege. How could any remain fair and impartial? They cite several precedents – including a case when Windeyer himself won a similar judgement.

To support this argument Scott lodges an affidavit incorporating all of his favourite themes; the prejudice of the local press who have branded him as the 'notorious criminal Scott', a 'scoundrel' and an 'incorrigible villain'. He states he is not prepared for his defence – 'the depositions of the witnesses for the Crown have only been supplied to me lately – some, indeed, were only delivered to me in the afternoon of yesterday'.

It is a compelling argument. But Wisdom opposes any postponement of the trial and Justice Windeyer is quick to agree.

—

There will be few victories for Scott and his men in the courtroom. But one of them will come from the Gundagai doctor, Robert McKillop. When Webb-Bowen died McKillop had told the committal hearing that the bullet he found lodged near the trooper's spine came from a rifle. But in Sydney he changes his evidence, saying he is now certain it came from a Colt revolver. A weapons expert will also support McKillop's evidence. It blows apart the police evidence – including two officers who swear they saw Scott shoot Webb-Bowen with a rifle.

But such a small win is of little comfort. Justice Windeyer becomes visibly distressed when mention is made of Wantabadgery – the pride of his brother who died earlier in the year.

Windeyer also has little time for forensic detail or Scott's cross-examination methods. When Scott interrogates one of the constables who claims he saw Captain Moonlite shoot Webb-Bowen with a Snider rifle, Scott begins by asking the trooper about the events at Wantabadgery earlier that day. Windeyer interrupts, telling Scott he has not been charged with any violation of the law at that station, but with committing murder at the McGledes' farm.

Scott: 'If I can prove to your Honour and the jury that the witness is perjuring himself in his evidence upon matters at Wantabadgery, it is proof that he might perjure himself in his evidence of what took place at McGledes'.'

Windeyer: 'I fail to see how your questions will prove perjury in any respect. If I thought your line of cross-examination could do your case any good I would not think of interfering with you.'

At the end of the third day, a tired Scott asks the judge to allow him to begin with his defence witnesses the following morning. 'At this hour of the night I am unable to speak or open a defence. I cannot enter into such voluminous depositions tonight, and would very earnestly and respectfully beg of your Honour to adjourn, and allow me to look through these depositions tomorrow morning.

'Since this trial has commenced I have been long hours here, and when out of the dock have been confined in my cell, and have not had one minute's time to look through the depositions or over my notes. I am physically unable to go on tonight . . . I throw myself on the Court, and ask you to adjourn the case till the usual hour tomorrow morning.'

Windeyer is having none of it. 'It is not at all usual to adjourn . . . I have had to conduct a defence myself after midnight.'

Scott tells him he has been on confined rations. 'I remain in the dock until the court rises and I am in again before the court sits. I am taken out and brought in by the police and have only a few minutes left to myself and therefore have had no time to prepare my defence . . . I am physically and mentally unable to enter into my defence tonight with any hope of doing justice to myself . . .'

Even Wisdom says he does not oppose Scott's application for an adjournment.

Windeyer asks if Scott has any witnesses to call.

Scott: 'Yes, your Honour.'

Windeyer: 'Then I will take witnesses tonight.'

—

The following day Scott launches into an impassioned two-hour address to the jury. There are matters concerning his *honour* and *dignity* that require addressing. His life has not been one long stretch of premeditated crime, but an unfortunate sequence of events peppered by constant police harassment and false claims. He goes into depth about the events at Wantabadgery and McGledes' and how the young men with him were simply following his orders.

There are men on the jury, says Scott, who are surely fathers themselves and understand how one rash act might lead to their own sons appearing in such a dock. Therefore they should apply that old rule to those young men who had simply been doing what he told them: 'Whatsoever ye would that others should do unto you, do ye unto them.'

He says he is disappointed that Rogan hid under the bed at McGledes' and has already told the young man that he holds him responsible for James Nesbitt's death; Rogan could have shot Constable Gorman before he fired the fatal shot at Nesbitt, a man whose life he would have done anything to save, even if it meant shooting a dozen persons, his Honour included. Several of the police were not only cowards who had run at the first sight of Scott advancing on them, but had been willing to perjure themselves.

But he keeps returning to Rogan, Bennett and Williams.

'If the law has been so broken that it must be avenged by a human life, then let me be the victim and spare these youths – God created them for something nobler than the gallows.'

In the Ladies Gallery several women are dabbing handkerchiefs at their eyes. At least one has begun to weep loudly. Bennett and Williams are sobbing.

The case continues until 11pm when Windeyer finally calls an adjournment. The following morning his Honour sums up and his directions to the jury are unmistakeably clear.

They will, he says, have no difficulty in concluding that the fatal shot was fired not by the police or some of the volunteers supporting them during the battle at McGledes', but it was 'fired by one of the party who were there engaged in resisting the police'.

When the case resumes after lunch, Scott says he understands that a member of the jury, John Stroh, does not understand written English. If the man is an alien or cannot understand the evidence, Scott must object to the man's presence on the jury.

Windeyer: 'You cannot submit that point now.'

Scott: 'I desire to be tried by a jury of my own countrymen.'

Windeyer: 'So far as I know the gentleman is competent to sit on the jury. Seven years' residence would be sufficient.'

Scott: 'I understand that the gentleman has not been here seven years.'

Windeyer: 'That will be for you to prove.'

When Windeyer returns to his summing up, John Want, the barrister for Williams, Rogan and Bennett, also interrupts to say one of the jury is clearly not a British subject and 'evidently could not understand what his Honour was saying'.

Windeyer says such an issue 'should have been mentioned earlier' and that he 'had nothing whatever to do with that'.

When the jury retires to consider its verdict there is a long discussion in the court about the juryman's nationality and ability to understand the evidence given over the past four days. Want questions whether a large amount of evidence tendered to the trial was admissible and argues there are grounds for the jury to be dismissed because of Stroh's inability to understand the language.

Windeyer merely says he will make a note about the objections.

Two hours later the jury returns with a clear verdict. All four prisoners are guilty. But they recommend mercy for Rogan, Bennett and Williams.

—

Do the prisoners have anything to say before judgement is passed? No-one is surprised when Scott is first to his feet. Clearly, he says, public opinion has been against the prisoners ever since they arrived handcuffed in Gundagai. Yet Nesbitt was the kindest and gentlest soul he had ever known and because he himself had no fear of death he could now 'follow a brave and true spirit to eternity'.

Scott thanks the jury for their recommendation of mercy for the three others and that he hopes Windeyer will act on their counsel. 'Do not let them remain so long in gaol – in a living tomb – that when they come out they have no hope for the future.'

And then Scott summons up his remaining strength for one final speech. It might be the finest of his life.

'Your church bells toll on Sundays, and you all preach charity. But tell me. Where does that charity exist? Do you not all disgrace the name of Jesus Christ? Show me the number of homeless children in your streets, and the number of prisoners that pass from Darlinghurst and meet with no charity.

'You may give your sixpences, and your names are put in the paper. But who goes and speaks one kindly word, or tells them to look up with hope? Don't run them to misery and the gallows. Don't issue tickets when human beings with immortal souls are in danger – are being tried for their lives – as if they were on exhibition.

'Pass a law that when a prisoner is charged before a criminal court that no evidence be published, that no remarks be published; brand as a murderer any person who in print will put a slander about a man in the dock.'

Scott points to Rogan. 'This young fellow there I saw once in Melbourne and not having a farthing in his pocket, he took his coat off his back, went and pledged it, and gave me the money. He followed me, would have worked for me and has come to the dock and perhaps the grave with me.'

Scott is crying now, wiping away tears.

'Men who swear lies are not the men to be entrusted with the safety of your colony. Constables watch the criminals but you do not watch the constables. I know what I have said of your penal establishments to be truth, and tell you, as a dying man, I have experienced it. Before your dignitaries visit a gaol a telegram is sent to the official and everything is prepared to receive them, and no-one but themselves and the poor prisoners know what is practised there.

'Talk about protection and free trade – look at the former in a criminal point of view. If he leaves the colony he is arrested and convicted for being in another whereas if he remains he is hunted by the police. The only resting place is the dock and the gallows where I am going.

'Make your reformatories real reformatories. Don't teach the inmates that they must be at war with society. Don't teach them to look upon a judge as the greatest savage in creation.'

Despite his exhaustion, Scott recites a verse from Longfellow's 'A Psalm of Life'.

Lives of great men still remind us,
We can make our lives sublime,
And, departing, leave behind us,
Footprints on the sand of time.

Scott: 'Though I stand on the verge of eternity, I assert that there is a sand upon which I will leave my footprints.

'I regret that I have broken the laws of the country but I regret far more the fact that poor Nesbitt lies in his grave than the brave Bowen lies in his. I am sorry for Bowen but more sorry for Nesbitt and Wernicke, and far more for these boys beside me.

'I am not mad and never was mad. You have all brought me to the gallows and left me there and I will die a man looking at God, fearless of my fate. If it is not wrong for me to make the request, I should like my body to be given to my friends. Is that right, your Honour?'

Windeyer says he has nothing to say to such a suggestion.

'Is it outside the law? Is it a necessary part of your sentence that I should be buried within the precincts of the gaol?'

'It is not part of the sentence,' says Windeyer. 'It rests entirely with the Executive.'

'I should like to make the request because I should like my body to be buried in Gundagai. I think I have some friends who will send it up there, if it is not much expense.'

Rogan is then allowed to address the court. He is brief. He is thankful to the jury, he says, for recommending mercy for himself, Williams and Bennett. But he wants to make something very clear. George Scott has been represented as a notorious villain. But in all his time with him, the man had shown himself to be straightforward and honest.

Justice Windeyer has been sitting through all of this, his temper rising. He has listened to Scott's eloquent speech and put up with all his posturing throughout the trial. Now it is time for Scott to hear a few hard truths.

'The evidence shows that from the time you commenced this career of crime – and when you thought you had arrived sufficiently far in the interior of this country to be away from the supervision of the police and those whose duty it is to maintain the law – your whole course has been marked by a determination to outrage and abuse all those who opposed you.

'Your whole career is marked by conduct as outrageous and as horrible as ever disgraced any band of bushrangers in this country. That you should act as you did – shooting Beveridge's horse and brutally outraging those persons as you did . . . was one of the most shocking and horrible outrages ever perpetrated by a band of bushrangers.

'Pricking a man with a knife and kicking him – outraging him in that manner is as brutal conduct as ever was committed by any felon that ever stood in that dock. And you have the hardihood to stand there and say that you have done nothing you are ashamed of?'

'I apologise,' says Scott.

Windeyer: 'I will not be interrupted! It is an outrage to hear any man in your position speak as you have spoken. You have that veneer of education, that facility of speech, and capacity for theatrical exhibition which deceive those who are ignorant in the ways of the world.

'But they do not deceive me or any sensible man. They will not impose upon any but those who sympathise with crime. The exhibition we have seen from you did nothing but indicate your bad and malignant heart.'

Windeyer has worked himself into a fury. The pitch of his voice has risen and he has to pause several times to regain control.

'With all your affectation of bravery and the rest, what do I see? I see you attack everybody who went against you. You have accused these young men, who have given their evidence as fairly and honestly as anybody of witnesses in a court of justice could ... you have branded them with perjury ... no-one could doubt that you started deliberately from the neighbouring colony with this band of young men, and apparently from a natural love of crime, commenced a course of plunder and violence in this country.'

Windeyer turns to a piece of paper and reads the sentence.

'The sentence of the court is upon you Andrew George Scott, upon you Thomas Rogan, upon you Thomas Williams, and upon you Graham Bennett, that you be ... taken hence to the place whence you came, and on an appointed day hereafter to be fixed for the purpose, to the place of execution, and that there each and all of you be hanged by the neck until your bodies be dead, and may God almighty help you to repent of your crimes.'

Windeyer has ignored the jury's recommendation. There is no hint of mercy for the three young men.

Scott rises and begins to say something but is ordered to be quiet. He tries to interject again.

Windeyer ignores him. He rises from the bench and walks out of the court. His work at removing another stain on the colony is done.

30

ALL THE BEAUTIFUL FLOWERS

Nosey Bob steps carefully. He holds a burning candle in one hand, its flickering light guiding his visitor along the path into his neat garden. The two men wander beneath an arch heavy with thick vines and grapes. Such a pity, says Bob, that the grapes are not quite ripe. But there are plenty of other sweet things to be found in the backyard of state executioner Robert Rice Howard.

He lifts the candle high so his visitor can peer into the darkness of this January evening. There is pride in his voice. A swelling of the chest. The fluttering flame reveals a garden bursting with swollen cabbages and row upon row of flowers, their fragrance filling the warm night air.

'If you ever come down in the daytime I'll give you as many as you like,' Bob tells his visitor. 'I can't see to pick 'em now. Just you fetch down your lady any day and whether I'm at home or abroad all you've got to do is say I sent you and you'll be given the flashest bouquet out.'

No-one in the suburb of Paddington can boast a garden like this. The man who is paid 12 pounds and 10 shillings a month to extinguish the lives of sinners is also expert at bringing life into the world.

It is a talent once shared by his late wife Jane. But even his prized garden must run a poor second to the job of raising his brood of boys and girls and ensuring they receive the education Jane would have demanded.

They can say what they like about how Robert Howard earns a living, but no-one can find fault with Nosey Bob's offspring.

'I bring up my children well,' he tells his visitor. 'I send 'em to school every day and the children belonging to the first gentleman in Paddington aren't neater, no cleaner, nor more mannerly. They always says "thank you" and "if you please" when they gets anything or wants anything.'

It might be the darkness. Or it might be Bob's tendency not to remember faces. What is certain is that Bob has no idea that the man he has taken into his garden and is now inviting into the parlour of his home is J. F. Archibald, the journalist who only six months before had followed him to Mudgee for the hanging of the young Aboriginal man, Alfred.

Archibald has moved on from *The Evening News* – he and a business partner are now preparing their first edition of a new weekly publication, *The Bulletin* – and he is determined to give readers a detailed account of the impending hanging of two of the Wantabadgery bushrangers.

Archibald needs something from Bob. Because of this, there is no way he will admit to being the man who described Robert Rice Howard on the day of Alfred's execution as 'frowsy . . . spider-legged, with arms like a gorilla, a flat face without a nose, and huge feet . . .'

That description had stuck in Bob's craw like few other insults hurled his way. He had considered launching a libel action. He had even consulted friends in high places (and enemies of *The Evening News*) like the great judge and former Lieutenant Governor Sir Alfred Stephen as well as the Premier Sir Henry Parkes, who both offered to back any court action.

But even though the comments had cost Bob work – other colonies and even New Zealand were often calling on his skills to dispatch their condemned – he had ultimately decided against it. Who needed more aggravation?

Now it is Archibald who needs Bob. He wants to gain access to Darlinghurst Gaol so he can report on the colony's latest execution and close the final chapter on the bushranging era. The public outcry over Alfred's hanging – all those thousands of protestors on the streets with their candles and cries over the injustice of it all – has spooked the colonial administration. As a result no newspapermen will be allowed to watch Captain Moonlite swing on Tuesday morning, the 20th of January. There will be no more articles about the harsh brutality of death at the end of a rope, or the brutal harshness of a noseless executioner.

Inside Bob's cottage Archibald admires the Bible sitting on a nearby table and a copy of Thomas Gainsborough's classic oil painting of 'The Blue Boy'. He is obsequious and careful not to give Bob any hint of his strong opposition to capital punishment.

'Do you think both these men will be hanged?' Archibald asks.

Nosey Bob isn't sure. 'Moonlite's sure to go but I don't know as Rogan will.'

Weeks of court appeals and pleas for clemency have come down to this: the architect of the Wantabadgery siege and its climactic shootout, George Scott, will be accompanied to the gallows by the man who never fired a shot in anger – Tom Rogan.

An appeal for clemency had centred on claims that Justice Windeyer had unduly influenced the jury. But the colony's Executive Council had determined 'that the sentence of the Law should not be interfered with'. On Christmas Eve, though, the new Governor, Lord Augustus Loftus, made it clear he would not sign the death warrants for Graham Bennett and Thomas Williams.

The two youngsters, he said, were mere 'striplings . . . [and] have never been committed before for any misdemeanour.

'Scott and Rogan are hardened criminals, who have already undergone conviction and punishment which has been without effect on them. Scott is undoubtedly the most guilty of all, for he was the planner, the instigator of the crime and the seducer of his young accomplices.

'There was no doubt organisation and premeditation on his part but it is not certain that his plans were clearly revealed to the younger prisoners. He commanded, they obeyed, whether willingly or from compulsion of fear is not clearly proved. They were led into the affray, their blood was heated, they had not the reflection and moral courage to draw back . . .'

Rogan, the young bootmaker with soft hands whose short criminal record consists of larceny and the theft of a horse, will hang alongside Scott for the offence of hiding beneath a cot in the McGlede hut. It is a decision still being debated in the pulpits and the press. But all that public and government fury that swirled around the trial has subsided. Petitions are being drawn up, sermons delivered and even the press is wondering if Rogan deserves a reprieve. But the clamour for leniency is nowhere near the level it reached six months earlier with Alfred's execution.

'I hope Rogan's reprieved,' Archibald tells Bob.

'Well, poor unfortunate devil, I hope he is.'

Archibald is taken aback. 'Then you don't particularly want to hang them both?'

'No indeed,' says Bob. 'Would you? I don't get any more for doing the work. It's a lot of trouble to me I can tell you. I spends all the time in preparations, for if anything goes wrong, here's the man as gets the blame. I've never had a mishap yet and I hope I never will have.'

Archibald senses an opening, an opportunity to get Bob to talk about his grisly work. 'What do you mean by a mishap?'

'Well, d'ye see, it wouldn't, for instance, do to put the knot under the chin. If you did that there would be the chance of scratching the man's neck and drawing blood, and if there was a single drop of blood the Press'd be down on me.'

Archibald expresses surprise that hanging a man requires such meticulous preparation.

'Oh ain't there!' says Bob. See, people have no appreciation for the subtleties and science required to send a victim plummeting through the trapdoor.

'I tell you there's a lot of trouble. The night before I fixes all the things as I remember, and then I takes my pipe in my mouth and I walks up and down and says to myself "Is there anything more?" and if there's anything more I thinks of it.

'It doesn't do to get flurried, for the day you gets flurried that's the day as you makes the mistake. And then when I sees the people walking in I thinks again and makes sure that everything's as nice and ready as a kid glove.'

Any decent journalist knows that one of the quickest ways of disarming an interview subject is to get them talking about their passions. It never fails. Even the shyest and most modest of men will become expansive. Archibald can see the enthusiasm of the man. Who in polite society ever dares to even imagine – let alone ask – what skills and subtle intricacies are required to bring a man's life to an end? From here it will be nothing for Archibald to ask Bob to get him into Darlinghurst Gaol. And sure enough, Bob promises he will secure a couple of passes from the Sheriff.

His work is almost done. Archibald stares across the room and studies the noseless face of Bob in the flickering candlelight.

'What do you think of Scott as a man?' he asks him. 'Do you think he'll be afraid of you?'

Bob considers the question. He is yet to meet Scott or Rogan. He prefers it that way. He is always given the condemned prisoners' height and weight well before execution day. Who knows how they might react if they were told the hangman was paying them a visit. And with two men standing next to each other on the gallows . . . well, you can never quite predict just how things might go.

'Well, it all depends,' says Bob. 'If him and Rogan have to stand up together and swing together, I think he'll not be much frightened. But if he loses his mate – that is to say if Rogan's let clear – he'll . . . not be the same man. There's a lot in company.'

—

Could they have chosen a crueller day to hang him? The 20th of January will be the 65th birthday of George Scott's father, Thomas. Hasn't the man suffered enough?

George may have his shortcomings – and many consider a lack of self-awareness to be high on the list – but even he is only too aware of the pain and grief he has caused his family.

Thomas and Bessie have stayed in touch and sent word through an old friend from New Zealand that he is in their prayers and not forgotten. But surely a day must never pass without them dwelling on how quickly they have fallen.

From those heights in Rathfriland – the manor at the very top of the hill, the positions of influence and respect – to life as a poorly paid Christian minister in a far-flung outpost of the empire with a son soon to hang from a rope like a common tawdry criminal.

It defies belief. What has a family devoted to the Lord and to justice done to deserve such a descent? It must surely have tested Thomas Scott's faith because his son's belief in a benevolent God has also been challenged and found wanting.

Today, the eighth day of January in the Year of Our Lord, 1880, is George Scott's 35th birthday. He has spent most of it in much the same way as every other day since the trial ended, hunched over a small table in his death cell, furiously writing on whatever scrap of paper he can obtain. There are people to farewell, memories to share and gratitude to be expressed to those who have helped or supported him down the years.

One of them is Claude McDonald, the young brother of Falconer. Scott was captivated with the man from the moment they met during that first tense evening at Wantabadgery. There had been an instant connection, something almost approaching what he had felt for James Nesbitt, and his esteem for Claude has only grown since then.

It was Claude who had ensured Nesbitt's body had been treated with care and buried in Gundagai. It was Claude who had visited George on one of his first nights in the Gundagai Gaol and warned him he should prepare for death and to face his God.

Scott is running out of paper on the evening of his birthday. But he is determined to thank Claude for his kindness – and to ask a favour.

'Facts are stranger than fiction is a truth I have often proved during the varied changes of my life,' he writes to Claude. 'But the present case surpasses them all; here I am in a condemned cell, within fifty feet of the gallows; within a few days of my death, writing to you who are the innocent victim who suffered most by the crime which led to my sentence.

'I write to you as a man to a man. I write to you as the man who has left me indebted for more than I can say. To tell you what I feel, I must wait till I meet you where truth cannot be misconstrued and where the helpless and unfortunate are beyond insult, where a man will be valued his worth, without prejudice, and judged by him who reads all hearts.

'This is my 35th birthday and my last and as I review the past I feel very sad. Two months since I had friends who loved me well, we were happy though poor and oppressed. Now some are dead, one is to come with me and the other[s] to be confined for life. I have done all I could to save them. I have taken more than my share of guilt and responsibility . . . my dearest friend Nesbitt was my comfort while living and my guardian angel in his death. His cruel fate I bitterly deplore, his memory I fondly cherish.

'I have had some friends worth dying for and now find some who are almost worth living for . . . when I review the past I see those who I treated kindly desert and deceive me while I found out your kindness by robbing you. But God knows after the first few minutes of our acquaintance, I liked you and you had an influence over me. I felt I could have trusted your honour. I felt you were a manly generous man. I feared that your manhood might dictate some act which might have endangered your life. I knew how to disarm and conquer you. I appealed to your honour and my confidence and appeal were justified and answered.'

On he goes. It is like one of his many speeches. When he pulls together a purple passage of prose he becomes nothing more than a sentence in search of a full stop. He goes on to extol Claude's many other virtues before getting to his request – the monument he wants to sit above the grave he and Nesbitt will hopefully share.

'The only thing I long for is the certainty that I may share his grave; once assured of this I am satisfied.'

He tells Claude he wants a 'rough unhewn rock . . . one that skilled hands could have made into something better. It will be like those it covers, as kindness and charity could have shaped us to better ends.'

Scott also includes instructions for the epitaph on the rock. 'This stone covers the remains of two friends,' it should say, before including their names and how they were separated by death on 17/11/1879 and united by death on 20/1/1880.

'I will enclose a slip of paper giving a few dates to be cut on it,' writes Scott, 'and Mrs Ames will ask you to find out for her how I can be sure to fill the grave of him I fondly love.'

—

Loyalty. Honour. Dignity. The very attributes that George Scott prizes above all else are all said to be found in Mary Ames, who had disembarked from the 1200-ton steamer *Ly-ee-Moon* during the middle of his trial.

Scott had told the court of a telegram he had received from Melbourne that a credible witness was coming to Sydney to speak in his favour. Two days later she had arrived. Mary Ames told reporters that Scott had lived with her brother-in-law for a time and that she could give 'very material evidence for the defence'.

Within days more details emerged. Mrs Ames was a 'lady about 30 years of age, who is most elegantly dressed, and rather of prepossessing appearance'. She was a rich widow with a nine-year-old son. She was a teacher to the children of some of Melbourne's wealthiest families. On the night of her arrival in Sydney she had gone looking for Richard Thatcher. Unable to find him, she had set out for Darlinghurst Gaol the next morning to visit Scott before his appearance in court. It was said she was deeply in love with the man.

There were suggestions the two were betrothed and that if she could help secure his release she would marry him immediately.

But Mary Ames never took the witness stand. Instead, she began campaigning behind the scenes. When the suggestion arose that a member of the jury, John Stroh, was suffering from a bout of insanity and did not understand English, Ames had visited the man's wife and asked if she would sign an affidavit confirming her husband was not 'in his right mind'.

Now, five days before the execution, a member of the Legislative Assembly, Angus Cameron, has risen to his feet and told the colony how he had learned 'that a woman who had interested herself in behalf of Scott had offered a large sum of money to the wife of one of the jurymen to commit perjury by swearing that her husband was not in his right mind'.

On the eve of Scott's execution, a letter appears in *The Evening News* from 'THE WOMAN REFERRED TO'.

'Having reason to think that I am "the interested person" referred to, I beg herewith to most emphatically deny the accuracy of that information,' she writes.

Ames says she had spoken to Mrs Stroh, who had told her 'that her husband had been previously out of his mind, and had returned home after the trial in a very excited state and to all appearances not in his right mind'.

Ames had asked the woman to go with her to the office of the solicitor, Robert Burdett Smith, and sign an affidavit to that effect. 'Mrs Stroh said if she went with me to make the affidavit there would be no-one to mind their place of business, her husband being unwell. I thereupon promised to pay whatever expenses her absence would incur, and thought at the time I had the perfect right to do so.'

But Mrs Stroh soon had second thoughts and 'gave as her reason that, if it became known that her husband was out of his mind, it would injure their business and rather than that, she would see all the bushrangers hanged.

'I distinctly deny asking her or offering her any sum of money to commit perjury but requested her, if she went, only to tell the truth of what she knew concerning her husband's state of mind.

'Heaven knows my mission here is painful enough in itself and it is made more than doubly so when statements for which there is no foundation in fact are promulgated about me.'

For those who have watched Scott closely throughout the trial, his relationship with Mary Ames, who is described by one newspaper as 'the mysterious lady in black', is a curious one. They have watched Moonlite repeatedly weep over the loss of his 'true friend' Nesbitt. But when it comes to a woman devoted to securing his reprieve from the gallows, the man seems appreciative but coolly detached. In all the letters Scott writes from his prison cell – missives that will be seized by gaol authorities and never sent – he only refers to Ames sparingly and without any hint of affection.

She is always, simply, 'Mrs Ames' or 'Mrs Mary Ames'. If there is a bond between them, it pales next to the relationship Scott enjoyed with Nesbitt.

Among those letters he has sent from his cell is one to a relative of Jim Nesbitt's mother. The press has never been shy in highlighting the curiously close relationship between the two men and, three days before the scheduled execution of Scott and Rogan, *The Evening News* prominently publishes a copy of the correspondence.

'I can assure you when poor dear Jim Nesbitt died in my arms it was worse to me than death,' writes Scott. 'God alone knows how much I loved him, and He knows how the dear fellow loved me. We never had an unkind word, never had an unkind thought; we were one in heart and soul. We shared everything.

'I had a very severe illness in Ballarat and he attended me with the care and love of a mother. Since then he has been to me all that man could wish for. I was often miserable but he always comforted me and taught me to hope for a brighter future . . . I have some of his hair – part of it I got years since, part of it I cut from his head before he died. This hair I value more than I can tell.

'I have one pleasure left, that is, I am to share his grave. We promised to sleep together, and not long before his death he made me promise it again. We will fill the same grave, and I hope and trust we shall be together forever . . . let me lie with him, and I can die happy.'

Scott writes countless letters like this. They carry an intensity and openness rare for the time. Scott is adamant. When Nesbitt died 'my heart was crushed, my life blighted'.

If Mary Ames does not fill the heart of George Scott in the same way as Jim Nesbitt, she remains dogged in her support of the man. She is a frequent visitor to his cell in his final weeks and an unceasing campaigner for him outside the gaol's walls. Her efforts do not go unnoticed, and provide a more palatable storyline for the newspapers than a deep and abiding love between two bushrangers.

'And so there was a romance, one – if not more – in Scott's lifetime,' writes someone to the small Victorian rural newspaper *The Castlemaine Representative*. Their pen drips with cynicism and facetiousness. 'He loved and was beloved. And the lady, described as young, rich and beautiful (mind, I am not responsible for the gush) expressed her willingness to marry him if he were set free.'

It's an observation *The Evening News* is quick to leap on: 'In this connection it may be remarked that in older days a curious law existed in England,' it writes. 'A man condemned to be hanged had not only his life spared but was liberated if any woman would marry him under the gallows. The last time this privilege was exercised, the condemned man was ungallant enough to refuse the hand of the woman who offered to save his life, and while mounting the gallows expressed his conviction that death was preferable to matrimony.'

Left unsaid is the view that George Scott, too, might prefer death and the opportunity to lie with Jim Nesbitt to a reprieve and a marriage to Mary Ames. But the woman is doing her best. There is no-one she won't turn to in her efforts to save him, including a man as scorned and ridiculed as the condemned bushranger for whom she professes so much love.

—

Throughout his life John Alexander Dowie has felt the Lord by his side. The first encounter occurred when he was a child in Edinburgh, Scotland. A local barrister had forsaken a wealthy career in the courts for a 'quaintly constructed street pulpit'. Each night he climbed on to this platform and preached to the neighbourhood about God's endless love. One evening, just as twilight descended, he lifted young Dowie into his arms and together they sang 'Long hath the night of sorrow reigned'. Little Johnny could see the stars twinkling and hear his own voice echoing up and down the street and he knew, oh how he knew, that Christ had touched him and he would never be the same.

The family emigrated to Australia and God booked a berth with them. He would never leave Dowie's side. When Johnny turned 16 there was another case of divine intervention when the Lord stepped in and cured him of chronic dyspepsia. What else could he do but devote his life to God?

He became a pastor with the Congregational Church. One evening Dowie was sitting in the study of his humble chapel in Newtown, feeling helpless as a contagious illness noted for a wicked fever began to spread among his flock. There was a rapid series of knocks on his door and Dowie heard voices summoning him: 'Oh, come at once, Mary is dying; come and pray'. Dowie rushed hatless down the street to Mary's home where he found 'the dying maiden . . . she lay groaning, grinding her clinched teeth in the agony of the conflict with the destroyer, the white froth, mingled with her blood, oozing from her pained distorted mouth.'

The anger began to burn inside Dowie. If only he had a sword to slay this cruel foe 'strangling that lovely maiden like an invisible serpent'.

Lo, there was a sword. It was his hands. He lay them on poor Mary and the maiden suddenly lay so still in her sleep that her poor mother had turned to Dowie and, in a low whisper, asked, 'Is she dead?'

'No,' answered Dowie in an even lower whisper. 'Mary will live. The fever is gone . . . He touched her and the fever left her.'

Inspired by that encounter, Dowie left the traditional church to form his own. There would always be doubters,' of course. For years the newspapers have scorned him as a charlatan and an endless publicity seeker. A few months ago they had revelled in the news that the good reverend had attracted barely 100 votes in a humiliating end to his campaign to win a seat in parliament. But he remains steadfast. He will show all the doubters. In the years to come he will emigrate to America, purchase 10 square miles of land outside Chicago and lay the foundations for the city of Zion, Illinois. He will attract tens of thousands of followers and proclaim himself reborn as 'Elijah the Restorer' and, for a time, become the richest and most famous evangelist preacher in the world.

But all that is to come. Right now Reverend Dowie is appalled. He has tried to visit Scott and Rogan in their cells to tell them how much the Lord loves them. But the prison authorities refused to let him through the gates and he has had to rely on Mary Ames to pass on his messages of support.

He has knocked on the door of Governor Lord Loftus, who listened patiently as Dowie told him how deplorable the death penalty was and why Scott and Rogan should not hang. He has helped print leaflets and organise petitions for clemency. One of them has attracted more than 3000 signatures calling for poor Rogan to be spared.

But no-one in power wants to listen to Reverend Dowie. And so he has taken to the pulpit on one of the last nights before the executions. If the influential will not listen, then he can at least influence those loyal listeners who turn up each week to his small room in Castlereagh Street and sit through his fiery sermons.

'Scott damaged his own cause wilfully at the trial, making his own guilt blacker that he might give his companions a chance at their lives,' he tells the crowd.

'Another chivalrous act was that he stayed . . . in Victoria after his release because he was devoted to a noble-hearted lady, who is now working for his release, and would have married him and supported him had he allowed it. He worked on, under persecution, hoping to gain a position of independence, and thus be able to marry her. He was not one whit more guilty than his companions, but a great deal more honest.'

Dowie is adamant. The state is about to hang two men who, while guilty of a serious crime, deserve to have their lives – and their souls – saved by the Lord. If only he could visit both prisoners. He could lay his hands on them so they, too, could feel the presence of Him.

But time has run out. For the first time in his life, Dowie is about to discover that the sword the Lord placed in his hands, a sword of mighty power and healing, is sometimes no match for a length of hessian rope.

31

FALLING FROM A GREAT HEIGHT

Come now. Let us gaze upon the condemned man who has known what it is to love and be loved, to hold and be held and to hate and be hated.

His last few hours are spent in awful silence.

Everyone has left – the friends from New Zealand, who have taken with them a signed Bible and a poignant letter of farewell to his ageing parents; the widow Mary Ames, who has given him a solemn promise to care for his body after his death; the gaol officials, who have taken his final weight and height so that Nosey Bob might make his final calculations. Gone, too, are the two men who have tried to provide comfort in these past few days; prison chaplain Reverend Canon Rich and the Reverend Henry Macready, who knew the Scott family during their days in Rathfriland.

Everyone who has filled his small cell in these last frenetic days has gone. Even God has deserted Andrew George Scott.

He confided as much three days ago. 'In the silent hours of the night, when I believe myself unobserved by the gaoler, I go down on my knees and try to pray,' he told a visitor. 'But all my efforts have failed.

'I have tried several times but find that I cannot pray with that earnestness and fervour with which I used to pray when I was a boy.'

Gone is the belief that God will welcome him to paradise and an everlasting afterlife. All those well-meaning sermons he delivered as a lay preacher, all those hymns he sang as a child in Northern Ireland, all those lessons he learned at the feet of his father . . .

Lies, all of them.

He would prefer to be an infidel after what he has seen of Christianity since his trial. So many mock Christians – pseudo preachers, journalists and even his old agent, Richard Thatcher – have been asking to see him, hoping to get in a word or two so they might use them for their own selfish reasons.

They all disgust him. They are hypocrites without honour, charlatans without dignity.

Just as bad are the penal authorities. Scott has learned they have been confiscating many of the farewell letters he has written to friends and old colleagues. They still fear him, these cowards, frightened by the truths he is committed to reveal.

He keeps telling everyone he is not afraid to die. The declaration is made in countless letters and to every visitor to his cell. But the rope worries him.

'I could now go into that yard and command a company of soldiers to fire at me,' he has told a visitor. 'But I cannot bear having to die an ignominious death on the gallows . . . why should they pinion me, and why place over my head that abominable garment, the white cap? I should like to see how I am dying, for I am not afraid of death.'

He had wanted to make one more speech. He had wanted to stand on the gallows and let everyone look him in the face as he told them what he really thought. But last night Tom Rogan, who had just said goodbye to his distressed mother and sister, had passed on a request through his priest.

Please, he had said. Let us go to our deaths silently. A speech might make me lose my nerve. Scott, assured the audience for the hanging would be small and no press men would be admitted, had reluctantly agreed.

Now Scott waits in this tiny cell, pale and exhausted, listening to the final sounds of the world he is about to leave – the footsteps of heavy boots, the clanking of chains, the muffled shouts and cheers coming from somewhere in the distance. Crowds outside Darlinghurst Gaol have been gathering since well before sunrise. Some have climbed trees outside the eastern wing, hoping to catch a glimpse of the gallows. Scott has tried to sleep. But it has never come easily to a man with a wild drop of blood always simmering, always ready to explode.

All those visitors have seen the best and worst of him in these past few days. They watched in amazement and with growing respect as he worked furiously, hunched over the small table next to his hammock, holding conversations, issuing commands and making jokes even as he continued to write.

There was so much to do. Piles of prison paper are scattered throughout the cell; letters of gratitude, requests to see fellow prisoners and constant declarations of his love for Jim. He has taken that lock of Nesbitt's hair and attached it to his letter to Jim's mother.

He has also just finished a long statement denying his involvement in the Mount Egerton bank robbery. *The Sydney Morning Herald* had published a long and error-filled account of the heist that had thrown him into a fit of rage. He had paced his cell in a fury over its contents. How could they continue denigrating his name and his honour with such slanderous lies? Did they think Andrew George Scott was some common criminal?

It was a final insult that demanded a lengthy and detailed reply. It had followed a letter from the lawyers of that spineless little coward Julius Bruun. They had had the temerity to draft a confession stating he had solely been responsible for the theft. The confession sits unsigned among all the other correspondence.

But there is one more letter to write.

Scott sits on a small wooden stool and takes up his pen for the final time.

He addresses it to 'W Nesbitt, Esq.'. Scott has still not had it confirmed that he will be buried with Jim in his grave in Gundagai. Mary Ames, who has been a constant presence in the Sheriff's office, crying and pleading for George not to be buried within the precincts of the gaol, has been promised his body will be given to her after the execution. But no-one has given him a guarantee that he will be reunited with his greatest friend.

Willie Nesbitt, who is no relation to James Nesbitt, is a humble shopkeeper in the small town of Carcoar in the central west of NSW. He might be Scott's last hope.

Willie had known Scott and his family in New Zealand. A fellow immigrant, he had stayed in touch with the Scott family after moving to Australia to run a general store and provide forage for horses used by the local police. A week ago Willie had written an impassioned note to *The Evening News* to tell the world it was mistaken. Andrew George Scott was not the man they believed him to be and deserved to be saved from the gallows.

'As to Scott, does his acceptance of responsibility, prompted by vanity and a desire to appear a martyr, justify those blessed with more wisdom than he in hanging him?' asked William Nesbitt. 'I believe I am almost the only one in this colony who knows Scott well, as also his father and mother, at whose house I spent many days in company with the unfortunately condemned man.

'During my career I have met very few men possessed of better qualities than Scott; bad ones he has too, as we all have, and to make him fare worse than the others, because his good points have not been brought to life, would be a state of things I hope never to see come to pass in a community of which I am a member.'

It had been a rare voice of support and Scott was grateful.

'My dear Willie,' he writes. Scott's handwriting has deteriorated and some of the words are almost illegible. 'I want to rest in the grave of my friend, gratify this my last wish if you can afford, do it in the cheapest manner possible.'

The next sentence is scrawled, written in haste and with a fatigued hand. But it seems to say: 'Be a friend to Mary.'

And with that George Scott signs off for the final time.

'Farewell my dear Willie,' he writes. 'I have only one hour to live.'

—

They come for him just before 9am.

Outside the prison a man has clambered up a tall tree and declared to the envious crowd below that he can see the ropes. But now to his dismay he is being ordered down by a policeman. Others are standing on the roofs of nearby homes. Thousands line the streets. An optimistic few press their ears to the walls and listen. The stone whispers to them. Death is coming.

The prison blacksmith knocks away the leg irons and Scott says: 'That's a relief.' The Sheriff arrives and leads Scott and Rogan from the cells. The gallows are only 20 steps away, perched on a small balcony facing the southern wall of the prison.

As they step on to its wooden platform, Scott looks down and is startled. There is a small garden below the gallows. But he has no time to admire its poplar and locust trees. He had been told only a select few would be present to watch him die. But there must be 50 people below, all of them staring at him.

He turns to Canon Rich. 'What does this mean? What do these people mean? I think I ought to speak.'

Rich shakes his head to remind him of his promise to Rogan.

Down there, amid that sea of faces staring back at Scott, is J. F. Archibald. Nosey Bob, it turns out, has been true to his word.

—

Archibald can't help but fix his eyes on Scott and Nosey Bob as they meet for the first time.

Scott is pale. Gone is the luxurious beard and moustache. He has not been shaved for several days and the stubble on his face makes him appear even more haggard. Archibald can tell the man wants to die bravely but Scott's stricken features – 'a fixed appearance of utter helplessness and despair' – betray him.

'I have now seen men expire under almost every variety of circumstance, and have learnt that death by the hands of the executioner is the most terrible of all spectacles,' Archibald will write. 'But however unnerving the sight of a fatally-wounded man may be to the ordinary spectator, that indescribable, livid ashen pallor which comes over the criminal as he faces the hangman is still more sickening and awe-inspiring.'

Archibald glances back and forth between Scott and Nosey Bob, who is sporting a black frock coat with a white tie. Bob likes to dress right for occasions like this, particularly when so many important people – the politicians and gaol officials and the odd international visitor – will be scrutinising his work.

The hangman has been charitable toward the reporter for *The Bulletin*. He might even have risked his job by providing the man with tickets. But Archibald is in no mood to return the favour.

'If Scott's face was terrible to look on – if over his features came that strained, grave-like stare, that hopeless look which I have seen almost blanch the cheek of a black man as the hangman seized him – the appearance of the executioner was still more fascinatingly horrible.

'The creature looked what he lives to be – a human ghoul, a fiend incarnate. Were he to hang a million murderers no-one from among them would or ever could compare with him in bodily hideousness . . . no nightmare ever presented to the dreamer a spectre so hell-like.'

—

As the men are pinioned, Scott reaches out to Rogan.

They touch hands. 'Goodbye, Tom,' he says. 'We've made a sad mistake.'

Nosey Bob places the white cap over both men's heads. He adjusts the noose. He checks to make sure the knots remained greased and ready to slip and tighten when the moment comes.

He steps back gently and nods to his assistant who has his hand resting on the bolt that releases the trapdoor.

—

Archibald once knew a man who suffered from smoker's heart. He had been forced to camp with him during a long night in the bush and the old codger kept waking everyone with sudden loud shrieks. Then he would lie motionless until someone reached over and lay a hand on him to make sure he was still alive. Too much nicotine in the blood, Archibald thought.

The old man told him that he could feel his heart stop beating and that even though he was aware he was still alive, 'he thought that he was falling, and was unable to speak until touched by someone.

'So it must be with the man who drops from the scaffold; he feels himself falling, not six or seven feet, but ten thousand feet. At last his fall is broken – he comes to the end of the rope. The hand of death is laid upon him and he wakes – in the other world.'

The assistant executioner pulls the bolt. The trapdoor rattles.

George Scott and Tom Rogan are falling.

—

Falling.

—

Hessian ropes strain on overhead beams.

Now they creak. One of them shakes. Rogan's body is jerking and convulsing. His legs spasm.

Not to worry, a doctor will soon assure everyone. He is in no pain.

—

Rogan's body twitches for several minutes. Then the seizures stop and he is finally still.

Next to him, swaying gently, is the motionless body of Andrew George Scott. He has fallen a long way.

But he has landed safely, back into the waiting arms of James Nesbitt.

EPILOGUE

The bodies of Andrew George Scott and Thomas Rogan were left hanging for 20 minutes before being cut down and removed to the gaol's morgue. The ropes were incinerated to prevent them being sold as souvenirs. The bodies were washed and shaved before a sculptor on the government payroll, Walter McGill, made plaster casts of their heads.

McGill, an amateur phrenologist who had previously taken casts of the heads of 23 executed criminals, told reporters that Scott's features were the worst he had seen and their only redeeming feature was 'slight benevolence'.

The Evening News reported McGill's findings: 'It was morally impossible for him to tell the truth or be honest . . . he was void of all moral courage, very secretive and would keep up to the last anything he once said.'

McGill told the newspaper that Rogan's head 'shows great animal propensities, great cruelty and dishonesty'.

Shortly after midday a black mourning coach carrying Mary Ames and a friend pulled up outside Darlinghurst Gaol's walls. As the two coffins containing Scott and Rogan were placed inside it, some in the crowd noticed a large man in a black suit and gloves running toward the hearse. Unable to gain access to the execution, the Reverend Alexander Dowie had been waiting on the private porch of a local hotel, shielding his face from the crowd with an umbrella.

Dowie, dubbed 'the mercy agitator' by some in the press, was forced to race through a jeering crowd as the coach departed, finally pushing his way through to take a seat next to Ames. The hearse then made its way into the city before the coffins and a small mourning party arrived at Haslem's Creek cemetery.

Scott and Rogan were buried in unmarked graves, more than 200 miles from Gundagai.

—

One hundred and fifteen years later, the remains of Andrew George Scott were removed to Gundagai.

After learning about Scott's request to be buried with James Nesbitt, two women – Christine Ferguson and Samantha Asimus – began to lobby the New South Wales Government and the Anglican Church to have Scott disinterred from what is now Rookwood Cemetery and reburied in Gundagai.

On 13 January 1995, a group of locals dressed in colonial period costumes formed a funeral procession that followed a horse-drawn carriage carrying Scott's coffin from the town's old gaol to North Gundagai cemetery.

The coffin was lowered into its new grave beneath an old gum tree. The tombstone, as Scott had requested, was a rough, unhewn rock, 'one that skilled hands could have made into something better. It will be like those it marks as kindness and charity could have shaped us to better ends.'

The final resting place in the cemetery of James Nesbitt is unknown.

—

Robert Rice Howard – 'Nosey Bob' – carried out more than 66 executions during his time as NSW hangman. He left his home in Paddington toward the end of the 1880s and moved to a small cottage on Ben Buckler Point on the northern headland of Bondi Beach, where he occupied his spare time gardening, fishing for sharks and raising pigs.

His pigs had to be sold at market at discount rates because of the stigma attached to his occupation. The council refused his application for a licence to slaughter them at home.

His three daughters – one of whom, Emily Jane, died a few months after the Moonlite execution – never married because it was said no man wanted a hangman as a father-in-law.

In 1887 he was assaulted by four young men at a public house in Bondi. According to a statement Howard made later, a man behind the bar said to him: 'You are the bastard hangman . . . you are the one who put the rope on the neck of Moonlite and Rogan . . . he then took my beer, for which I had paid, and pitched it out into the sand.' Howard told police four men then bashed him and threatened to burn down his cottage.

'I have now been in the Government service for many years but I have never been assaulted in this way. I have been insulted and people have refused to serve me. Sometimes when I have been travelling by coach up country, they have refused to serve me with meals. But this is the first time that I have been maltreated.'

Two years later he oversaw the execution of Louisa Collins, the last woman to be hanged in NSW. That same year he travelled to Wagga Wagga to hang a cousin of Ned Kelly. The cab drivers refused to take Howard and his luggage into town and he was forced to walk several miles, accompanied by jeering and hooting from locals.

A year before Howard retired on a pension in 1904, *Truth* reported that Howard was standing on a crowded tram bound for his home in Bondi when an elderly male passenger called out to the conductor to object to Nosey Bob's presence. Howard reportedly smiled and told the man: 'Don't you get excited, mister. One of these days I'll have you standin' before me, and then you'd be glad of any company you can get.'

He died in 1906 at the age of 73. He was laid to rest with his wife, Jane, in Waverley Cemetery.

—

James Nesbitt's father continued to make several court appearances in the years following his son's death. In December 1879 – midway through the trial in Sydney of the Wantabadgery bushrangers – he was charged with using threatening and abusive language toward his wife. According to a report in *The Argus*, Nesbitt senior told the court that he 'had not known what he had been about since his son's untimely death'.

He was gaoled after being unable to pay a surety of 25 pounds guaranteeing he would keep the peace for six months.

The following year he was gaoled for two months for stealing a set of tradesman's tools. Shortly after being released, he was charged with the theft of more than 200 newspapers from a local newsagent. The court heard that Nesbitt offered to return the newspapers if the agent gave him liquor. He was returned to prison for a month.

He died in Melbourne Gaol in 1892 while serving six months' imprisonment for vagrancy. An inquest heard he was suffering from brain disease and recorded a verdict of death by natural causes.

—

The Reverend Thomas Scott, the father of Andrew George Scott, died in Coromandel, New Zealand, in July 1882. He was 67. He had changed his will three years earlier, shortly after Captain Moonlite was released from Pentridge and just before the events at Wantabadgery. The will made no mention of his second-born son.

—

Thomas Williams, whose real name was Frank Johns, was hanged in July 1885 for attempting to murder a fellow prisoner in Parramatta Gaol. He pleaded temporary insanity, claiming the prisoner had made a derogatory remark about a woman he had become attached to who was a regular visitor to the prison.

Williams refused counsel and conducted his own defence, according to the *Daily Telegraph*, 'marching up and down the box . . . with an action very similar to that of his former head, Captain Moonlite. The language used abounded in high-flown phrases.'

Williams told the court his life in crime had begun with Captain Moonlite. 'I was led astray by the oily tongue of a scoundrel who meretriciously portrayed the romantic life we were to lead. I was deceived. I have suffered, and am now suffering, a bitter punishment.'

He addressed the jury for more than 40 minutes, telling them: 'Gentlemen, when I love, my passionate nature compels me to do so in such a degree that, if it is not reciprocated, earth and its enjoyments no longer present any attraction to my spirit. The only desire of my heart is to sink in rest in death's oblivion.'

He was sentenced to death by Justice Windeyer, the same man who had sentenced him to be hanged six years earlier. His execution was accompanied by loud public protests against the death penalty. Williams made a speech on the gallows, breaking down at times as he said he hoped he would be the last man hanged in New South Wales. 'Speak to my poor mother and tell her that Frank died loving her till the end, and that her name was the last on my lips . . . my poor mother!'

—

Graham Bennett, whose death sentence had also been commuted to life imprisonment following the trial of the Wantabadgery bushrangers, was released from Goulburn Gaol four months after the hanging of Thomas Williams. His freedom was granted after the government decided 'that it was not, as was thought at the time of the trial, through the barrel of his revolver that the bullet passed into the brain of the unfortunate constable'.

An impassioned letter written by Thomas Williams shortly before his execution is also thought to have played a significant part in Bennett's release.

Williams – the young man Scott had hired in Ballarat during his public lecture tour – wrote a lengthy statement claiming that Bennett had been an unwilling participant during the siege and subsequent shootout.

Williams wrote that Scott believed Bennett would make a sixth member of their gang. 'No man would then be alone, he said, but we could always be in twos when doing anything.' According to Williams, Scott then told Bennett he was Captain Moonlite, showed him his revolvers and told him he was planning to stick up Wantabadgery Station.

'As near as I can remember he used these words, then: "You must do one of two things, either join us of your own accord and we will all share alike, or you must join us by compulsion."

'I know it was reported that Bennett shot Bowen; but I don't believe it. There was a favourite Colt revolver of Scott's which I noticed did not appear in any of the courts after the affair. I thought at the time, and still think, that Scott probably shot the man and then threw this revolver away into one of the paddocks.'

—

Seven months after the death of Gus Wernicke during the shootout at McGledes' hut, his stepmother, Isabella, died at the age of 22.

Gus' father Ernest, the proprietor of the County Court Hotel in Melbourne, died early the following year.

In 2017, *Lawless* – a television program about Australia's bushrangers – claimed that Wernicke had fired the shot that killed Senior Constable Webb-Bowen.

The claim was made after the show's producers and a team of scientists carried out extensive archaeological work at the site where McGledes' hut once stood.

Using contemporary Terrestrial Laser Scanning (TLS) systems to identify the various participants and reconstruct the gunfight, they concluded that Wernicke was the only gang member using a Colt revolver to the left of Constable Webb-Bowen.

The findings were published in the journal of *Forensic Science, Medicine and Pathology* in October 2017.

—

The widow of Senior Constable Edward Webb-Bowen struggled to come to terms with her husband's death, despite her generous gesture of forgiving Scott when she visited him in Gundagai.

Granted an annual pension of 78 pounds, Marion Webb-Bowen told newspapers in 1881 that 'the pension generously granted to me by the Government is barely sufficient for the maintenance of myself and family'.

A failed stint as the landlady of the Bay View Hotel in Double Bay was followed by a long-running battle with the trustees of a benefit set up with public funds for her son. At one stage a trustee wrote to her saying: 'Madam, I must ask you not to cause so much trouble, repeatedly answering the same questions about the money we hold on your son's account.'

She moved to Adelaide in the 1890s, where she battled problems with alcohol. She was charged several times with public drunkenness, using indecent language and causing a public disturbance. In 1896 she was fined 20 shillings for breaking a window of the Royal Hotel at eight o'clock on a Sunday morning after being refused a drink.

She died alone at about the age of 70 in a boarding house in Melbourne in 1911. The coroner recorded the cause of death as 'heart and kidney disease, probably accelerated by alcohol'.

—

Edward and Marion Webb-Bowen's only surviving son, also named Edward, was sent to a military school in England in the early 1890s. He was said to have served in the Boer War. He returned to Australia and in 1903 served three months in prison for uttering a valueless cheque.

In 1904 a police warrant was issued for his arrest for fraudulently obtaining five shillings. He was listed as 'clean shaven, minus two upper front teeth, scars on right side of head and left forearm from bullet wounds . . . other charges pending'. In 1909 a Sydney solicitor advertised for information about his whereabouts, saying he was 'very much addicted to drink'. He died an unmarried station hand at the age of 60 of heart disease.

—

The first edition of *The Bulletin*, which included J. F. Archibald's interview with Nosey Bob and an account of the hanging of Scott and Rogan, sold out quickly.

Under Archibald's editorship the publication launched the careers of several of Australia's greatest literary figures, namely Banjo Paterson and Henry Lawson. It also drove – and reflected – the emerging national character. It was unapologetically pro-republican and xenophobic, and encouraged Australians from all over the country to contribute stories, poems and observations.

Neurotic and obsessive about his work, Archibald suffered a mental breakdown in 1906 and was committed to the Callan Park Asylum. He was discharged several years later and sold his interest in *The Bulletin* in 1914.

He died in 1919 and was buried in Waverley Cemetery, not far from Nosey Bob. His will provided for an endowment for an annual painting award, now known as the Archibald Prize.

—

Justice William Windeyer continued to earn a reputation as a controversial judge long after the case of the Wantabadgery bushrangers. He presided over the trial of a group of larrikins in 1886 known as the 'Waterloo Push' who were charged with the gang rape of a 16-year-old girl. Windeyer sentenced nine men – almost all under the age of 20 – to death.

The decision sparked an outcry among large sections of the public and became a critical moment in the colony's history. Dubbed the 'Mt Rennie Outrage', several of the accused had their sentences commuted. But in early 1887 four of those found guilty were hanged together inside Darlinghurst Gaol, three of them slowly strangling to death after the drop was misjudged.

The botched execution was overseen by Robert Howard.

Windeyer died a decade later from a heart attack while travelling in Italy at the age of 62.

—

New South Wales carried out its last execution in 1939. It became the last Australian state to abolish the death penalty for all crimes in 1985.

—

Ned Kelly was hanged in Melbourne in November 1880, 10 months after the execution of George Scott and Tom Rogan.

The Kelly gang had staged raids on two small Victorian towns – Euroa and Jerilderie – and eluded the Victorian police for more than two years after shooting dead three policemen in 1878 near Stringybark Creek.

In June 1880 the gang damaged the train tracks outside Glenrowan and took 62 of the town's inhabitants hostage at the local hotel. A train carrying police reinforcements from Melbourne and Benalla approached Glenrowan at 3am the following morning and was flagged down by a hostage Kelly had earlier released in the belief he was a sympathiser.

Gun battles continued through the night and one of the gang, Joe Byrne, died after a stray bullet severed his femoral artery. At dawn, with steam rising from the ground, Kelly attacked the police from their rear wearing heavy armour and carrying three handguns. Laughing and taunting the police, Kelly was shot six times in the legs, feet and groin before being captured. His armour showed 18 bullet marks. The bodies of two other members of the gang, Dan Kelly and Steve Hart, were found in the smoking ruins of the hotel after it was set alight by police. Four civilians also lost their lives.

Kelly was tried in October before Sir Redmond Barry – who died two weeks after the court case – and ordered to be hanged. More than 32,000 people signed a petition for clemency, while thousands attended street rallies throughout the city to oppose the execution. He was hanged at the Melbourne Gaol at 10am on 11 November, 296 days after George Scott's death in Sydney.

The era of the bushrangers was finally over.

AFTERWORD

Astronomers and historians spend their lives peering into the past. But surely historians have the tougher job.

Astronomers, by comparison, have it easy. Their research is governed by one immutable fact. Light travels at close to 300,000 kilometres per second. Many of the stars and galaxies captured by state-of-the-art telescopes are so far away it takes billions of years for their light to reach earth.

But when it does arrive it provides a startlingly accurate depiction of the universe at a certain time in the past. A photograph of the sun shows what it looked like eight minutes earlier. An image of the nearest galaxy to our Milky Way – Andromeda – represents its condition 2.5 million years ago. The most distant object ever seen is 13 billion light years away, a time when the universe was nothing more than a newborn.

The science and the images are genuine and irrefutable.

Historians have no such luck. When they peer into our human past there are few clear images shining back at them. Instead, they must penetrate a thick fog of prejudice, opinions, claims and the outright lies, not only of history's participants, but all those historians too.

All those documents, letters and thoughts left behind by the dead are written by human hands and stained with bias and partisanship. The French poet Jean Cocteau worked it out best. 'What is history after all?' he asked. 'History is facts which become lies in the end. Legends are lies which become history in the end.'

So how to assess the relationship between Andrew George Scott and James Nesbitt? Have the facts become lies because our desire for legends makes us want to believe that Captain Moonlite was a gay bushranger? That both men loved one another is indisputable. But were they physical lovers? Was their friendship far more than just a deep affection and respect for one another? Did it go well beyond the tenderness and emotional intimacy that defined many attachments between men in the 19th century? And does it matter, anyway?

Of course it does. George Scott's sexuality is important because sexuality is such a complex and defining feature of our lives and personalities. There is no escaping it. If Scott was homosexual in an era that severely frowned on physical same-sex relationships, surely it would have added to the furnace of frustration blazing inside him.

The Australian historian Garry Wotherspoon has written extensively on gay issues in Australia. He was among the first to examine the extensive batch of letters written by Scott in his death cell. The letters were seized by gaol authorities and remained in the archives until the early 1990s. Uncovered, they revealed an intensely passionate love by one man for another that borders on the obsessive. In them Scott repeatedly declares his love for Nesbitt. He wants to be buried in the younger man's grave. He wants to spend eternity resting in the younger man's arms. 'We were one in heart and soul,' is a typical phrase Scott often used. 'He died in my arms and I long to join him where there shall be no more parting, no more injustice . . . When he died my heart was crushed.'

Wotherspoon was the first historian I sought out when I began researching this book. His work has included extensive research into the relationship between Matthew Flinders, the first man to circumnavigate Australia, and his close friend and British naval surgeon,

George Bass. 'What did exist then . . . are what are termed "romantic friendships" between men of the same sex, high in passionate expressiveness but not necessarily or usually sexual in a physical sense,' Wotherspoon once observed when writing about the pair. 'Among the sources for such friendships might be classical ideas of platonic love, aspects of medieval chivalry (such as the relationship between a knight and his squire), and direct experiences of male bonding in sex-segregated institutions, notably English public schools. Such love was designated "manly love".'

History is replete with instances of this 'manly love'. Were those heroic biblical figures David and Jonathan more than just good friends? Aristotle described the friendship between Alexander the Great and one of his generals and lifelong companions, Hephaestion, as 'one soul abiding in two bodies'. Even that other bushranging gang, the Kellys, have not been immune to speculation. Joe Byrne and Aaron Sherritt 'had known a David and Jonathan friendship' according to one noted historian. When Sherritt was accused of betraying the gang, he is said to have told Byrne's mother: 'I'll kill him and before he's cold I'll fuck him.'

In 1992 Wotherspoon penned an influential essay in the *Journal of the Royal Australian Historical Society* that assessed whether Scott and Nesbitt were just another example of 19th-century 'manly love' or were, in fact, in what we would regard today as a homosexual relationship. He concluded: 'Even if we accept that nineteenth century friendships may have represented something not understood in the terminology and concepts of the early to mid-twentieth century, it would still seem that the friendship of Moonlite and Nesbitt was one of those "special friendships", a case perhaps of "the love that dared not speak its name".'

I would drop the word 'perhaps'. I'm not an historian like Wotherspoon but the evidence that has come to light since Wotherspoon's first glimpse at the death cell letters is overwhelming. If Andrew George Scott was not gay, then he was at least what we might call today sexually ambiguous. His relationship with Allan Hughan, who sailed with Scott to Fiji after the Mount Egerton bank robbery, was clearly an intensely emotional one – at least from the married Hughan's point of view. Even putting aside the florid prose of the time, Hughan's letter to Scott calling him 'my darling' is a flourish that was rare by the second half of the 19th century.

More of the evidence, aside from the overt language in Scott's letters, comes to us in hints and asides we find in the reports of the Wantabadgery siege and the subsequent trial. Scott and Nesbitt's relationship was clearly a talking point in an age when homosexual relationships were carefully couched in euphemisms. For example, we have the letter to a newspaper referring to the Moonlite gang, which states: 'One phase of the inner life of prisoners and boys of the reformatory class is quite unknown to most of your casual reader of newspapers, and it is only to such as myself, and a comparatively few persons gifted with a desire to acquire positive knowledge of the dark side of human nature for the purpose of aiding in the amelioration of it . . . that the terrible knowledge weighs with the oppression of a nightmare.' The writer reminds readers about the case of Marks and Feeney in the Treasury Gardens – two men involved in an intense relationship that scandalised Melbourne just as Scott was beginning his sentence in Pentridge. We have the colourful reports of how police watched Scott passionately kiss Nesbitt after he had been shot. We have the newspaper stories of Scott becoming 'intensely passionate' and shedding tears in the courtroom when referring to his Nesbitt. We also have the sarcastic asides of William Baynes, the manager of Wantabadgery Station who, having observed Scott and Nesbitt together, labels Nesbitt a 'puff' – a common slang word of the era for a male homosexual.

This is why the sexuality of Captain Moonlite is important. Male culture in colonial Australia was steeped in swaggering machismo. The 'manly love' to be found in British private schools and among the aristocratic set was a rare thing in the Australian bush. It was there, among the callused hands of loggers and shearers and drovers, that many believe the idea of Australian mateship was first formed before being catalysed in the furnace of World War I. If they were regarded as homosexuals, it also helps explains much of the loathing directed toward Scott after his capture. Being an accused cop killer was one thing. But a practitioner of the unnatural act as well?

Lies become facts that mature into legends. Long before he was sentenced to death, Scott always had an eye on how history would remember him. He told a Ballarat court he was unable to say where he had been on the night of the Mount Egerton bank robbery, because he had been with a woman whose honour he had to defend and whose identity he had to protect. I think the book you are now reading has dealt with that attempted alibi – along with several others. The appearance of the mysterious Mary Ames during his trial in Sydney is another potential red herring. There is no doubt a woman called Mary Ames existed. Scott briefly refers to her in a couple of his death cell letters, and without any of his usual emotional flourishes. But searching for details about her life is a frustrating exercise that leads to a series of dead-ends.

I spent a lot of time trawling through records in Melbourne and Sydney and could find no trace of her. The Ballan Historical Society conducted an intensive search through records in the Ballarat region and also came up with nothing. A professional genealogical research company also failed to find any evidence that she existed under that name – or had a nine-year-old son and had been betrothed to Scott for years. By 1880 it was getting more difficult, although not impossible, to have lived and died and never earned even the smallest of mentions in history's pages, much less a birth or death certificate.

In all the voluminous correspondence and documents dealing with Captain Moonlite there is nothing to support the view that he was ever engaged to the woman. Might she have been a ruse by Scott to deflect the speculation about his relationship with Nesbitt? Richard Thatcher, Scott's agent from Melbourne, had extensive contacts in the theatrical world. Given his impresario abilities, it would not have been beyond him to hire an actress to elicit sympathy for a condemned man and try and secure a reprieve.

The weight of evidence strongly supports the view that Captain Moonlite was gay. It also overwhelmingly suggests he suffered significant mental health issues. Narcissism lay at the heart of his personality. He craved attention but when he finally gained it, he became flustered and exhausted by its demands. He was prone to outbursts of irrational anger and was consumed by a rigid code of honour that, while often getting him into trouble, allowed him to make sense of a world he often, clearly, found bewildering.

Andrew George Scott was by far the most fascinating Australian bushranger. For all his failings he was erudite, chivalrous and imaginative. Compared to Ned Kelly, who has been mythologised down the years but was little more than a thuggish horse thief with a limited intellect, Scott had genuine charisma and an ability to turn a noisy room suddenly quiet.

Not, like Kelly, out of fear. But because of his mere presence.

The story of Captain Moonlite is extraordinary, even by the remarkable standards of the 19th century. Perhaps he was not a man most of us would have liked to meet. But he was a man who played a part in shaping what we have become. And while history is replete with lies and legends, that much is fact.

ACKNOWLEDGEMENTS

Many thanks to Garry Wotherspoon, who gave up his time to talk about Captain Moonlite during the early phase of research for this book and encouraged me down paths I might otherwise not have taken. Thanks also to Jill Baker, who patiently read drafts and suggested new directions when the narrative encountered brick walls. Deborah Beck, archivist and collections manager at the National Art School, which is housed within the precincts of the old Darlinghurst Gaol, was incredibly helpful. One morning she gave me a personal tour of the prison and allowed me to stand under the exact spot where George Scott was hanged. The hair on the back of my neck is still standing. Historian and acclaimed author Kiera Lindsey played more of a role in the shape of this book than she can imagine. A long chat over coffee on the campus of the University of Technology in Sydney provided the inspiration that kept me going.

Thanks also to the efforts of Richard Biden from the Ballan Shire Historical Society and Phoebe Wilkens from Born and Bred Historical Research in Victoria. In New Zealand, the Collections Manager of Pioneer Village Kaikohe, Delwyn Walker, helped unearth a synopsis of the diary of Alfred Alexander, a passenger on the

Black Eagle that carried the Scott family from Ireland to New Zealand in 1861. Andrew Weglarz, the museum manager for NSW Corrective Services, led me into a cold storage room in Cooma and directed me to an old but very valuable box of Moonlite correspondence and related documents. As always, the staff of the NSW and Victorian state libraries were helpful. So, too, those at the National Library of Australia and at the NSW State Archives in Kingswood, where the original letters penned by George Scott in his death cell are kept. At Penguin Random House Australia I've been fortunate to have the enthusiastic backing and trust of the wonderful Alison Urquhart, and the incisive editing skills of Michael Epis and Patrick Mangan. But most of all I thank my wife Maria. She provided food, coffee, love and daylight when all I could see was Moonlite.

Garry Linnell

October 2020

A NOTE ON SOURCES

The elderly gentleman seemed sincere when he rose to ask a question. A previous book of mine – *Buckley's Chance* – had just been published. It told the story of William Buckley, an English convict who escaped from a fledgling Port Phillip settlement in 1803 and went on to live for more than 30 years with the Wadawurrung Aboriginal people.

I was giving a talk at a Queensland library about the book when the man stood up to pose an innocent inquiry.

'How much did you make up?' he asked.

'Nothing,' I replied. 'It's called non-fiction. Everything in the book must be sourced.'

I told him there were dozens of pages of endnotes, as well as an extensive bibliography, that explained all the sources I had relied on. He nodded politely. But I'm certain he didn't quite believe me.

Moonlite, too, is a work of non-fiction. And while I have tried to write it in a style that borrows heavily from novels and movies – using character development, pacing, dialogue and sub-plots – everything in it relies on thousands of pages of reports, memoirs, diaries and other archival material sourced from the 19th century.

I've decided not to list every one of them because I despise foot-notes. This might dismay academics and earnest devotees of detail. But footnotes interrupt the flow of a story, not to mention being a typo-graphical annoyance that leave a page littered with what appears to be small flies crawling over the end of sentences. And let's be honest. Who reads them anyway? Certainly not the old fella I met in Queensland. A lengthy footnote section is often little more than a brag sheet so authors can show off how much research they have undertaken.

So when it comes to Captain Moonlite, you and that elderly gentleman in Queensland will just have to take me at my word. Hand on heart. I haven't made anything up.

You don't need to when it comes to documenting the life of Andrew George Scott.

In doing so I relied to a great extent on two key sources – his death-cell letters and hundreds of contemporaneous newspaper reports, most of which can be found using Trove, that brilliant online resource provided by the National Library of Australia.

The death-cell letters are held by NSW State Records and Archives and were also published in a limited collection by Popinjay Publications called *The Moonlite Papers: the letters and statements of A.G. Scott written in the death cell, Darlinghurst Gaol* (1988–1991). Additional correspondence previously unseen is held in Cooma by NSW Corrective Services.

The Public Record Office of Victoria also holds extensive docu-ments relating to Scott, including the letter he wrote to his father in 1872. These can be found in the PROV's *Kelly Historical Collection – Part 5: Miscellaneous Records (VPRS 4969/ PO unit 4, item 95)*. Some of the accounts of Scott's early days in Rathfriland come from the reminiscences of W. A. Osborne in the *Victorian Historical Magazine (27, 1955–57)*.

His enrolment in the British Navy is contained in a report to the House of Commons titled *Return of Nominations to cadetships in Royal Navy, 1854–59*. His family's departure from Ireland in 1861 was extensively covered by *The Newry Telegraph* and other County

Down journals of the time. His father's involvement in the Dolly Brae affair is referred to during a parliamentary debate in the House of Lords (*Hansard HL Deb 18 February 1850 vol 108 cc886–968*) and in other parliamentary reports.

Records relating to Scott's military service in New Zealand and his application to join the constabulary can be found in Archives New Zealand (*Army Dept files, letter CD64/318 and application CD67/3955*). The experiences of the Scott family, including Thomas Scott's role as a reverend, are listed in many publications of the era, which I accessed through the NZ government's Papers Past website.

Scott's time in Victoria in the lead-up to the Mount Egerton bank robbery is referenced in countless newspaper reports of the era. Those wishing to read an example of his prodigious letter writing can find one on page three of *The Bacchus Marsh Express* on 12 December 1868 (https://trove.nla.gov.au/newspaper/article/88374016?searchTerm=A.G.Scott&searchLimits=l-decade=186). His role in a séance while undertaking the journey to Fiji on Allan Hughan's *Pilot* is related by a contributor to the *Ballarat Courier* on 6 January 1880 (https://trove.nla.gov.au/newspaper/article/232149935?searchTerm=silver pen%20A.%20G.%20Scott%20Fiji&searchLimits=). Biographical information about Hughan was drawn, in part, from the extensive and richly detailed Hughan Genealogy family blog (https://hughanhistory.blogspot.com/). The letters written to Scott by Hughan, along with other documents relating to his Pacific Islands visit, were sold at auction in Melbourne in 2012 and detailed in Paul Terry's commendable *In Search of Captain Moonlite*.

His arrest and subsequent imprisonment in Maitland Gaol were covered extensively in several Sydney publications. Scott's time in Pentridge is reported in various Victorian newspapers of the time, as well as his and James Nesbitt's official prison records. The trials and tribulations of Nesbitt's father are chronicled in Melbourne newspapers throughout the 1870s and 1880s.

The siege at Wantabadgery and the subsequent shootout at McGledes' farm was reconstructed using dozens of sources, including police reports, eyewitness testimony and newspaper accounts of the battle and the subsequent trial.

Descriptions about the life and times of Nosey Bob – who surely deserves a rich biography of his own – are also largely drawn from contemporaneous sources. For instance, a detailed report about Howard's horse and how he trained it to fetch his beer from the pub appeared in *The Australian*, 11 November 1905. His tendency to drown himself in drink in the lead-up to an execution is also extensively documented, including a reference in the *North Australian* (Darwin), 18 July 1884, p. 5. A file relating to Nosey Bob held in the Local Studies Collection of the Waverley Library was also of enormous assistance.

J. F. Archibald's reports on the Mudgee hanging of Alfred can be found in *The Evening News* of the time, as well as in his lengthy reminiscences contained in the *Archibald Papers* in the Mitchell Library in Sydney. I relied to a great extent on Archibald's account of the hanging of Scott and Tom Rogan from the first edition of *The Bulletin* of 31 January 1880.

Details and anecdotes about Ned Kelly and other bushrangers have been drawn from the considerable library of material written about them over the past century.

Those wanting further information about the research for this book can contact me through Penguin Random House Australia. A more extensive list of selected reference material can be found in the bibliography.

BIBLIOGRAPHY

Alexander, Alison. *Tasmania's Convicts: How Felons Built a Free Society*. Allen & Unwin, 2010.

Alexander, Alison, ed. *The Companion to Tasmanian History*. Centre for Tasmanian Historical Studies, Hobart, 2005.

Asimus, Samantha Anderson. *Captain Moonlite: Victim or Villain?* Ginninderra Press, 2012.

Beck, Deborah. *Bailed up: Bushrangers at Darlinghurst Gaol*. National Art School, 2014.

Beck, Deborah. *Hope in Hell: A History of Darlinghurst Gaol and the National Art School*. Allen & Unwin, 2005.

Beckett, Ray and Richard. *Hangman: The Life and Times of Alexander Green, Public Executioner to the Colony of New South Wales*. Nelson, 1980.

Bennett, John Michael. *Sir Alfred Stephen: Third Chief Justice of NSW, 1844–1873*. The Federation Press, 2009.

Boxall, George. *An Illustrated History of Australian Bushrangers*. Viking, 1988.

Brennan, Martin. *Police History of the Notorious Bushrangers of New South Wales and Victoria, 1910*, State Library of NSW A2030/CY934.

Burdett-Smith, Robert. *Papers of Robert Burdett-Smith*. NSW State Library.

Burgess, Richard. *Guilty Wretch that I Am: Echoes of Australian Bushrangers and the Death Row Memoirs of Richard Burgess*, with historical notes by Ken Byron. Macmillan, 1984.

Byard, Roger, and five others. 'Line of Fire: What Happened at the Wantabadgery Siege?', *Forensic Science, Medicine and Pathology*, October 2017.

Calderwood, George. *Captain Moonlite: Bushranger*. Rigby, 1971.

Carey, Peter. *True History of the Kelly Gang*. University of Queensland Press, 2000.

Castieau, John Buckley. *The Difficulties of My Position: The Diaries of Prison Governor John Buckley Castieau, 1855–1884*. National Library of Australia, 2004.

Coupe, Robert. *Australian Bushrangers*. New Holland, 1998.

Eburn, Michael. 'Outlawry in Colonial Australia: The Felons Apprehension Acts 1865–1899', *Australia and New Zealand Law and History E-Journal*. Vol. 2005, pp. 80–93.

FitzSimons, Peter. *Ned Kelly*. Penguin, 2015.

Galbally, Ann. *Redmond Barry: An Anglo-Irish Australian*. Melbourne University Press, 1995.

Garden, Don. *Victoria: A History*. Thomas Nelson Australia, 1984.

Gatrell, V. A. C. *The Hanging Tree: Execution and the English People 1770–1868*. Oxford University Press, 1996.

Gillespie, Raymond. 'A Manor Court in Seventeenth Century Ireland.' *Irish Economic and Social History*. Vol. 25, 1998.

Glen, Frank. *For Glory and a Farm – the Story of Australia's Involvement in the New Zealand Wars of 1860–66*. Whakatane Historical Society, 1984.

Gott, Richard. *Britain's Empire: Resistance, Repression and Revolt*. Verso, 2011.

Harris, Alexander. *Settlers and Convicts Or Recollections of Sixteen Years' Labour in the Australian Backwoods* [1847]. Melbourne University Press, 1953.

Harris, Steve. *The Prince and the Assassin, Australia's First Royal Tour and Portent of World Terror*. Melbourne Books, 2018.

Hirst, John. *Freedom on the Fatal Shore: Australia's First Colony*. Black Inc, 2008.

Hocking, Geoff. *Wild Colonial Boys: Tall Tales & True Australian Bushrangers*. Five Mile Press, 2012.

Hughes, Robert. *The Fatal Shore*. William Collins Sons and Co Ltd, 1987.

James, John Stanley. *The Vagabond Papers*. Edited by Michael Cannon, 2016.

Jinks, Catherine. *Charlatan: The Dishonest Life and Dishonoured Loves of Thomas Guthrie Carr, Stage Mesmerist*. Penguin, 2017.

Karskens, Grace. 'This Spirit of Emigration: The Nature and Meaning of Escape in Early New South Wales', *Journal of Australian Colonial History*, ISSN 1441-0370, 2005, Vol. 7, pp. 1–34.

Karskens, Grace. 'The Dialogue of Townscape: The Rocks and Sydney, 1788–1820', *Australian Historical Studies*, 1997, 27:108, pp. 88–112.

Keenan, Desmond. *Pre-Famine Ireland: Social Structure*. Xlibris Corp, 2001.

Kercher, Bruce. *The Unruly Child: A History of Law in Australia*. Allen & Unwin, 1995, pp. 22–42.

Kociumbas, Jan. *The Oxford History of Australia, Vol. 2: Possessions 1770–1860*. Oxford University Press, 1992.

Lindsay, Gordon. *John Alexander Dowie: A Life Story of Trials, Tragedies and Triumphs*. Christ for the Nations, 1980.

Malcolm, Elizabeth and Hall, Dianne. *A New History of the Irish in Australia*. New South Books, 2018.

Macintyre, Stuart. *A Concise History of Australia* Second Edition. Cambridge: Cambridge University Press, 2004.

Maddox, Neil P. 'A Melancholy Record: The Story of the 19th Century Irish Party Procession Acts.' *Irish Jurist,* Vol. 24.

Maxwell-Stewart, Hamish. The Bushrangers and the Convict System of Van Diemen's Land, 1803–1846. PhD Thesis, University of Edinburgh, 1990.

McHugh, Evan. *Bushrangers: Australia's Greatest Self-made Heroes.* Penguin Australia, 2011.

McKenna, Neil. *Fanny and Stella: The Young Men Who Shocked Victorian England.* Faber, 2014.

McKenry, Keith. *More Than a Life: John Meredith and the Fight for Australian Tradition*. Rosenberg Publishing, 2014.

McQuilton, John. *The Kelly Outbreak 1878–1880: The Geographical Dimension of Social Banditry.* Melbourne University Press, 1979.

Mendham, Roy. *The Dictionary of Australian Bushrangers.* Hawthorn Press, 1975.

Mickleborough, Leonie. *William Sorell in Van Diemen's Land: Lieutenant Governor, 1817–24: A Golden Age?* Blubber Head Press, 2004.

Morgan, Patrick. *The Vandemonian Trail: Convicts and Bushrangers in Early Victoria.* Connor Court Publishing, 2016.

Morrissey, Doug. *Ned Kelly: A Lawless Life*. Connor Court Publishing, 2015.

Morrissey, Doug. *Ned Kelly: Selectors, Squatters and Stock Thieves.* Connor Court Publishing, 2018.

Nixon, Allan M. *Stand and Deliver!: 100 Australian Bushrangers 1789–1901*. Lothian, Melbourne, 1991.

Noonan, Rodney. 'Wild Cathay boys: Chinese Bushrangers in Australian History and Literature', *Journal of Australian Studies*, 24:65, pp. 127–35.

O'Farrell, Patrick. *The Irish in Australia*. NSW University Press, 1987.

O'Malley, Pat. 'Class Conflict, Land and Social Banditry: Bush Ranging in Nineteenth Century Australia', *Social Problems*, Vol. 26 No. 3, February 1979.

Prest, Wilfrid, Kerrie Round and Carol Fort, eds. *The Wakefield Companion to South Australian History*. Wakefield Press, 2001.

Pobjie, Ben. *Mad Dogs and Thunderbolts*. Affirm Press, 2019.

Purcell, Anna. *Bushrangers: A History of Australia's Outlaws*. New Holland Publishers, 2018.

Reynolds, Henry. *A History of Tasmania*. Cambridge University Press, 2012.

Richards, Jonathan. *The Secret War: A True History of Queensland's Native Police*. University of Queensland Press, 2008.

Roope, Colin and Patricia Gregson. *An Organised Banditti*. Self-published, 2002.

Ryan, Lyndall. *The Aboriginal Tasmanians*, 2nd edition. Allen & Unwin, 1996.

Ryan, Lyndall. *Tasmanian Aborigines: A History Since 1803*. Allen & Unwin, 2012.

Seal, Graham. *The Outlaw Legend*. Cambridge University Press, 1996.

Select Committee on Transportation, Report, 1838.

Sheldrake, Edna Miller. *The Personal Letters of John Alexander Dowie*. Creative Media Partners, 2015.

Smith, Peter. *The Clarke Gang: Outlawed, Outcast and Forgotten*. Rosenberg Press, 2015.

Smith, Peter. *Tracking Down the Bushrangers*. Kangaroo Press, 1982.

Statham, Commander E. *The Story of the Britannia*. Cassell and Co., 1904.

Terry, Paul. *In Search of Captain Moonlite*. Allen & Unwin, 2013.

Tranter, Bruce and Jed Donoghue. 'Bushrangers: Ned Kelly and Australian Identity', *Journal of Sociology*, 2008 Vol. 44: pp. 378–9.

Tranter, Bruce and Jed Donoghue. 'Ned Kelly: Armoured Icon', *Journal of Sociology*, 2010 Vol. 46: pp. 187–205.

Ward, Russel. *The Australian Legend*. Oxford University Press, 1958.

White, Charles. *History of Australian Bushranging*. Rigby Limited, 1975.

White, Henry. *Tales of Crime and Criminals in Australia*. Ward and Downey, 1894.

Williams, Stephan. *Dictionary of Australian Bushrangers*. http://pandora.nla.gov. au/nph-wb/20010131130000/http://www.whiskershill.dynamite.com.au/ newpage1.htm.

Williams, Stephan. *The Book of a Thousand Bushrangers*. Popinjay Publications, 1993.

Williams, Stephan. *The Moonlite Papers: The Letters and Statements of A. G. Scott Written in the Death Cell, Darlinghurst Gaol, Vols 1–4*. Popinjay Publications, 1988–91.

Wisdom, Sir Robert. *Papers of Sir Robert Wisdom*, NSW State Library.

Woollacott, Angela. *Settler Society in the Australian Colonies: Self-government and Imperial Culture*. Oxford University Press, 2015.

Wotherspoon, Garry. 'Moonlite and . . . Romance? The Death-cell Letters of Captain Moonlite and Some of Their Implications', *Journal of the Royal Australian Historical Society*, Vol. 78, Parts 3 and 4, December 1992.

INDEX

Aboriginals 95
  conflict with 66, 95, 221
  convictions 5, 191
  defence of 54, 80
  massacres 221–2, 248
Age of Exploration 18
Albert, Prince 45, 163–4
Alfred 5–6, 188–91, 267–8
Alfred, Prince (Duke of Edinburgh) 6, 45–7
  assassination attempt 47–50, 56
Allen, Edward 35
Ames, Mary 82, 280, 283, 284, 289, 303
  campaign to free Scott 273–6
  Reverend Dowie, and 278
Archibald, John Feltham 156, 190–1, 267–70
  The Bulletin 267, 296
  execution of Scott 284–6
  final years 296
Arthur, Lieutenant-Governor George 113, 114
Asimus, Samantha 290

astronomy 299
Australia 17–18
  anti-Irish sentiment 50
  myths and legends 20
Australian Arms hotel 213, 215, 217
Australian identity 21–2

Bacchus Marsh 58–60, 71, 127
Bacchus, William 58
Baker, Thomas *see* Rogan, Tom
Ballan 82
Ballarat 39, 66, 71
  Captain Moonlite's public lecture 182–6
  Circuit Court 78
  Gaol 124–6, 130
Barrow, Louisa 79
Barry, Constable Alexander 230
Barry, Justice Redmond 78–80, 81, 83
  Mount Egerton bank robbery trial 131–2, 134, 135, 138
  Ned Kelly, trial of 298
  prison inspection 169–71

Bass, George 301

Bates, Frank 193, 194

Baynes, William 204–5, 207–10, 214–15, 243, 302

Bennett, Graham 11, 202–3, 208, 210, 236, 246, 252
arrest, following 237–8
Darlinghurst Gaol 251–2
McGlede homestead shootout 228, 231
release from gaol 293–4
reprieve 268
trial of Moonlite gang 260–1, 264, 265

Benz, Karl 18

Berry, Graham 201

Bertrand, Henry Louis 117–19

Beveridge, John 216, 217–19

Bingham, Lord 26

Birkmyre, William 135

Black Eagle 32–3, 35

Boulton, Thomas (Stella) 163, 164–5

Bowden, Detective 106

Boyle, Richard 132

Brady, Matthew 113–14

Britannia (HMS) 34, 74

Brown, Reverend James 166

Brownlow, Mary Ann 54

Bruun, Julius 62–4, 74–7, 120, 282
Scott, relationship with 75–6, 77, 84–5, 120
Scott's trial 132, 133–5
trial 77, 78, 83

Bruun, Ludwig 136–7

Bugg, Mary Anne 112

Burgess, Richard see Hill, Richard

Burrangong 66

bushrangers 11–12, 14, 19, 21, 31, 54–5, 67, 73, 91, 92, 112, 113, 256 see also by name
death of last 297–8
media portrayals 19–20, 235, 253

myths and legends 19–20, 52–3, 92, 110, 113–15, 130
New Zealand 38, 40
police, clashes with 87–8

Byrne, Joe 297, 301

Byron, Lord 86, 87

Cameron, Angus 274

capital punishment 5, 9, 291
abolition 297
botched hangings 89, 187, 246, 297
protests against 187–8, 268, 269, 278, 293, 296–7, 298

Cappisoti, Giovanni 112

Captain Moonlite see Scott, Andrew George (Captain Moonlite)

Carey, Eleanor 104–5, 106

Carr, Dr Thomas Guthrie 50–1

Carroll, Senior Sergeant John 224, 226–8, 239

Cassin, Sergeant Henry 232

Celestia 106

Clarke, Jack 53

Clarke, John 21, 50, 53
trial 52–6

Clarke, Marcus 179–81, 197
For the Term of His Natural Life 179

Clarke, Thomas 21, 50, 53
trial 52–6

Clinton, Lord Arthur 165

Cocteau, Jean 300

Collins, Louisa 291

Comet 103–6

Connell, John 58–9

Contemporary Terrestrial Laser Scanning (TLS) 294–5

convicts 9, 12, 17, 19, 39, 45, 65, 122, 255

Courtenay, William 24, 25

Cowper, Charles 4

Crawley, Fred 223

Crom Dubh 23
Crook, James 58, 60, 64
Crook, Robert 64–5, 68, 82

Darling, Ralph 248
Darlinghurst Gaol 247, 248
  Scott inside 10–13, 145–6, 247,
    249–50, 271–3, 280–2
Darwin, Charles 97, 130
Davidson, Charlie *see* Williams,
    Thomas
Delany, Officer 110, 111
Dermoody, Jack *see* Harris, Jack
Dick, John 189–90
Dillon, Charles 106
Disraeli, Benjamin 25
Dolly's Brae 30, 41
Dowie, Reverend John Alexander
    277–9, 290
Dullahan 24, 31
Duncan, George 142, 154, 174

Edward, Prince 45
Eleven Mile Creek 69, 107
Esmond, James 66
Ethan Allen 42
Eugowra robbery 88, 114
Eureka rebellion 66, 78
Excellent (HMS) 34

Feeney, Edward 161–3, 164, 165,
    302
Felons Apprehension Act 53, 55
Fenianism 49
Ferguson, Christine 290
Fiji 86, 94, 98, 106, 126, 137, 159,
    192, 302
Flinders, Matthew 300–1
flogging 151
Flying Dutchman (horse) 121
Foy, William 105
Freemasons 121, 122
Freud, Sigmund 44

Gainsborough, Thomas
  'The Blue Boy' 9, 268
Galatea 46
Gall, Franz 43–4
Gardiner, Frank 'The Darkie' 87–93,
    113, 114
  San Francisco, in 92
  trial 90
Gardiner gang 88, 114
Gardiner, Superintendent 172, 173
Garibaldi, Giuseppe 28, 34
Gately, Michael 151–2, 156–7, 172
Geldern, Count 105, 121, 122
Glenny, Henry 185–6
gold 86, 138
gold rush
  America 66
  Australia 65–7, 221
  New Zealand 38
Goon, Ah 211, 241
Gorman, Constable Patrick 230, 246,
    260
Green, Alexander 248–9
Gundagai 223, 290
  Moonlite gang hearing 237–44

Hall, Ben 55, 56, 88, 113, 114–15
Hammill, Julius 133
hangings 245–6, 248, 269–70
  botched 89, 187, 246, 297
  rope 3, 5, 8, 187, 190, 286, 289
Harding, Samuel 41, 59
Hargraves, Edward 66
Harris, Jack 127
Harrison, George 35
Hart, Steve 297
Hartigan, Edward 'The Snob' 95–6
Harwood, Dodson 132
Haselden, Reverend John 41
Haughton, Reverend Samuel 245
Hayes, Bully 98, 104, 105
Headley, Constable Henry 239–40,
    241

Heathorn, Hanna 133
Heathorn, Henry 133
Hemans, Felicia
  'The Lady of Provence' 15
Hill, Richard 38–40, 67
history 299–300
  sources 300, 307–10
Hobbs family 103–4
Holworthy, Francis 98–9, 101, 103,
  106
homosexuality 159–67
  'manly love' 300–1
Horner, Eliza Jane 106
Howard, Jane 7, 8, 267, 292
Howard, Robert Rice (Nosey Bob)
    3–9, 16, 280, 285, 290–2, 297
  coachman 47–8
  death 292
  execution of Scott and Rogan 284–6,
    291
  family 267
  garden 266
  hanging, on 268–70
  Mudgee, hanging in 5–6, 187–91
Hughan, Allan 94–7, 103, 106
  New Caledonia 99
  Scott, and 97–8, 101–2, 301–2
Hughan, Phoebe 94

Ireland 23, 28, 31
  England, relationship with 22, 25–6,
    49
  land leases 24–5
  mass evictions 26
  potato famine 23–5, 26, 27–8, 30
  sectarian violence 29–31, 46
Irwin, William 125–6

James, John Stanley 171–2
  Scott, assessment of 172–4
  The Vagabond 171–2
Johns, Frank see Williams, Thomas
Johnson, William 193–4

Kelly, Chief Prison Warder 172–3, 184
Kelly, Dan 297
Kelly, Ellen 69–70, 72, 108
Kelly, Jim 70
Kelly, Ned 11, 19, 21, 39, 67–72,
    107–9, 139, 304
  apprentice to Harry Power 39,
    68–72, 107–8
  Beechworth Gaol 107, 109
  execution 297, 298
  Pentridge 139, 140–2
  snitch, as 72, 107–8
  war on police 141–2
Kelly, Red 70
Kelly, Thomas 39
Kelly gang 19, 183, 194, 196, 201,
    202, 213, 223, 235
  Glenrowan siege 297–8
Kidd, Dr Robert 41
Kinder, Ellen 117–18
Knatchbull, John 248

Lambing Flat riots 66, 87
Lancefield bank robbery 196
Lawson, Henry 296
lay readers (Church of England) 57
Lewis, C. S. 28
Lindon 207, 208, 213
Lloyd, Jack 108, 109
Loftus, Lord Augustus 268, 278
Long Depression 201
Love, William 238–44

McClelland, Dr 29
McCormick, Catherine 109
McCormick, Jeremiah 109
McDonald, Claude 205, 209, 210–11,
    215
  Scott, relationship with 271–3
  testimony 241–2
McDonald, Falconer 205, 209, 210,
    211, 213, 215, 271
  testimony 242

McDonnell, John 132
McGill, Walter 289
McGlede, Edmund 217–18, 224
McGlede, Hannah 224, 228, 229
McGlede, Henry 224
McGlede homestead shootout 225–33,
    258
McKenna, Thomas 133
McKillop, Robert 237, 258
Mackston, Constable 81
Macready, Reverend Henry 280
Manchester Martyrs 49
Maniapoto, Rewi 37
Manns, Henry 88–9
Maori 36–7, 41, 74, 77
Marietta 221
Marks, Charles 161–2, 164, 165, 302
Martley, James 128–9
mateship 302–3
Maungakaramea 36, 41
Metcalfe, Alexander 188
Mitchel, John 26
Monckton, Constable 81, 83
Moonlite gang 11, 197–8, 200
    trial *see* trial of Moonlite gang
    Victoria, travelling around 200–4
Morgan, John 133
Morgan, Mad Dog 21, 55
Mount Egerton 65, 127, 185
    bank robbery 62–4, 74–7, 83–4,
        120, 123, 131–8, 282
Mudgee 5, 188–91
Mutter, Joseph 187

Naylor, Thomas 166
Nesbitt, Catherine 147–50
    letter to 14–16, 282
Nesbitt, James 12, 21, 158, 217
    burial 237, 271, 273, 290
    character 12, 13, 202
    death 13, 14, 231–3, 236, 263
    final gun battle 12–13, 14, 226–8,
        231–3

ghost 252–3
harassment by police 193–4, 196–7
Pentridge, in 12, 148, 150–1,
    158–9
Scott, and 12–14, 152–4, 158–60,
    167, 168, 175, 183, 184, 193,
    199, 202, 210, 238, 242, 262,
    273, 275–6, 290, 300, 302–3
Wantabadgery siege *see* Wantabadgery
    Station
Nesbitt, James (Senior) 12, 147–50,
    158, 168, 169, 292
Nesbitt, Willie 283–4
New Caledonia 98, 99, 100, 137
New Zealand 33, 36–8, 137, 196
    bushrangers 38, 40
    Wars 37
Norfolk Island 166
Nosey Bob *see* Howard, Robert Rice
    (Nosey Bob)
Nulty, Thomas 26

O'Farrell, Henry James 48–51, 52
Orakau, Battle of 37
Orange 66
Orangemen 30, 46
Otago 38, 39
outback 18

Park, Frederick (Fanny) 163, 164–5
Parkes, Sir Henry 50, 188, 253, 257,
    267
Parramatta Lunatic Asylum 116–19
Parramatta River murders 122
Paterson, Banjo 296
Patterson, Isabella 214, 215
Patterson, Jack 213–14
Patterson, Thomas 100
Peisley, John 88
Pentridge prison 12, 68, 109, 140–5,
    150–5, 158
    homosexual relationships 159–60
    punishments 151–2

Scott's complaints about 168–71,
  181
solitary confinement 152, 154, 173,
  175
'The Vagabond' report 172
Perry, Charles 56–7, 79
phrenology 43–5, 50–1, 238, 289
Pilot 86, 94–5, 96–7, 99, 102, 106
Plummer, Charlie 222
Plunkett, James 124–6
police
  establishment of police force 87
  harassment of Scott 193–4, 196–7,
    200–1, 243, 260
  McGlede homestead shootout
    225–33, 235–6
  Wantabadgery siege 215–16, 223–4,
    245
potato famine 23–5, 26, 27–8, 30
Pottinger, Sir Frederick 88–9
Power, Harry 39, 67–72, 107, 109
Price, John 39
psychoanalysis 44

racial tensions 66–7, 87
Rathfriland 27–8, 33
Rea, Thomas 144–6
Read, John 254
Ribbonmen 30
Rich, Reverend Canon 280, 285
Rogan, Tom 11, 12, 198, 202, 252,
    262, 268–70, 278, 284
  arrest, following 237–8
  burial 289–90
  Darlinghurst Gaol 251–2
  hanging 281, 285–7, 289
  McGlede homestead shootout 228,
    230, 236, 239, 260
  mock trial 218
  trial of Moonlite gang 260–1, 264,
    265
  Wantabadgery Station siege 208, 217

Rowe, Constable George 216
Rowe, John 70

Sadlier, Superintendent John 201
Saladin (horse) 121
San Francisco 66
Sandhurst 128, 185
Sarah Pile 100–1, 137
Scott, Andrew George (Captain
    Moonlite)
  alcohol 41, 59, 104
  Australia, move to 42, 51, 56
  Australia, return to 99, 100–1, 102
  Ballarat Gaol, escape from 124–30,
    159
  Bendigo, capture near 126–8
  birth 27
  Bruun, and 75–6, 77, 84–5, 120,
    133–5
  burial 263–4, 283, 289–90
  bushranger, recognition as 19,
    21–2
  cadetship in the Royal Navy 34
  Catherine Nesbitt, letter to 14–16,
    282
  celebrity 21, 119–20, 128–30, 186,
    246–7, 285
  character 35–6, 42, 44, 60–1, 74,
    117, 119, 152–3, 168, 169, 174,
    192, 210, 304
  cheques, bouncing 106, 132, 133
  childhood 29
  Comet 103–6
  contempt, gaoled for 83
  cotton plantation 98–9
  cross examination of witnesses
    132–7
  Darlinghurst Gaol 10–13, 145–6,
    247, 249–50, 271–3, 280–2
  early employment 40–1
  emigration 34
  engineer 41, 59–61
  execution 10

Fiji, journey to 86, 96–7, 302
final gun battle 12–13, 14, 225–33
God, and 280–1
Gundagai courtroom, in 237–44
gunshot wounds 37
hanging 271, 280, 284–7, 289
harassment by police 193–4, 196–7,
    200–1, 243, 260
honour 10, 14, 38, 75, 77, 81–2,
    83, 84, 138, 192, 199, 205, 244,
    260, 272, 304
Irish heritage 21–2, 44
lay reader 58–9, 61, 65, 76, 127,
    159
letter to father 120–3
mental health 35–6, 106–7, 116–19,
    173, 192, 304
military service in New Zealand
    37–8
mock trial 218–19
Mount Egerton bank robbery 62–4,
    74–8, 81–4, 120, 123, 131–8,
    282
myths and legends 28–9, 34, 41–2,
    74, 78, 104–5, 130
Nesbitt, and 12–14, 152–4, 158–60,
    167, 168, 175, 183, 184, 193, 199,
    202, 210, 231–3, 238, 242, 262,
    273, 275–6, 290, 300, 302–3
New Zealand, in 36–8, 40–1
orator 58, 60, 155, 169, 184, 238,
    242–4
penal system, comments on 180–6,
    192, 194–5, 211, 243–4, 258,
    262–3
Pentridge 12, 139, 140, 142–5,
    152–5, 168–75, 181
plaster cast death mask 43
poetry, love of 15, 74, 140, 263
police surveillance 191
policeman, death of 10, 11
public lecture (Ballarat) 182–6
sexuality 300–4

showman 58, 131–2, 137–8, 154,
    155, 172–3, 182–6, 242–3
smuggling 104, 121, 159
storyteller 153–4, 159, 184–5
trial see trial of Moonlite gang
Wantabadgery siege see Wantabadgery
    Station
Weechurch, witness for 154–6, 172
wildness 29, 35–6, 41, 103, 105,
    129, 174, 175, 192, 199, 205,
    209, 228, 240
Scott, Bessie 27, 28, 33, 271
Scott, Sir Walter 179
Scott, Thomas (brother) 27, 121
Scott, Thomas (father) 27, 28, 30–1,
    45, 271, 292
    emigration 32–3, 36
    letter from George 120–3
    magistrate in New Zealand 36, 40–1
    reverend 41, 121, 292
    Seneschal of the Manor 27, 32–3
Scott-Siddons, Mary Frances 180
Second Industrial Revolution 18, 51, 97
sectarian issues
    Australia 46, 50
    Ireland 29–31, 46
sexual repression 164
Seymour, George 211–12
Shanklin, Laurence 143
Sherritt, Aaron 301
Simpson, James 75, 77, 78, 83, 135
Simpson, Justice 107
Sly, George 120
Smith, Robert Burdett 251, 254, 274
sodomy 164–7
spiritualism 97
state executioner 4
    media portrayals 5–8
Stephen, Sir Alfred 50, 80, 88, 117–18,
    267
    bushrangers, attitude to 52–6, 90–2,
        114
    Mudgee hanging 188, 191

Stroh, John 261, 274
Stuart, Peter 152
Stuart, Robert 166
Sullivan, John 174
Sydney 255–6
Sydney International Exhibition 255–6

Taylor, John (Weechurch) 142–3,
    154–7, 172, 185
Thatcher, Richard 180, 192–3, 196,
    250–3, 273, 281, 303
Thomas, Julian *see* James, John Stanley
Thunderbolt, Captain *see* Ward,
    Frederick (Captain Thunderbolt)
Tommy the Nut 152
Treasury Gardens shooting 160, 161–3,
    302
Trevelyan, Sir Charles 25
trial of Moonlite gang 10–11, 20,
    256–65
  address to jury 260
  adjournment, case for 257–8
  appeals 268
  cross-examination of witnesses 258–9
  directions to jury 260–1
  Mary Ames, campaign 273–4
  Scott's defence 257, 258, 261
  Scott's final speech 262–3
  tickets 256
Turpin, Dick 88, 92
Twain, Mark 39, 181

Victoria, Queen 37, 45, 163–4

Waikato 37
Walker, Alex 112
Want, John 261
Wantabadgery Station 11, 203–5, 211,
    258
  departure from 216–17
  police retreat 215–16
  siege 14, 207–16, 241–3
Ward, Ada 180

Ward, Frederick (Captain Thunderbolt)
    21, 56, 87, 114
  career 110–13
  death 110, 112–13
  song 111
Waterloo Push 296
Webb-Bowen, Edward 220–4, 230,
    234–6
  death 244, 263
  shooting 230, 231, 238, 239, 241,
    257, 258, 294–5
Webb-Bowen, Edward (son) 295–6
Webb-Bowen, Marion 223, 234, 244,
    295
Weechurch *see* Taylor, John
    (Weechurch)
Weir, David 203, 208, 210, 214,
    217–19
  McGlede homestead shootout 227
  mock trial 218
Wells, Jane 65
Wernicke, Ernest 198, 294
Wernicke, Gus 197–8, 202, 226, 294
  burial 237
  death 233, 236, 263
  McGlede homestead shootout 228,
    230, 231–3
  Wantabadgery Station siege 210,
    217
Wernicke, Isabella 198, 294
White Boys 25, 30
Why Not 106
Wild West 92, 113
Wilkinson, Charles 188
Williams, Thomas 11, 183–4, 198,
    202–3, 232, 236, 252
  arrest, following 237–8
  Bennett, letter in support of 293–4
  Darlinghurst Gaol 251–2
  death 292–3
  McGlede homestead shootout 228,
    229
  reprieve 268

trial of Moonlite gang 260–1, 264, 265

Wantabadgery Station siege 217

Windeyer, Justice William Charles 252, 253, 256–65, 293, 296–7

death 297

directions to jury 260–1

judgement 265

Windeyer, Walter 204–5, 252, 258

Winter, George 99

Wisdom, Robert 253, 256–7, 258, 259

Witherden, Edward 133

Witherden, Margaret 133

Wotherspoon, Garry 300–1

Wright, Wild 141

Yarra Track bushranger *see* Sullivan, John

Yuill, Captain William 100, 102

Discover a
new favourite